Foreword

This Bulletin for Comparative Labour Relations contains monographs dealing with equality and the prohibition of discrimination in employment. Two monographs describe international rules and instruments as they are developed both by the International Labour Organisation (ILO) and by the European Communities (EC). 13 Monographs examine the situation in the following countries: **Belgium, Canada, France, FR Germany, Great Britain, Hungary, Italy, Japan, The Netherlands, Sweden,** the **United States** and **Yugoslavia.** The introductionary remarks and general overview tries to give a comparative and panoramic picture of the state of the art, of similarities and differences, as well as of trends and prospective developments and a summary evaluation of the exercise in equality.

As Laszlo Nagy, President-Elect of the International Society for Labour Law and Social Security, in his report on Hungary rightly indicates, the actual assertion of equality of rights or of fact cannot be separated from the political, social, economic and cultural circumstances in which the quest for equality evolves. The different rapporteurs could - for reasons of space - not always provide this global societal framework in detail. For this we can fortunately refer to the **International Encyclopaedia for Labour Law and Industrial Relations,** which contains that background material, enabling one to put the different reports into an overall integrated national picture.

We would even go a step further than L. Nagy - as one outcome of our comparative overview - and say that, as for other rights, rights of equality of opportunity and equality of treatment can only become a fact of life if society at large is really motivated and engaged to reach that goal.

May I also express my gratitude to the authors and to the English language editors F. Millard and M. Smith, who have made this study another positive result of friendly and rewarding international collaboration.

R. Blanpain
November 1984

List of Abbreviations

AFL-CIO	American Federation of Labor - Congress of Industrial Organisation
AP	Arbeitsrechtliche Praxis
BAG	Bundesarbeitsgericht (Federal Labour Court)
CGT	Confédération Générale du Travail (France)
ETUC	European Trade Union Confederation
GG	Grundgesetz (Constitution)
IELL	International Encyclopaedia for Labour Law and Industrial Relations
ILO	International Labour Organisation
NLRB	National Labor Relations Board (USA)
OJ	Official Journal EC
UN	United Nations
UNICE	Union des Industries de la Communauté Européenne

Notes on Contributors

ASSCHER-VONK, Irène, is Lecturer of Labour Law at the University of Amsterdam (The Netherlands)

BIRK, Rolf, is Professor at the Faculty of Law of the University of Trier (FR Germany)

BLANPAIN, Roger, is Professor of Labour Law at the University of Leuven (Belgium) and Visiting Professor at the European Institute of Business Administration, Fontainebleau (INSEAD) (France)

BRAJIC, Vlajko, is Professor of Labour Law at the University of Beograd (Yugoslavia)

EGGER, Johann, is Lecturer in Labour Law, Faculty of Law of the University of Innsbruck (Austria)

FLODGREN, Boel, is Associate Professor of Civil Law, Faculty of Law of the University of Lund (Sweden)

HANAMI, Tadashi, is Professor of Labour Law at Sophia University, Tokyo (Japan) and a former Dean of the Law School

HEPPLE, Bob, is Professor of Law, University College, University of London (England)

JAIN, Harish C., is Professor of the Personnel and Industrial Relations Area, Faculty of Business, McMaster University (Canada)

JONES, James E., Jr., is Professor of Law and Industrial Relations, Law School, University of Wisconsin (USA)

NAGY, Laszlo, is Professor of Labour Law at the University of Szeged (Hungary)

ROJOT, Jacques, is Professor of Management at the University of Rennes (France), as well as holding an appointment at the European Institute of Business Administration, Fontainebleau (INSEAD)

ROSSILLION, Claude, is Head of the Equality of Rights Branch in the International Labour Office (ILO)

TREU, Tiziano, is Professor ordinarius of Labour Law at the University of Pavia, as well as holding an appointment in the Department of Economics at the Catholic University of Milan (Italy)

WALGRAVE, Jo, is Social Conciliator at the Belgian Ministry of Labour and a Member of the Committee of Women at Work (Belgium)

Table of Contents

1. General Introduction: A Comparative Overview

R. Blanpain

EVOLUTION

Although the goal of equality and the prohibition of discrimination constitutes a long-standing and fundamental aspiration of many nations and even a universally accepted human right, it is only recently that a number of countries have taken positive steps aiming at its concrete implementation.

No doubt international organisations, like the International Labour Organisation and the European Communities, have contributed greatly to that end as they translate a profound concern and respect by the international community for human rights, not only **in abstracto,** but also **in concreto.**

At the same time, however, one can discern, beneath these great humanistic ideals, more self-centred economic undertones, reflecting the down-to-earth interests of groups and nations, wrapped in the garb of unfair competition, special protection and the like.

France may be one country, illustrating such a development. The French Declaration of Human Rights of 1798 - almost 200 years ago now - deems men to have been born and to remain free, with equal rights; all citizens have equal access to all honours, positions and public employment according to their capacities without any difference other than their virtues and their talents. The preamble of the Constitution of 1946 reiterates that all human beings possess sacred and inalienable rights, without distinction of race, religion or beliefs.

For a long period these national sources were the only available basis of judicial protection against discrimination of all kinds. **France** ratified the Equal Remuneration Convention (100) in 1952 and the Discrimination (Employment and Occupation) Convention (111) of the ILO in 1983.

France was also instrumental in seeing to it that the Treaty establishing the European Economic Community contained the principle of equal pay for equal work. It was convinced that being ahead in that area in relation to other countries, it would suffer unfair competition due to the unequal pay practices in some other EC countries at the time of the negotiation of the Treaty.

It is only recently however that **France** has adopted a large number of legal texts covering different kinds of discrimination namely in 1972, in 1975 and especially in 1982 and 1983.

Another example is the **USA,** which bravely declared in 1776 that all men are created equal and endowed with inalienable rights of life, liberty and the pursuit of happiness, but continued at the same time to enforce a system of slave-labour, which led to civil war and the Emancipation Proclamation in 1865. One had to wait some 100 years

1

more before laws with some teeth were adopted, supported by public opinion, to tackle the problem. In the **USA** the complexities, generated by the unfortunate legacy of slavery, far more than the example set by internatonal organisations, led to a plethora of laws and programmes directed at equal opportunity, which has no parallel in any other of the industrialised countries.

Other examples can be found, illustrating the recent preoccupation with ensuring that the ancient goals of equality prevail in development in **Belgium, Great Britain, Italy, Sweden, The Netherlands,** and the like.

These developments may be at a turning point. Although in no way have the goals of equality been reached, the equality movement is likely to become at best blocked, at the worst eroded, by the overall embracing deregulation mood, urging for market flexibility for the very sake of employment and job creation and thus doing away with protective legislation, also in the name of freedom.

This does not however detract from the fact that important steps have been taken in a number of countries and that consequently a lot can be learned regarding equal treatment from a comparative exercise, especially in the area of follow-up, enforcement, remedies and affirmative action. The lesson indeed is clear and loud: without effective implementation procedures, the results seem meagre and in reality, discrimination is thus, stronger than law.

DEFINITION

Given the universal appeal of the equality principle and the ease of paying lip-service to great causes, Convention 111 of the ILO has been ratified by more than 100 countries. There is no doubt that the definitions used in that convention have had a wide ranging impact on national legislation, especially in countries such as **France** and **Belgium**, in which ratified international conventions may supersede national law.

Convention 111 and especially later instruments tackle, expressly or by implication, both direct and indirect discrimination. This does not however mean that the word 'discrimination' has the same meaning everywhere.

Direct discrimination in general refers to differential treatment, which is 'less favourable' on prohibited grounds. In the **Netherlands** however it is not yet clear whether every distinction is forbidden, or only less favourable distinctions. In the **USA** it does not matter whether the treatment is better or worse. In **Great Britain** case law has established that any deprivation of choice can amount to 'less favourable treatment'. Indirect discrimination is 'discriminiation by effects'.

For some direct discrimination covers both equal opportunity and 'equality of outcomes'. This may not be fully the case in all countries. **British** legislation, for example, is based rather on the notion of equal opportunity. B. Hepple remarks: 'it aims to remove all formal and deliberate impediments to opportunity on the basis of ability or individual merit.'

In general legal as well as **de facto** situations are covered.

The definition of direct discrimination in most cases covers both intentional and unintentional practices. This is however not the case in **Canada:** direct discrimination involves searching for a motive or an intention to discriminate on any of the prohibited grounds of discrimination; intention to discriminate must be proved. Direct discrimation is open and intended, the **Swedish** author, B. Flodgren, reports. In **Yugoslavia** both discrimination (intention) and unequal treatment (non-intention) are prohibited. In the **USA** disparate treatment or prohibited discrimination requires a showing of intent or purpose.

Indirect discrimination, what H. Jain calls systemic discrimination, is in **Canada** the result of measures or practices unrelated to any discriminatory criterion but which, in the circumstances in which they apply, result in adverse impact on minority groups.

In the **USA** the concept of indirect discrimination was articulated by the Supreme Court in the Griggs v. Duke Power Co. case in 1971. In the **USA**, J. Jones says, the 'disparate impacts or disparate effects, or the consequences theory holds that a facially non-discriminatory employment practice that disproportionally screens out a higher percentage of protected class members is an unlawful employment practice unless it can be demonstrated ... that the practice is required by business necessity or has a manifest relationship to job performance. The disparate impact concept has been used to invalidate a wide range of recruitment, assignment, hiring, promotion, discharge, testing and supervisory selection practices.

In order to establish indirect discrimination the complainant in **Great Britain** must prove that the respondent applied a requirement or conditions, applied to all work-seekers or employees and which constitutes an absolute bar; the proportion of the complainant groups, who can comply with that requirement is considerable smaller than the proportion of persons who do not belong to that group. It is then up to the respondent to prove that the requirement or condition is 'justifiable'. The **British** concept of justifiability is far broader than the **American** touch stone, which is 'business necessity'. B. Hepple rightly remarks that if the defence of justifiability is too wide, the objective of the legislation will be easily defeated. In the **British** context, some of the most important examples of indirect discriminatory requirements or practices would include minimum height requirements; prohibition on wearing certain types of clothing (such as turbans by Sikhs); language proficiency in manual jobs; a refusal to accept foreign qualifications; maximum age limitations; experience or training in Britain; recruitment by personal referrals within the existing workforce, sometimes called 'word of mouth hiring'; and recruitment through a network of contacts which excludes ethnic minorities, women, etc.

The **US** Griggs approach has been adopted in **Canada** in both equal pay and equal employment cases. The final resolution of impact vs intent as an element of the definition of discrimination is now before the Supreme Court of Canada.

In other countries, for example **Japan**, the difference between direct and indirect discrimination has been less discussed. There is, however, according to T. Hanami, no doubt that any indirect discrimination which brings separate treatment as a result without reasonable grounds is regarded as prohibited discrimination.

3

Sweden's B. Flodgren indicates another form of indirect discrimination: when rules aimed at helping certain categories of employees (as with the right for foreign employees to study Swedish at the employers' expense) have the effect that those employees become less attractive on the labour market.

Another element of the definition obviously refers to the areas and persons to which it applies: to employees as wel as the self-employed, to all or only some aspects of the employment relationship. The **ILO** and the **EC** instruments cover a wider field. Recommendation No. 111 specifies as follows the matters in respect of which all persons should, without discrimination, enjoy equality of opportunity and treatment (paragraph 2):

(i)   access to vocational guidance and placement services;
(ii) access to training and employment of their own choice on the basis of individual suitability for such training or employment;
(iii) advancement in accordance with their individual characters, experience, ability and diligence;
(iv) security of tenure of employment;
(v)   remuneration for work of equal value;
(vi) conditions of work including hours of work, rest periods, annual holidays with pay, occupational safety and occupational health measures, as well as social security measures and welfare facilities and benefits provided in connection with employment.

It also points out that there should be no discrimination in respect of admission to, retention of membership in or participation in the affairs of employers' and workers' organisations.

An **EC** Directive No. 76/207 of 9 February 1976, as J. Egger indicates, deals with equal treatment as regards access to occupation, vocational training and promotion and working conditions.

In **Canada** the relevant statutes apply to employers, employment agencies, trade unions and in some jurisdictions to self-governing professions. Discrimination is prohibited with respect to advertising, the terms and conditions of employment, including promotion, transfer and training.

In other countries one may have different instruments, which cover each different area and/or actor. For **Japan**, the courts protect workers against discrimination only after employment, but not in hiring.

GROUNDS

Some grounds, which do not justify different treatment, are more or less universally covered.

In the international rules and countries studied race and sex are most prominent on the list of prohibited grounds. Religion, political opinion and marital status (which is closely linked with sex), rank second. Then follow colour (close to race), nationality and related grounds as national extraction, ethnic origin, as well as social origin, trade union involvement and age. Handicap is gaining in importance as a prohibited ground, as well as private life.

EXPLICIT FORBIDDEN GROUNDS

	ILO	EEC	Belgium	Canada	France	FR Germany	Great Britain	Hungary	Italy	Japan	Netherlands	Sweden	USA	Yugoslavia	Total	Subtotal
I. Race	×	×	×	×	×	×	×	×	×	×	×	×	×	×	14	
Colour	×			×		×	×				×	×	×		7	
Ethnic origin		×		×	×		×	×			×	×			7	
Language									×						1	
Nationality			×	×		×	×		×	×	×	×	×		9	
National extraction	×			×					×	×	×				5	
Social origin	×			×	×		×		×	×	×	×			8	
Social status										×				×	2	53
II. Sex	×	×	×	×	×	×	×	×	×	×	×	×	×	×	14	
Family responsibilities	×	×	×		×				×						5	
Marital status	×	×	×	×	×		×	×	×	×				×	10	
Pregnancy	×								×						2	31
III. Ideological opinion									×						1	
Political opinion	×			×	×			×	×	×	×	×	×	×	10	
Religion	×			×	×	×			×	×	×		×	×	9	
Trade Union Involvement	×		×	×	×	×		×					×	×	8	28
IV. Age	×		×	×	×	×		×					×		7	7
V. Handicap			×	×				×					×		4	4
VI. Pardonned offences													×		1	
Private life			×	×	×						×	×			5	
Sexual orientation					×								×		2	8
TOTAL	12	5	9	14	12	7	7	8	12	9	10	8	11	7	131	

Less prominent are pregnancy (also related to sex), ideological opinion, social status, family responsibilities, sexual orientation, pardonned offence and language. But most of these grounds can however be brought under the umbrella of other more widely prohibited grounds.

This brings us to the first problem, namely the fact that the meaning of some of the terms employed is not at all clear, so that different words are used to point to a diversified reality, which may contain shades of differences in relation to one other. This leads to the possibility of grouping certain grounds. One can distinguish the following groupings:

1. Race, colour, ethnic origin, national extraction, nationality, social origin, status;
2. Sex, pregnancy, marital status, family responsibilities;
3. Political and ideological opinion, religion and trade union involvement;
4. Age;
5. Handicap;
6. Private life, sexual orientation, pardonned offences.

Let's consider some of these grounds, which due to the vagueness of the terms do to a certain extent overlap, in more detail.

1. Race, colour ... nationality

A common feature of these various grounds of discrimination is the fact that they are generally linked to the existence of different ethnic groups.

The words 'ethnic origin' have, so B. Hepple reports, been given a wide interpretation as meaning a group which is a segment of the population distinguished from others by a sufficient combination of shared customs, beliefs, traditions and characteristics derived from a common or presumed common past, even if not drawn from a common 'racial stock'.

The concept of race stems from perceptions in difference of primary stock, J. Jones remarks. Even though 'race' and 'colour' refer to two different kinds of human characteristics, it is the visibility of skin colour - and of other physical traits associated with a particular colour or group that marks individuals out. 'Most people', Jones states, 'do not know the difference between race and ethnic groups, between nurture and nature. It makes for an economy of thought to ascribe peculiarities of appearance, custom, values, to race. It is simpler to attribute differences to heredity than to juggle all the complex social grounds for diffences that exist.'

National origin includes in the **USA** 'the denial of employment opportunity because of an individual's, or his or her ancestors', place of origin; or because an individual has the racial, cultural, or linguistic characteristics of a national origin group. It also includes consideration of whether opportunities have been denied because of marriage to or association with persons of a national origin group, or membership in or association with an organisation so identified, attendance or participation in schools, churches, temples or mosques generally used by persons of a national origin group and because an individual's name or spouse's name is associated with such a group.'

The term 'national origin', which is a protected class under the principal federal law, does not prohibit a private employer from discriminating on the basis of an employee's lack of citizenship. However, the failure to include the term 'ancestry' does not reduce the scope of coverage as the term national origin is considered to include ancestry.

Social origin refers to situations where there exist divisions of society into classes or castes or hierarchic traditions or distinctions resulting from the educational methods which are employed.

National extraction, as C. Rossillion of the ILO office indicates, covers distinctions with reference to naturalised persons of foreign origin or between communities with ties to different national cultures.

Access to most labour markets is restricted for foreigners, who need a work permit in order to take up a job. A notable exception is to be found in the **EC** treaty which provides for the right of free circulation of workers inside the Community, with as **ratio legis** the establishment of a Common Labour Market. Nationals of the Member States can claim admission to vacant positions on the same basis as native workers. Foreign workers are to be treated equally. Convention No. 143 (1975) of the ILO providing for equality of opportunity and treatment of migrant workers has not been widely ratified (only 13 countries).

The **EC** treaty specifies that only discrimination on grounds of nationality is forbidden. The Court of Justice has indicated however that indirect discrimination, referring **e.g.** to origin or domicile are equally prohibited. Equal treatment in the EC also benefits family members.

The knowledge of a given language may be a permitted ground if justified objectively. In **Sweden** the labour court dit not accept an employer's argument that Swedish was a prerequisite for safety reasons.

2. Sex

As C. Rossillion observes, discrimination based on sex - which means in practice discrimination against women - is certainly the form of discrimination which is most freqently encountered, both in the area of equal pay and equal treatment. The legal protection in many countries, mainly due to the action of the ILO and the EEC, seems at first glance quite complete and covers not only direct, but also indirect discrimination, including that linked to pregnancy, marital status and family responsibilities. In many cases the legislation concerned represents an attempt at 'social engineering' in a situation in which there is no real consensus.

Marital status is defined in **Ontario** (Canada) as the status of 'being married, single, widowed, divorced and separated' and expressly includes 'living with a person of the opposite sex in conjugal relationship or outside marriage'. In **Italy**, to give another example, act 7/1963 nullifies any clause in agreements or factory rules providing that the employment relationship be terminated because of marriage or for any dismissal of a female employee occuring between the banns and one year after the marriage. In **Great Britain** dismissal on grounds of pregnancy is not covered by legislation on discrimination on grounds of sex since that legislation applies legally to men and women and men cannot become pregnant. In the **USA** an amendment to the 1964 Civil Rights Act was added in 1978 defining the terms 'because of sex' to include on the basis of pregnancy, childbirth or related medical condition.

Notwithstanding wide ranging legislation, discrimination because of sex still exists. Differentials in income remain in certain cases considerable. The reasons for these differences, as T. Treu indicates, depend on historical tradition and are multi-dimensional. The problem is to overcome historical sex segregation by opening up traditionally male professions to women through education and training; another aspect is the under-valuing of certain kinds of jobs, which are female-dominated. Lack of social organisation my be another factor. These factors, Treu concludes, can only be redressed by positive action rather than by the legal prohibition of formal discrimination.

Discrimination on grounds of sex is perhaps the most significant field of discrimination in contemporary **Japan,** also due to a constant increase of the number of female employees. Not only is legislative protection regarding equal treatment not forthcoming; the traditional practice of discrimination continues. Some companies employ women mainly for temporary, part-time or lower jobs. Some of them still have earlier retirement, compulsory retirement for women on marriage, pregnancy or childbirth. Most companies discriminate regarding promotion. Average wage differentials are still considerable. The **Japanese** Government is rather hesistant given the serious divisions in Japan on how to tackle the problem. Labour strongly opposes attempts to abolish protective provisions (**e.g.** concerning night work), while employers insist on them, except for maternity protection. Certain groups of women workers (**e.g.** managers, professionals) favour the abolition of protection, which they view as obstacles to their promotion.

Obviously economic crisis and especially rising unemployment have an impact. R. Birk reports for the **FR Germany** that the courts tend toward the view that the decision of an employer does not represent inadmissible discrimination against a married woman if he terminates her employment contract instead of that of a married man when she is in a secure economic position due to her husband's job.

In other instances commercial interests are in play: in **France** the dismissal of an employee whose husband was hired by a competitor was deemed justified. This may be remedied by recent legislation which protects against dismissal for reason of marital status.

3. Political opinion ... religion and trade union involvement

These grounds relate to the right to freedom of opinion and conscience in general. In some countries discrimination on those grounds is forbidden on the basis of general, fundamental legal principles; thus in **France** the civil code provides that all persons should enjoy the right of protection to their private lives. Thus when hiring, inquiries

8

concerning political opinion or political and trade union affiliation are forbidden. In other countries these grounds are explicitly prohibited. Thus the **Italian** workers' statute of 1970 stipulates that 'it is unlawful for an employer, with a view to admitting a worker into his employment, and for so long as the employment relationship continues, to conduct or cause to be conducted any inquiry into the worker's political, religious, or trade-union opinions, or concerning any fact not connected with an assessment of the worker's aptitude for this occupation.'

In **Canada** there is - and this is probably true for most countries - no clear indication whether religion and creed include only beliefs in a supreme being or a broader spectrum including a personal philosophy, political beliefs, agnosticism, atheism and others. Legal decisions have thus far only addressed a narrow range of issues such as dress and safety requirements, sabbath observance and the like.

In the **USA** the Civil Rights Act of 1964 was amended in 1972 to define the term 'religion' to include all aspects of religious observances and practice as well as belief, unless an employer demonstrates an inability to accommodate reasonably an employee's or prospective employee's religious observance or practice without undue hardship.

In a number of countries it is accepted that enterprises with a special political, religious or ideological vocation may demand specific requirements from their employees to match their purposes. Those exceptions to equality are however to be interpreted in a restrictive manner.

In **Sweden** women are now allowed to hold positions as clergy within the Swedish Church. The question remains whether clergymen may refuse to hold services together with female colleagues.

4. Age

In times of growing unemployment the question of age becomes increasingly important in the discussion who should get and retain the jobs that are available. In quite a number of countries there is no specific protection against discrimination because of age, interpreted to include younger workers, as well as older ones.

Canadian laws set varying protected age groups: 45 to 65, 40 to 65, 18 to 64. In the **USA** age groups 40 to 69 are protected. In **France** the Labour Code provides that job offers cannot include an upper age limit. In **Japan** there are special measures to promote the employment of aged workers (45 to 65 years) and some quota have been set by the government for workers olders than 55 years.

Seniority benefits and compulsory retirement seem exempted from prohibited discriminatory practices, notwithstanding the ILO recommendation regarding the latter; lately in many countries older workers have been pushed out, voluntarily or involuntarily, in order to make room for younger workers, for whom, in many countries preferential measures are taken. Neither seem different retirement ages for men and women to be looked upon as contrary to the goals of equality. The Supreme Court of **Canada** (1982) ruled that in order for employers to deny employment on the basis of age, two standards must be met. One is subjective (**i.e.** honestly imposed) based on production and economic reasons and the other is objective, related to employee, fellow employees and general public safety. There must be objective evidence relating to performance in order to claim exception.

5. Handicap

Specific protection of handicapped people, from the point of view of equality, is a more recent concern, as expressed in the 1983 ILO Convention No. 159 and Recommendation 168.

In **France,** as in some other countries, handicapped persons benefit from positive discrimination, as legislation imposes a quota of 3 per cent of the work force to be compulsorily hired in enterprises of over 10 employees. In **Japan** the government has set a quota, a prescribed percetnage of handicapped workers, as well as providing funds to employers who employ or train them. In **Yugoslavia,** V. Brajic reports, certain jobs and working tasks are reserved exclusively for disabled persons. In de **USA** certain contractors with the Federal Government and recipients of federal funds are prohibited to discriminate against the handicapped and some 47 of the 50 states have some form of handicapped law.

6. Private life

In most countries discrimination in employment for reasons related to an employee's private life is not covered by specific texts and therefore is covered by the general principles of law providing that all persons enjoy protection in their private life. One consequence is that recruitment tests and inquiries have to be job related.

Although private lives and jobs are to be treated separately, one cannot escape the fact that they have an important impact upon each other. This differs from person to person and job to job. It differs for a priest teaching religion in a religious school on the one hand and for a painter in an automobile factory on the other. Just as a job may make certain demands upon an individual's private life, so privacy must also be protected at the workplace: thus the right of non-smokers to fresh air, freedom of dress (within reasonable limits). The rule which is more and more generally accepted is that private life is only relevant to a job if in consequence the adequate performance of the job is seriously threatened and/or undermines considerably the credibility of the employee. Examples of such facts include criminal charges, extra-marital relationship(s), or homosexuality. Sexual harassment at the workplace has been recently highlighted as a form of unacceptable conduct at the workplace.

Alcoholism, drug addiction and gambling may also have an important impact on job performance and may constitute reasons for disciplinary action, including dismissal. In **Sweden,** however, the Labour Court (1979) distinguishes between chronic alcoholism and other forms of drunken behaviour. The Court has ruled that an employee who is chronic alcoholic is ill and could therefore not be subject to damages, dismissal or disciplinary sanctions.

It seems 'that the original moralistic approach is giving way to the reverse attitude, aiming at rehabilitating the addicted to normal working life'.

EXCEPTIONS

Both international and national regulations do indicate measures which are not deemed to be discriminatory; or put otherwise, constitute differences in opportunity or treatment which are justified.

First there come to mind **bona fide occupational qualifications** (BFOQ). In **Belgium**, J. Walgrave indicates, a limited list of professions for which the gender of an employee is a decisive element due to the particular nature of the job was drawn up: actors, singers, dancers, artists and models and also jobs which are reserved for a particular sex in countries which are not members of the EC.

In **Great Britain**, the list also includes toilet attendants, hospital and prison staff, personal welfare counsellors, The Race Relations Act allows exceptions for jobs for which a person of a particular race is required 'for reasons of authenticity' (**e.g.** Chinese restaurants). In **Japan**, it is not yet clear whether youth and beauty (**e.g.** T.V. announcers) are BFOQ's.

Also in **Italy** BFOQ's are related to the nature of the work: it would be illegal to exclude women as salespeople for reason of insufficient agressiveness or unsuitablility of the business invironment. Certain physical requirements such as minimum height or weightlifting were considered to be irrelevant.

In **Sweden** moral or cultural values or respect for integrity justify that only women are employed in the social home service. It is in **Sweden** uncertain whether an employer may select a person of a certain sex simply because of a belief that his business would so benefit. As in **Great Britain** natural origin (**e.g.** of ethnic chefs) may be a BFOQ in **Sweden.** Similarly, political and religious opinion may be a BFOQ for instance for a political secretary of a political party, a chief editor of a newspaper, a clerical position of different kind. Following the ILO a religious requirement should not apply to the holding of all jobs in an institution connected with the religion concerned; the nature of the particular job must be taken into account.

In the **USA** while the 1964 Act recognises a BFOQ for religion, sex, and national origin, there is no BFOQ exemption for race or colour. The law declares that it shall not be an unlawful employment practice for an employer or other covered entity to classify on the basis of religion, sex, or national origin in those certain instances where religion, sex, or national origin is a **bona fide** occupational qualification reasonably necessary for the normal operation of that particular business or enterprise. The age discrimination laws also contain specific **bona fide** occupational qualification exceptions.

The burden of proof of a BFOQ rests with the employer. In **Canada** the Supreme Court found that mandatory retirement of firefighters at age 60, although honestly imposed, was not objectively based and constituted discrimination on the basis of age.

In **Yugoslavia** there are additonal requirements for certain jobs; **e.g.** judges, public prosecutors and policemen should have moral-political

11

capabilities in conformity with the Discrimination (Employment and Occupation) Convention.

Security of state is another ground justifying separate treatment. Following the ILO this exception relates to individual activities and not merely to the basis of membership of a particular group or community; the concept of State security must be interpreted in a sufficiently strict sense. Criticising the policy of the Government is not in itself an activity against the security of the State.

Usually civil service jobs are reserved to nationals. The **European** Court of Justice has ruled that this exception to the free movement of labour in the EEC has to be interpreted restrictively and only concerns functions which have to do with the exercise of public power. In **Hugary** the safety of the State emphasises Hungarian citizenship and a clean record. In **FR Germany** civil servants are expected to have a positive attitude towards the Constitution. In **Japan** the National Civil Service and the Local Service law disqualify from employment those who engage in activities which extend to destroy by violence the Government based on the Constitution. Public employees should be politically neutral. In the **Netherlands** security reasons were explicitly mentioned by the government in the case of a homosexual who applied for a job as social worker in the Royal Household; he was rejected on the grounds that he had kept his homosexuality secret in the course of the selection procedure and that a homosexual who keeps his nature a secret is vulnerable and thus can be considered a security risk. In **Sweden** certain positions which are 'essential for the total defence of the country or for the security of the State in general' may be classified as sensitive positions. For those functions checks are made regarding civil reliability and may be reconsidered every five years.

In the **USA** members of the Communist Party are looked upon as security risks. One should in the context of this exception to equal treatment mention that the ILO advocates the guarantee of the existence of a right of appeal to a competent body.

A third category of exceptions may be found in special measures of protection. The **ILO** indicates that each country may define as non-discriminatory other 'special measures designed to meet the particular requirements of persons, who for reasons such as sex, age, disablement, family responsibilities or social or cultural status are generally recognised to require special protection or assistance'. Also the **EC** accepts special provisions for the protection of women, especially the protection of motherhood. It is above all in the area of discrimination on the basis of gender that problems have arisen and the question arises whether some protective measures are still justified in the light of the goals of equality and modern technological evolution.

In **Belgium**, J. Walgrave notes, maternal protection is confined first to the 14 weeks of compulsory rest in case of childbirth; education of children, in the sense of leave of absence for family reasons, parental leave and the like are not covered and equal treatment is the rule. In **Belgium** a list of jobs which are considered to be dangerous for mother and/or child has also been drawn up. In such a case the employer must do the utmost to provide another (healthy) job.

There are also specific rules on night work. In this area there reigns a lack of consensus: trade unions distrust social regression for the sake of equality; employers want equality for the sake of more flexibility and female night work.

In the **FR Germany** the legislature has embodied a series of additional protective measures for women, juveniles and severely disabled persons. Also in **Great Britain** the Sex Discrimination Act and Equal Pay Act preserve the special protective legislation which applies to women; much of the nineteenth and twentieth century legislation relating to the hours of work, holidays and safety of women in factories, mines and certain other places of employment remains in force. The absolute prohibition of employment underground has been modified. However, it is still impossible for a woman to become a face-worker in a coal mine but she could become an engineer or join any other occupation which does not involve spending a significant proportion of her time underground. In **Hungary** special protection concentrates on pregnant women, mothers, and the handicapped. In **Italy** too protective measures in favour of women workers were traditionally rather widespread. The criticism claiming that this legislation was at least partly responsible for women's disadvantaged position and thus indirectly conducive to discrimination, has been almost totally accepted by the law. Italian law now, Treu reports, encompasses more than is required by the EC. The way the changes are introduced is interesting: a flexible arrangement is set up by an interplay between the law and collective bargaining. Thus the prohibition of heavy work was lifted by Act 903 but at the same time the law empowered collective agreements to restore the prohibition of 'particularly heavy jobs'. A different approach was followed with respect to night work: Act 903 maintains the prohibition but empowers collective agreements to deviate. For heavy work no more than 20 agreements were reported; for night work over 200.

The major protective legislation still in force in **Italy** concerns pregnancy and maternity. Some rights reserved to the mother have been granted to the father when the children are in his custody.

In **Japan** traditional special protective measures remain unchanged: the Labour Standards Law provides protection for women, restricting overtime, holiday work, prohibiting night labour, underground and other dangerous work and providing maternity leave, menstruation leave and nursing periods. In **Sweden** equality prevails: both parents have a right to parental leave. The only difference which remains on grounds of gender is the obligatory rest in case of maternity and time for breast-feeding.

In **Sweden** there are also important protective measures for those employees who lack adequate formal schooling, or do not speak Swedish or for youngsters (18-20 years). In the **USA** generally speaking, special protective laws directed toward women in the employment area are relics of the past.

It thus seems that there is still an urgent need in some countries to review the justification of a number of protective measures in the light of the UN declaration of 1975 on equality for women workers: that special measures for the benefit of women should be taken up only for work proved to be potentially prejudicial to reproduction and that such measures should be reviewed periodically in the light of advances in scientific knowledge.

LEGAL CONSEQUENCES

The question arises as to the legal consequences of rules or acts that are discriminatory. The **EC** regulation on free movement of labour provides that provisions in individual labour contracts, workrules and collective agreements which are discriminatory are null and void. The same goes for **Belgium:** all provisions and practices contrary to the principle of equal treatment are void, which mean that they are null, **ex tunc,** and are to be invoked by the judge **ex officio.** Also in the **FR Germany** the sanction of illegal acts is nullity. The same is true for **Italy** and other countries.

AFFIRMATIVE ACTION AND REVERSE DISCRIMINATION

Affirmative action programmes are designed to correct the consequences of past and continuing discrimination. They involve a series of steps in order to remove barriers to employment and achieve measurable improvement in recruiting, hiring, training and promotion of worker groups who have in the past been denied assess to certain jobs. In **Japan** affirmative action is only a matter of theory. In other countries, like **Italy,** this area of law is hardly developed. In still other countries, like **Belgium, FR Germany** and the **Netherlands** the idea is accepted, but no concrete action of any importance is undertaken, except for some isolated actions in individual enterprises. In **Great Britain** the Commission of Racial Equality has issued a Code of Practice recommending trade unions and employers to take positive measures to provide encouragement and training where there is under-representation of particular groups in particular jobs. A similar Code has been drafted by the Equal Opportunities Commission in respect of sex discrimination but is not yet in force. In **France** temporary measures to the benefit of women, in order to re-establish equality of opportunity between men and women, and particularly to remedy current **de facto** inequalities, are allowed. They may be initiated by the government, by extended collective agreements or by enterprise plans. These plans can benefit from governmental subsidies up to 35 per cent of the capital investment needed and 50 per cent of other expenses.

It is especially in **Canada** and more so in the **USA** that substantial affirmative action programmes have been set up and tested in the courts. The Canadian National Railways, to give one example, was ordered by Court to hire women for one in four non-traditional (blue collar) jobs in the St. Lawrence Region until they hold 13 per cent of such jobs. The CN is also required to implement a series of other measures, ranging from abandoning certain mechanical aptitude tests to modifying the way it publicises available jobs.

The affirmative action programmes in the **USA** are impressive. Governmental rules require that companies take affirmative action to ensure equality of employment opportunity and prepare and maintain an affirmative action plan. This plan requires self-analysis and determination of areas of under-utilisation of women and minorities and the establishment of goals and timetables to achieve appropriate utilisation of the excluded classes in the job categories in which they are found lacking. The rules require the 'government contractor' to make an effort in good faith. J. Jones stresses that nothing in the plan requires the employers to hire unqualified individuals. Voluntary programmes - **e.g.** between a company and a trade union - are equally legal and it seems that the principle of affirmative action is constitutionally secure.

ENFORCEMENT

J. Jones rightly reports that the mechanism provided for the enforcement of any law is as important as the substantive rights sought to be protected by the legislation. Otherwise a law tends to be more symbolic than substantive, especially in an area where there is a likelihood of non-voluntary compliance with legal goals.

An analysis of the different reports confirms this observation. This is **e.g.** the case in **Belgium**, the **FR Germany**, **Italy** and **Japan**, where the normal, usual procedures apply. The limited implementation of the law, T. Treu remarks, is due in part to the weakness of the enforcement system.

1. Proof

A key point in the enforcement concerns the proof of discrimination. In quite a number of countries the normal rule **'actori incumbit probatio'**, namely that a plaintiff has to prove his or her point, has been reversed.

In **France e.g.** without going to the extreme of reverting the burden of proof (the employer would then have to prove that he did not discriminate) the law prohibiting sex discrimination now provides that the judge, who has knowledge of the elements of proof of discrimination claimed by the plaintiff, will also have the employer furnish elements of proof justifying the absence of discrimination. The judge, J. Rojot indicates, may order all provisions deemed necessary (experts and the like) before reaching a decision. If a doubt remains it should benefit the employee. In the **FR Germany** the burden of proof lies with the employer must prove that his decision was based on other reasons than sex, if the employee can satisfactorily show that there is a presumption of sex discrimination by the employer. In **Great Britain** the formal burden of proof is on the complainant; the tribunals however adopt a flexible attitude: if the primary facts indicate that there has been discrimination of some kind, the ball is in the camp of the employer.

In **Italy** courts appear reluctant to admit statistical evidence as **prima facie** evidence of discrimination. In **Japan** courts often switch the burden of proof to the dependant when the plaintiff has reasonably convinced the court of the probability of discrimination. Even with this shift, T. Hanami says, it is very hard to prove discrimination, especially in cases of hiring or promotion, since the courts acknowledge extensive freedom to employers in such cases. In **Sweden** an applicant who did not get a job (and who claims that sex discrimination has taken place) first has to make evident that he/she has better qualifications than the person of the opposite sex who got the job. If such is found to have been the case, the assumption is made that the employer has discriminated due to sex. The burden of proof then falls on the employer to exculpate him or herself. S/he must demonstrate that the decision was not due to the person's sex, or that it was part of a conscious affirmative action programme or that there was some other **bona fide** reason for the decision. If s/he does not manage to prove this, sex discrimination shall be found to have taken place.

In the **USA** the Supreme Court, in establishing the order and allocation of burdens of proof for disparate treatment under Title VII of the 1964 Act, has declared that the plaintiff in order to establish a **prima facie** case needs to show membership in a protected class, qualification for the position or promotion in question, application for consideration of some, and that he or she was passed over and some other unprotected class person accepted or that the employer continued to seek persons of the skills which the plaintiff has. Once a **prima facie** case has been established, the defendant may 'articulate a non-discriminatory reason for the action'. The burden would then shift to the plaintiff to establish that the purported reason is a pretext for discrimination or is unworthy of credence. For disparate impact - or effects discrimination, a plaintiff needs to show that a disproportionate number of his or her class is affected; the employer must prove that his action is job related and necessary.

2. Representatives of employees

France is one of the few countries where specific measures have been taken to enhance the role of the representatives of the employees in the pursuit of equality. In **France** recently certain steps have been taken, enhancing the role of the workers' representatives. First, the employer must give the works council a written report on the comparative situation regarding the general conditions of employment and training of women and men in the enterprise. This report must include 'a quantitative analysis evidencing, for all categories of employers the respective situation of men and women as far as are concerned "hiring, training, promotion, qualifications, classification, conditions of work and actual pay".' Besides, the report must enumerate all provisions taken during the past year with a view to ensuring occupational equality, objectives for the following year, and it must define quantitatively and qualitatively specific actions towards that goal and an evaluation of their cost. If actions asked for by the committee or forecast by the report of the preceding year did not take place, the report should also explain why. Also the works council has, in French law, the right to give its advice on the plan for employee training established by the employer, which must compulsorily amount to a minimum of 1.2 per cent of the wage bill. Before deliberating the council has to be given, three weeks in advance, a set of documents to which are now added the 'provisions to be taken to ensure occupational equality between women and men within the enterprise'. In **France** it is now compulsory to bargain annually over wages and every five years over scales. The parties are to examine them by sex.

16

Next trade unions are allowed to embark on law suits in favour of an employee without being empowered to do so by the employee, but only provided that the employee has been warned and has not opposed the suit within a period of 15 days. The employee retains the right to join the suit later.

3. Ombudsman

In **Sweden** an equality ombudsman tries to persuade employers to voluntarily comply with the equal treatment legislation. The policy of the ombudsman - in fact it is a woman - is voluntarism and co-operation.

4. Equal Opportunity Commissions

In a few member countries specific enforcement organs have been set up. In the **Netherlands** the officially established Committees for Equal Treatment have only very limited power and resources. Their judgment has no binding effect. Also in **Italy** a Committee for Equality has been set up. It has however only rather theoretical powers.

The **British** Equal Opportunities Commission and the Commission for Racial Equality are empowered to conduct investigations and to take action to remove unlawful practices. They may apply to an industrial tribunal and seek injunctions in the County Courts. The Commissions have made relatively little use of their powers.

In the **USA** the Equal Employment Opportunity Commission has substantial enforcement authority through the judicial process. The agencies have authority to investigate, hold hearings and to attempt to resolve disputes by conciliation. There are also substantial efforts to assist the parties voluntarily to resolve such issues.

5. Remedies

In many countries remedies remain rather weak. In the **FR Germany, e.g.,** the plaintiff is only entitled to the damage s/he can prove. If the plaintiff can prove s/he was not hired for reason of discrimination s/he is entitled to compensation for the costs of the application. The European Court of Justice (1984) has declared this sanction insufficient, without however indicating what constitutes an appropriate compensation.

In **Great Britain** the remedies which the tribunal may award under the terms of the Sex Discrimination and Race Relations Acts are far less effective than those to be found in corresponding USA legislation. The tribunal may
(i)   make an order declaring the rights of the party;
(ii) award compensation which is subject to a maximum at present of £7,500, including a sum in respect of injured feelings (usually in the vicinity of £150); and

(iii) recommend that the respondent take within a specified period action appearing to the tribunal to be practicable for the purpose of obviating or reducing the adverse effect of the unlawful discrimination on the complainant.

There is no power to order reinstatement or re-engagement or that the next job be offered to the complainant, although these measures may be recommended. If a recommendation is not complied with, without reasonable justification, the amount of compensation may be increased but not so as to exceed the overall limit of £7,500.

In **France** on the contrary the dismissed employee is to be reinstated, or at his or her choice be compensated by the usual severance pay, augmented by a sum equal to a minimum of six month's wages. In **Hungary** the employment relationship will be considered to continue in case of termination on basis of discrimination. In **Sweden** discrimination in the case of hiring may lead to damages; in the case of firing to reinstatement. Again, the **USA** provides for reinstatement - including orders for hiring - with back pay. Where reinstatement does not seem appropriate the individual is compensated in an adequate way.

EVALUATION

Even in countries where some positive efforts have been undertaken towards more equality, overall results are often meager. The earning gaps remain. Very little use is made of legal remedies. In **Great Britain** the number of cases are decreasing and those who use the law have little chance of success. Even in the **USA**, where substantial legal instruments are in place, attempting to ensure equality of employement, the macrofigures demonstrate clearly that much remains to be done. Inequality, more than equality, seems the rule.

The lesson is clear. As H. Jain concludes, equal opportunity legislation, although more than necessary, may not be sufficient for the elimination of inequality between majority and minority groups within the labour force. Legal approaches are limited because they operate only on the demand side of the problem (**i.e.** employer side) and do little to change supply, (**i.e.** education and training of minorities). V. Brajic rightly observes that free and equal access to education and professional training is the essential condition for the realisation of the right to work and employment. This suggests the need for supportive politics in education and training, together with continued vigilence.

2. ILO Standards and Actions for the Elimination of Discrimination and the Promotion of Equality of Opportunity in Employment

C. Rossillion

I. INTRODUCTION

1. The elimination of discrimination and the promotion of equality of opportunity in employment today accupy an important place in the standards and programmes of action of the ILO. They reflect a relatively recent growth of concern for fundamental human rights in the field of labour, a concern which was initially directed towards protection against abusive working conditions, the elimination of forced labour and guaranteeing trade union rights and collective bargaining.[1]

2. Since the foundation of the Organisation in 1919, provisions of the constitutional instruments have referred to the need to ensure opportunities for development and equitable economic treatment for all. But it was with the Declaration of Philadelphia, adopted in 1944 and subsequently incorporated in its Constitution, that the ILO proclaimed, as a fundamental constitutional principle, that 'all human beings, irrespective of race, creed or sex, have the right to pursue both their material well-being and their spiritual development in conditions of freedom and dignity, of economic security and equal opportunity'.

3. These principles have been put into effect through a number of Conventions and Recommendations adopted by the International Labour Conference and through various action programmes.

4. The broades standards are those of the Discrimination (Employment and Occupation) Convention (No. 111) and Recommendation (No. 111), adopted in 1958, whose aim is to deal with the overall problem of discrimination based on the various grounds most commonly encountered. Before that date, a number of instruments had been concerned with equality of rights in respect of certain matters or for certain categories of persons, for example those concerning freedom of association and the right to organise (1948, 1949), social policy in non-metropolitan territories (1947), migrant workers (1949) and equal remuneration for men and women (1951). Since 1958, the normative action of the International Labour Conference has continued on the basis of Convention No. 111 and Recommendation No. 111, expanding their principles in Conventions and Recommendations concerning particular categories of workers such as migrant workers (1975), older workers (1980), workers with family responsibilities (1981) and disabled persons (1983) and also in instruments dealing with certain matters such as employment policy (1964), human resources development (vocational training and guidance, 1975) and termination of employment (1982).

5. As will be seen further on, special support was given to the implementation of these standards - particularly those of Convention No. 111, which has been ratified by more than 100 countries - both through the normal procedures for supervising the application of conventions and recommendations and through the complaints and representations machinery which has been used on a number of occasions. Futhermore, shortly after the adoption of the 1958 instruments, the Organisation decided to supplement these regular methods by undertaking a special programme of practical activities designed to promote throughout the world knowledge of the problems of discrimination and of methods of combating it. In addition to these forms of broader action, the ILO has also tackled the problem of apartheid in South Africa through a Declaration on the subject, which was adopted in 1964 and updated in 1981, and through a special programme of action.

6. All these efforts form part of the overall action taken by the United Nations and the specialised agencies, with which the ILO has been associated, particularly in developing standards and procedures for their application. Instruments worth mentioning in this connection are the UNESCO Convention on the Eliminations of Discrimination in Education (1960) and, adopted under the auspices of the United Nations, the 1965 Convention on the Elimination of All forms of Racial Discrimination, the 1966 Covenants on Human Rights, the 1980 Convention on the Elimination of All Forms of Discriminations against Women and the Convention, currently in preparation, on the human rights of all migrant workers and their families.

II. GROUNDS OF DISCRIMINATION

A. Grounds referred to in Convention No. 111 and in Recommendation No. 111

7. The 1958 instruments concerning discrimination in respect of employment and occupation refer expressly to the following grounds of discrimination: race, colour, sex, religion, political opinion, national extraction and social origin (Article 1, paragraph 1(a), of the Convention.) They also provide that each country can include in its definition such other grounds of discrimination as it considers appropriate after consultation with employers' and workers' organisations (Article 1, paragraph 1(b)). It is thus clear that, while it appeared desirable to identify the most common and most disturbing grounds of discrimination by means of an enumeration such as that given above, the enumeration is not exhaustive and, generally speaking, the problem of discrimination results from any attempt to take account of factors having nothing to do with job requirements or personal abilities.

(1) Race, colour, national extraction and social origin

8. A common feature of these various grounds of discrimination is the fact that they are generally linked to the existence within a country of different ethnic groups or communities. It has been observed[2] that there is little difference between the criterion of race and that of colour, unless it is that racial barriers may exist between persons of the same colour. The term race does not have a very precise scientific definition, the essential point being the way in which the persons concerned consider their differences, and the attitudes resulting therefrom, in their relations with one another, particularly in so far as this concerns employment. Similar problems often arise, moreover, in the case of groups defined on the basis of religion, language or even regional origin or tribal associations (or other ethnic or cultural groupings); the latter ground is indeed expressly covered by the Social Policy (Basic Aims and Standards) Convention, 1962 (No. 117) which has reproduced the provision of the 1947 Convention on the same subject concerning non-metropolitan territories), in force in nerarly thirty countries, most of them in Africa. The United Nations Convention on the Elimination of All Forms of Racial Discrimination, adopted in 1965, and now in force in about 120 countries, refers generally to race, colour, descent and national or ethnic origin. As for the criterion of social origin, it may also result in similar phenomena where there exists a more or less rigid division of society into classes or 'castes'; in other cases the problem arises from hierarchic traditions or distinctions resulting from the family setting of from the educational methods employed.

9. Aside from avowedly discriminatory policies such as apartheid (see section VI) and manifestations of individual prejudice, problems frequently arise from the fact that certain social, racial or ethnic groups do not, in practice, enjoy the same opportunities for training and for economic and occupational advancement as other groups, **e.g.** for geographical reasons. As will be mentioned later, genuine discrimination may also exist if measures are not taken to remedy such situations.

10. The reference to national extraction in the 1958 instruments is designed to cover possible distinctions among nationals of a given country (for example, with reference to naturalised persons of foreign origin or between communities with ties to different national cultures), but not distinctions affecting foreigners as such. The position of foreign workers has also been considered to pose specific problems and is the subject of particular provisions in the Conventions and Recommendations concerning migrant workers (see below, paragraph 17).

(2) Sex

11. Discrimination based on sex - which means, in practice, discrimination against women - is certainly the form of discrimination that is most frequently encountered. This is why one of the first ILO instruments on equality of rights was the 1951 Conventions (No. 100) concerning Equal Remuneration for Men and Women Workers for Work of Equal Value . which is naturally one of the subjects also dealt with in Convention No. 111.

12. In the matter of access to and retention in employment, special questions have arisen with regard to the status of married women. The supervisory organs of the ILO have in fact considered that disqualification or exclusion of women on marriage constitute discrimination based on sex (in so far as they affect women and not men).[3]

As will be seen later, marital status or family situation as such were dealt with later in other instruments (see paragraphs 20, 21).

13. In 1975 - International Women's Year - , the International Labour Conference adopted a Declaration on Equality of Opportunity and Treatment for Women Workers which constitutes a sort of code of modern principles on the subject. This Declaration will be referred to later in connection with the question of 'protective' measures and the positive action that requires to be taken.

(3) Political opinion; religion

14. These two grounds of discrimination may be regarded as comparable in so far as they both apply to intellectual choices and are connected with protection of the right to freedom of conscience as it relates to employment. However, they also sometimes involve quite separate phenomena. Relations between communities of different faiths may give rise to problems similar to those which exist between racial or ethnic communities, as was mentioned above. In other cases the problem is more one of intolerance either in privacy practices or on the part of the State, as, for example, when there is a State religion or where the State is anti-religious, or again where activities of a public naturel are overly subject to the dictates of a single or dominant political party.

15. The supervisory organs of the ILO have pointed out that protection against discrimination based on political opinion must necessarily apply to the expression or demonstration of such opinion, since protection afforded for opinions alone, which were neither expressed nor demonstrated, would be pointless.[4] The same argument can be applied to religion and the practice of religion. Difficult problems have nevertheless arisen in connection with requirements which may be justified by the demands of certain types of employment (in the civil service, for example, or in religious institutions) or those of State security (in the case of political activities), as will be seen further on in connection with authorised 'exceptions'.

B. Other grounds

16. Among the other grounds of discrimination in employment, some of the most commonly encountered are trade union membershp and trade union activities: these are mentioned here only for the record, as this question is considered rather to be one aspect of the protection of trade unions rights, collective bargaining and the representation of workers; it is dealt with in Conventions and Recommendations concerning these matters, particularly in the Right to Organise and Collective Bargaining Convention, 1949 (No. 98).

(1) The situation of migrant workers

17. Because countries generally have special regulations governing employment of aliens, discrimination against migrant workers is dealt with in the instruments on that subject. Equality of treatment in the application of labour and social security legislation was called for in a special provision of the Migration for Employment Convention (Revised), 1949 (No. 97) (Article 6). Broader provisions were adopted in 1975 with the Migrant Workers' (Supplementary Provisions) Convention (No. 143) and the Migrant Workers' Recommendation (No. 151). As regards the promotion of equal opportunity and treatment in general practice, these standards are based on the concepts of the 1958 instruments. They also include provisions specially designed to take account of the special characteristics and needs of foreign workers (having regard to linguistic, cultural and other problems) so as to enable them to enjoy effective and not purely formal equality. They allow restrictions on certain aspects of the employment of foreigners (particularly employment in posts connected with the interests of the State), but they limit to two years, as a rule, any other restrictions on freedom of choice of employment (this rule is in advance of the legislation of a number of countries, including countries in Western Europe). Another important feature of these standards is the fact that they specify the minimum equality of rights which must be enjoyed even by migrant workers who are in an irregular situation (other provisions of the Convention deal with the repression of unlawful or clandestine practices involving migrant labour). Perhaps because its aims are set too high for the present, Convention No. 143 has not yet been widely ratified (13 countries), but, together with Recommendation No. 151, it has clearly had a major impact on the general trend of thinking, demands and practices in this field.

(2) Age

18. Discrimination based on age has become a matter of increasing concern in many countries in recent decades and the International Labour Conference dealt with this subject in a special part of the Older Workers Recommendation, 1980 (No. 162), which is designed to supplement the 1958 instruments on this point. The Recommendation applies to 'all workers who are liable to encounter difficulties in employment and occupation because of advancement in age'. It defines, in terms comparable to those of the 1958 instruments, the measures to be taken to prevent any discrimination in employment against older workers, having regard to the special nature of their situation due to age, the need for adjustment of working conditions and the nature of their problems of access to retirement.

19. Does the setting of a mandatory retirement age constitute discrimination based on age? It is interesting to note that Recommendation No. 162 tackles this question somewhat cautiously. It recommends adoption of the principle that retirement should be on a voluntary basis and that the age of entitlement to old-age benefits should be made more flexible; it also recommends that legislative and other provisions making mandatory the termination of employment at a specified age should be examined in the light of the principle of non-discrimination.

(3) Marital status, family situation and family responsibilities

20. These causes of discrimination, which are closely linked with the obstacles encountered by women in the area of employment, were tackled as such in the Convention (No. 156) and Recommendation (No. 165) concerning workers with family responsibilities, which were adopted in 1981. The Conference had earlier adopted (in 1965) a Recommendation concerning the Employment of Women with Family Responsibilities. This was made redundant by the new standards which relate to workers of both sexes in accordance with the modern concept of the sharing of family responsibilities. Under these new standards, men and women workers must be enabled to exercise their right to obtain or engage in employment without being subject to discrimination because of their family responsibilities and, to the extent possible, 'without conflict between their employment and family responsibilities'. Various measures are recommended with a view to avoiding 'direct or indirect' discrimination based on marital status, family situation or family responsibilities in the areas of training and employment and to encourage appropriate adjustments of working conditions (e.g. flexible working hours, parental leave), social security, child-care services and family aid.

21. It should be noted that the Termination of Employment Convention, 1982 (No. 158), includes among the causes which do not constitute valid reasons for termination of employment, in addition to those referred to in Convention No. 111, marital status, family responsibilities, pregnancy and absence from working during maternity leave (Article 5, paragraphs (d) and (e)).

(4) Disability

22. Persons whose capability is reduced by physical or mental handicap often encounter discrimination even in respect of jobs which their handicaps would in no way prevent them from performing adequately, and they also need special help in order to enjoy equality of opportunity in employment which is adapted to their particular condition. The Vocational Rehabilitation and Employment (Disabled Persons) Convention, 1983 (No. 159), and Recommendation, 1983 (No. 168), attacked, **inter alia,** these causes of direct and indirect discrimination and recommended various measures designed to ensure effective equality of opportunity and treatment for such persons - without distinction of sex. These standards deal in particular with the measures fo assistance and the adjustments needed in the areas of training, employment and working conditions and also with the encouragement to be given to employers. They do not refer expressly to the question of the obligations to employ handicapped workers which have been introduced in certain countries (and which seem generally more acceptable than quotas based on sex or origin), but they specify that 'special positive measures aimed at effective equality of opportunity and treatment between disabled workers and other workers shall not be regarded as discriminating against other workers'.

III. DEFINITIONS OF DISCRIMINATION

23. The Convention (No. 111) and the Recommendation (No. 111) adopted in 1958 define discrimination as 'any distinction, exclusion or preference (based on one of the grounds which these instruments enumerate) which has the effect of nullifying or impairing equality of opportunity or treatment in employment or occupation'. The subsequent instruments relating to particular types of discrimination have referred, expressly or by implication, to this definition.

24. In the light of this definition, there may be said to be discrimination whenever - for reasons which should not be taken into consideration - a person does not have the full benefit of the same opportunities or treatment as are enjoyed by other persons in respect of employment or occupation. The definition given in the 1958 instruments takes account of the fact that equality of opportunity or treatment may be effected not only by negative attitudes, which are the most obvious ones, but also by 'preferences' which are often more difficult to detect. It covers both situations in which the equality is 'nullified' and those - more difficult to identify - where it is only 'impaired'.

25. Two aspects of the definition deserve particular emphasis. In the first place it applies to 'any' distinction, exclusion or preference, which means both to those which are the result of legislation and to those which arise in practice, including private practices, where national policy must also aim to eliminate discrimination.

26. Secondly, the definition refers to the 'effect' of these distinctions, exclusions or preferences on equality of opportunity or treatment and it is therefore not restricted to intentional discrimination specifically 'intended' to nullify or impair this equality. It may thus be deemed to include indirect discrimination, which may be the result of measures or practices unrelated to any discriminatory criterion but which, in the circumstances in which they apply, result in an inequality of opportunity or treatment based on race, sex or some other characteristic - as for example when requirements which cannot generally be met by persons of a particular sex or group are needlessly laid down, or when possible measures are not taken to enable such persons to cope with the requirements. As was mentioned earlier, certain conventions and recommendations adopted subsequent to those of 1958 and dealing with particular causes of discrimination refer expressly to 'direct or indirect' discrimination.

27. Another element of the definition refers to the areas to which it applies: 'in employment or occupation'. Convention No. 111 indicates that these terms include access to vocational training, access to employment and to particular occupations, and terms and conditions of employment (Article 1, paragraph 3), which - as the supervisory organs pointed out - covers all matters relating to labour and employment.
Recommendation No. 111 specifies as follows the matters in respect of which all persons should, without discrimination, enjoy equality of opportunity and treatment (paragraph 2):
  (i) access to vocational guidance and placement services;
  (ii) access to training and employment of their own choice on the basis of individual suitability for such training or employment;
  (iii) advancement in accordance with their individual character, experience, ability and diligence;
  (iv) security of tenure of employment;
  (v) remuneration for work of equal value;
  (vi) conditions of work including hours of work, rest periods, annual holidays with pay, occupational safety and occupational health measures, as well as social security measures and welfare facilities and benefits provided in connection with employment.
It also points out that there should be no discrimination in respect of admission to, retention of membership in or participation in the affairs of employers' and workers' organisations.

28. Other instruments adopted later, in 1958, such as those mentioned above, contained similar listings of matters in respect of which there must be no discrimination, sometimes with adaptations necessitated by the nature of the subject dealt with (**e.g.** migrant workers and older workers).

29. The application of the principles of non-discrimination and equality of opportunity in certain matters is also required or explained by special instruments, such as those dealing with employment policy (Convention No. 122 and Recommendation No. 122), vocational guidance and training (Convention No. 142 and Recommendation No. 150) and termination of employment (Convention No. 158 and Recommendation No. 166).

IV. MEASURES WHICH ARE NOT DEEMED TO BE DISCRIMINATION

30. Instead of referring to 'exceptions', Conventions No. 111 and Recommendation No. 111 explain that certain measures 'shall not be deemed to be discrimination'. These explanations constitute more a definition of the features of the concept of discrimination than an indication of derogations: if there is a valid justification for a distinction, the latter is not a 'discrimination'.

(1) Qualifications required for a particular job

31. 'Any distinction, exclusion or preference in respect of a particular job based on the inherent requirements thereof shall not be deemed to be discrimination' (Article 1, paragraph 2, of the Convention and the corresponding provision of the Recommendation). It is necessary, therefor, to see in what cases and to what extent it is legitimate to take account of considerations of race or origin, of sex, of religion, etc., because of the inherent requirements of a particular job. The supervisory organs of the ILO have noted that there is no instance of a case where considerations of race or origin fall in this category (except cases related for example to establishments or artistic activities devoted to the culture of certain ethnic groups). As regards nationality, the Migrant Workers (Supplementary Provisions) Convention, 1975 (No. 143), recognises that this may lead to restriction of access to limited categories of employment or functions where this is necessary in the interests of the State (Article 14, paragraph (c)). Sex has more frequently been regarded as a legitimate ground for distinction in certain types of employment, but this issue is largely connected with the 'protection' measures which will be considered further on. Furthermore, the concepts in this area are by no means rigid and are in fact evolving rapidly. Many occupations in which only a few years ago it seemed perfectly legitimate to employ only men or only women are now generally accessible without distinction as to sex. The demands for equality of opportunity and, even more, simply for freedom of choice of employment have become increasingly determining. The supervisory organs of the ILO have had to deal in particular with the problems involved where account is taken of considerations of religion or political opinion.

32. As regards religion, national legislation may justifiably define as non-discriminatory measures restricting access to employment connected with a specific religion to persons belonging to that religion. However, in connection with a case which was the subject of a representation made under Article 24 of the ILO's Constitution, the Committee set up by the Governing Body to examine this representation observed[5] that regard must be had only to the inherent requirements of the particular job, in other words to the actual duties of the job in question and, when necessary, to the bearing of these duties on the employing institution's objectives. The exception clause should therefore be applied only in the case of jobs which by their very nature involve a special responsibility to contribute to the attainment of the institution's objectives. In other words, a religious requirement should not apply to the holding of all jobs in an institution connected with the religion concerned; on the contrary, the nature of the particular job must be taken into account.

33. As regards political opinion, the supervisory organs have recognised, for example, that this factor can be taken into consideration as one ofthe necessary qualifications for certain higher civil service posts involving special responsibility for the execution of governement policy. Beyond certain limits, however, this practice would come into conflict with the provisions of the Convention. The Committee of Experts on the application of Conventions and Recommendations has expressed the view that 'special requirements for certain specified forms of employment may relate to the reliability or restraint which may be expected from their incumbents in political matters', provided the scope of these requirements remains within limits compatible with the general meaning of the Convention (see paragraph 15). Representations made under Article 24 of the Constitution with regard to the situation in certain countries gave an opportunity for the Committee set up by the Governing Body to examine them to explain the scope of these principles, also in connection with the idea of protection of the security of the State, as will be seen below.

(2) Protection of the security of the State

34. Under the standards adopted in 1958 'measures affecting an individual who is justifiable suspected of, or engaged in, activities prejudicial to the security of the State shall not be deemed to be discrimination, provided that the individual concerned shall have the right to appeal to a competent body established in accordance with national practice' (Article 4 of the Convention and paragraph 7 of the Recommendation). This clause is designed to avoid the possibility that persons might actually engage in activities running counter to the security of the State under cover of the principles of non-discrimination, and also to establish conditions and safeguards to prevent measures taken on State security grounds from enfringing these principles.

35. In the first place, the measures in question must be taken in the light of individual activities, and not merely on the basis of membership of a particular group or community; the concept of State security must also be interpreted in a sufficiently strict sense. The supervisory organs of the ILO have drawn attention to the fact that 'in protecting workers against discrimination on the basis of political opinion, the Convention implies that this protection shall be afforded to them in respect of activities expressing or demonstrating opposition to the established political principles' (see paragraph 15). In connection with representations made under Article 24 of the Constitution, they held, for example, in one case, that endorsement by workers of a document criticising the policy of the Government should not be considered in itself as constituting an activity against the security of the State or incompatible with the requirements of their employment.[6] In another case they pointed out that investigation of the 'loyalty to the Constitution' of applicants for employment in the public service should not cause the applicants to be rejected simply on the basis of their membership of an organisation regarded as 'hostile' to the Constitution and that the investigation should be limited to special cases in which there are 'serious and justified doubts regarding the reliability or restraint which may be expected from applicants ... with particular reference to the nature of the posts which they are to occupy'.[7]

36. Another guarantee provided for is the existence of a right of appeal to a competent body. This guarantee naturally implies that the law

which the said body is to apply shall meet the necessary basic requirements. In connection with a complaint filed under Article 26 of the
Constitution of the ILO, the Commission appointed to consider it
concluded that the many dismissals which took place following a major
change of the political régime had not satisfied the requirements of
Article 4 of the Convention because the special bodies established 'were
not governed by clear provisions enabling them to examine the substance
of the case. They did not provide sufficient guarantees for the adequate
consideration of exonerating factors, nor did they facilitate the presen-
tation of evidence by the appelants ... Lthey] did not provide the
guarantees which should normally exist to prevent, or to obtain the
reversal of, dismissals based on political opinion rather than on activities
which were in fact prejudicial to the security of the State or on other
legitimate grounds for dismissal'.[8] The Commission requested that
these measures should be reviewed and the normal supervisory organs
have continued to follow this question.

(3) Special measures of protection

37. Article 5 of the Convention provides that special measures of
protection or assistance provided for in other ILO Conventions or
Recommendations shall not be deemed to be discrimination. Furthermore each country may define as non-discriminatory other 'special
measures designed to meet the particular requirements of persons who,
for such reasons such as sex, age, disablement, family responsibilities
or social or cultural status, are generally recognised to require special
protection or assistance'.

38. It is mainly in connection with grounds of sex that the problem has
arisen of the relations between the so-called 'protective' measures and
direct or indirect discrimination. In addition to the ILO standards which
prohibit the employment of women for tasks or for the handling of
substances prejudicial to maternity, there are others relating to such
matters as night work and underground work in mines. Some countries
have denounced the Conventions on these subjects on the ground that
they are no longer adapted to changing concepts of equality and
changing customs and working conditions. Other countries have remained
attached to these instruments and have pointed out that the requirements for elimination of the abuses these Conventions were designed
to deal with are still far from satisfied everywhere, particularly in the
developing countries. The prohibitions which are the result of national
legislative action vary in scope with local conditions, but the supervisory organs of the ILO have frequently draw attention to the need
to review the justification for many of them.
    The United Nations Convention on the Elimination of Discrimination
against Women adopted a rather restrictive position on this subject.
The Declaration on equality of opportunity and treatment for women
workers, adopted by the International Conference in 1975, calls for
protection aimed at improvement of the conditions of all employees
and states that special measures for the benefit or women should be
taken only for work proved to be potentially prejudicial to reproduction

- and that such measures should be reviewed periodically in the light of advances in scientific knowledge.

39. Special measures of assistance based on grounds such as social or cultural level may also be taken to meet the particular needs of certain population groups. In India such measures have taken the form, **inter alia,** of the reservation of jobs for members of certain castes (including the former 'untouchables'), on the ground that in the absence of such measures these persons would have no likelihood of gaining employment. This is a particular aspect of the more general problem of the justification for 'reserve discrimination', which is sometimes advocated as an active means of promoting equality of opportunity. This question is examined below, as well as that of special measures of preference or equitable representation (see paragraph 48).

V. POSITIVE MEASURES DESIGNED TO ELIMINATE DISCRIMINATION

(1) General principles

40. Under the 1958 Convention (Articles 2 and 3), each country has to 'declare and pursue a national policy designed to promote, by methods appropriate to national conditions and practice, equality of opportunity and treatment in respect of employment and occupation, with a view to eliminating any discrimination in respect thereof'. To this end, it is required:
(a)   to seek the co-operation of employers' and workers' organisations and other appropriate bodies in promoting the acceptance and observance of the policy;
(b)   to enact such legislation and to promote such educational programmes as may be calculated to secure the acceptance and observance of the policy;
(c)   to repeal any statutory provisions and modify administrative instructions or practices which are inconsistent with the policy;
(d)   to pursue the policy in respect of employment under the direct control of a national authority;
(e)   to ensure observance of the policy in the activities of vocational guidance, vocational training and placement services under the direction of a national authority.

41. Emphasis is thus placed on the positive aspect of the measures to be taken. Naturally, it is not sufficient for the State to refrain from practising discrimination itself in its laws and administrative practices. It must strive to eliminate it in relations between private individuals and it must encourage development of the basic conditions which will enable all to benefit from equality of opportunity to obtain training and employment, so as to eliminate any source of direct or indirect discrimination.

42. As was seen earlier, other conventions and recommendations have applied the same ideas, adapting them to particular types of discrimination (**e.g.** migrant workers and older workers) or specifying how they are to be applied in certain areas (such as vocational training).

43. As regards legislative and educational action designed to end discriminatory practices, Recommendation No. 111 states in its paragraph 4 that 'Appropriate agencies, to be assisted where practicable by advisory committees composed of representatives of employers' and workers' organisations, where such exist, and of other interested bodies, should be established for the purpose of promoting application of the policy in all fields of public and private employment, and in particular
a) to take all practicable measures to foster public understanding and acceptance of the principles of non-discrimination;
(b) to receive, examine and investigate complaints that the policy is not being observed and, if necessary by conciliation, to secure the correction of any practices regarded as in conflict with the policy; and
(c) to consider further any complaints which cannot be effectively settled by conciliation and to render opinions or issue decisions concerning the manner in which discriminatory practices revealed should be corrected.'

44. The link established here between legislative action and educational action is significant. Attention has been drawn[9] to the educational value of legal standards. Their public character and the fact that they emanate from the highest organs of the State or the economy, are usually the work of the sovereign representative body and draw their strength from an executive with wide powers over public and economic life, from the authority and prestige of the judiciary or from the will of the employers' and workers' organisations as expressed in their policies and negotiations covering wide sectors of economic and social life gives these standards, irrespective of their actual legal content, an exceptionally great potential influence and ability to attract public support and approval for a national policy of equality in respect of employment.

45. Educational action can and must also take over from legal standards or supplement them effectively: codes of practice have, for example, been circulated in various countries for the purpose of clarifying the scope of legislation and explaining to employers, trade unions and governmental agencies the measures they can take (voluntarily or under mutual supervision) in routine activities connected with employment and the determination of working conditions, in order to avoid direct or indirect discrimination and to promote equality of opportunity (see also paragraphs 49 and 57 below).

46. The national policies that will promote the means of establishing the practical requirements for equality of opportunity for different categories of persons are explained, **inter alia,** in the instruments on employment policy (Convention No. 122 and Recommendation No. 122) and in those on human resources development (Convention No. 142 and Recommendation No. 150). Human Resources Developments Recommendation, 1975 (No. 150), contains several detailed sections on the measures to be taken in respect of particular population groups: persons lacking schooling; older workers; linguistic and other minority groups; handicapped and disabled persons; women; and migrants. As was noted earlier, instruments concerned with certain of these categories contain provisions on this subject and on the adaptations of working conditions that are necessary in order to take account of the special needs of these persons and without which they could not enjoy genuine equality of opportunity (**e.g.** workers with family responsibilities, older workers, disabled persons).

(2) The question of special measures designed to give preference or ensure equitable representation

47. How acceptable are positive preferences as a means of promoting equality in respect of employment? Apart from their reference to special measures of assistance which, as was seen earlier, may involve, **inter alia**, the reservation of certain forms of employment for specific underprivileged groups, Convention No. 111 and Recommendation No. 111 of 1958 do not expressly regulate this matter. Nor do the other ILO instruments concerning equality of rights and opportunity in employment. However, the 1983 instruments concerning disabled persons make special provision for 'special positive measures aimed at effective equality of opportunity and treatment' and the 1975 Declaration on equality for women workers states that 'Positive special treatment during a transitional period aimed at effective equality between the sexes, shall not be regarded as discriminatory'.

48. The nature of the measures involved may vary considerably, ranging from special efforts to develop resources and infrastructures which certain groups lacked and thus to equalise certain basic conditions, to 'quota' systems or systems of systematic preference in access to training or employment. The first type of measures is certainly the least debatable (it is implicit, moreover, in the idea of promoting equality of opportunity and eliminating indirect discrimination); the second is sometimes termed 'reverse discrimination',[10] which implies that it is to be regarded somewhat unfavourably. This measure must be used prudently, in circumstances where it is justified and which make it generally acceptable to all groups, for otherwise it is liable to have effects which are the reverse of those in principle aimed at. The supervisory organs of the ILO have indicated that they intend to examine the validity of these systems on a case-by-case basis, identifying those which aim to ensure a fair degree of proportional representation in employment and those which aim to promote the advancement of groups previously disadvantaged in certain activities.[11]

49. An intermediate formula which may prove effective, without having the drawbacks of rigid quotas, is the setting of simple numerical targets to be used for statistical monitoring and with which the burden of proof may be reversed, the training organisation or employer being required to justify any imbalance by showing that they have made every effort to find qualified candidates in all groups or in either sex.

Such systems may be of value both as an incentive to encourage the elimination of imbalances or **de facto** segregation in employment and also as a means of evaluation and monitoring that is sufficiently flexible to be adapted to different circumstances. While there are no provisions of conventions or recommendations on this subject, such measures were among those advocated - in the light of the experience of a number of countries - in the context of the ILO's educational efforts designed to increase knowledge of practical means of applying the standards on equality of opportunity (see paragraph 57 below).

VI. INTERNATIONAL METHODS OF APPLICATION

(1) Methods based on the general procedures for international labour standards

50. Without going into the detail of these procedures, it is worth noting certain points regarding their use and their effectiveness in efforts to eliminate discrimination. The Constitution of the International Labour Organisation provides for various procedures designed to encourage ratification of the Conventions and application of standards generally (Article 19), including examination of the application of Conventions which have been ratified (Article 22).

These procedures involve action by a Committee of Experts on the Application of Conventions and Recommendations and a Tripartite Committee of the Conference on the same subject, which meet annually. In addition there are representation procedures (Article 24) and complaints procedures (Article 26), which allow not only governments but also employers' or workers' delegates or organisations to call for the examination of cases involving the application of Conventions which a country has ratified.

51. In order to promote ratification of Convention No. 111, it was decided, first of all, to request those countries which had not yet ratified it to furnish reports every four years under Article 19 of the Constitution. This special request is additional to the possibilities of normal use of this procedure, which enabled the Committee of Experts to submit comprehensive studies concerning the 1958 instruments on two occasions, in 1963 and in 1971, thus already encouraging ratification of the Convention. The above-mentioned decision was taken following the adoption by the Conference in 1977 of a resolution on human rights recalling that non-discrimination is a basic principle of the ILO's Constitution, whose furtherance constitutes a constitutional obligation for all the Member States. According to this decision, ratification should be a measure giving specific effect to the general obligation which already arises from the Constitution. These special quadrennial reports were examined by the Committee of Experts on two occasions, in 1980 and 1984. It should be noted that Convention No. 111 has now been ratified by 106 countries.

52. Secondly, the application of Convention No. 111 by the countries which have ratified it must be the subject of detailed reports made under Article 22 of the Constitution every two years (the same periodicity as for certain other basic conventions; whereas the periodicity is now four years as a general rule). In cases where special problems arise, a detailed report may be required every year. The Committee of Experts has always submitted numerous comments on the application of this Convention, with the aim, **inter alia**, of supporting or drawing attention to developments and progress and thus furthering the general efforts of the Member States. Convention No. 111 and Convention No. 100 are among those in respect of which the Committee has in recent years most frequently noted that national measures have been taken following its comments.[12]

53. Finally, the complaints procedures (Article 26) and the representation procedures (Article 24) have been used on several occasions in connection with Convention No. 111; they have enabled investigating commissions or committees set up by the Governing Body to examine cases that were particularly striking or which raised particularly important questions of principle, and to submit recommendations with a view to overcoming certain difficulties. The action taken on these recommendations is then considered by the normal supervisory bodies, which have been able to press for their implementation and, where appropriate, to note their impact.

54. The effectiveness of all these procedures is clearly based primarily on moral pressure, especially that exerted through discussion in the tripartite Committee of the Conference, but they do eventually produce results, particularly in matters connected with non-discrimination (as well as other fundamental rights), where there is particular sensitiveness to criticism.

(2) Special programmes of practical activities

55. Shortly after the adoption of Convention No. 111 in 1958, it was decided to establish a programme of special activities to further the practical application of the principles of non-discrimination in all countries.

56. A proposal to establish a complaints procedure comparable to the procedure for complaints regarding freedom of association, which would apply to every country, whether it had ratified the Convention or not, failed to secure adoption and it was considered more appropriate to undertake educational and promotional activities. These took the form of research, publications, the systematic dissemination of information, meetings of experts, symposia and seminars, all designed to increase knowledge of the problems of discrimination and inequality of opportunity and of the methods which may be used to overcome them. These activities are regularly monitored by a special committee of the Governing Body, the Committee on Discrimination.

57. Recent practical activities have involved the formulation of suggestions for guidelines or Codes of practice for avoiding direct or indirect discrimination and ensuring equality of opportunity in the various aspects of recruitment, selection, training and promotion and adapting working conditions and other terms of employment, in order to furnish international bodies, employers and trade unions with directives and methods of evaluation for use in everyday practice (see, above, paragraphs 45, 49 and 57). The dissemination and development of these suggestions have been supported by the holding of a series of triparte seminars, pending their publication in a more official form.

58. It is also necessary to bear in mind the fact that all the practical activities of the International Labour Organisation, and particularly its technical co-operation activities, take account of the need to promote equality of opportunity or to contribute directly thereto, and that many of them aim especially to promote the rights of migrant workers, women, the disabled, older workers and other special categories of workers.

59. In 1973 the Governing Body adopted - on a proposal by its Committee on Discrimination - rules for considering 'requests for special studies' which might be submitted by governments or employers' or workers' organisations on matters connected with the elimination of discrimination in employment. This procedure is not restricted to the case of countries which have ratified Conventions No. 111.

Later, it was indicated that it could apply, **inter alia**, in the case of migrant workers. This possibility might be compared with the procedure for complaints regarding the right of association, but it has not as yet seen any similar developments.[13]

60. In any case, special investigations ordered by the Conference or by the Governing Body (Article 10 of the Constitution) may have to be made by the International Labour Office in this field. This was the case in connection with the situation of Arab workers in the territories occupied by Israel since 1967, following resolutions adopted by the Conference in 1974 and in 1980. Annual reports on this subject have been prepared since 1978 on the basis of missions sent to the area with the consent of the various governments concerned.

(3) Special action against apartheid

61. It is possible to mention here only the main features of this action, a subject which in fact calls for a detailed review. [14] This action is based on the 'Declaration concerning the policy of apartheid in South Africa', originally adopted in 1964 and updated by the Conference in 1981. Apartheid was, quite naturally, firmly condemned in this Declaration as contrary to the fundamental principles of the Constitution of the ILO. Since 1964 (when South Africa withdrew from the Organisation), special reports have been submitted annually to the Conference on this subject for the purpose of study of the harm caused by this policy in the field of labour and promotion of international action for its elimination. Since 1981 the Declaration provides that governments, employers' and workers' organisations shall be requested to provide information on action taken to bring about a change of policy in South Africa, in accordance with recommendations made to them on this subject in an appendix to the updated Declaration. A special report on apartheid analysing this information is considered by a Committee on Apartheid which has since been set up at each session of the Conference. This Committee presents conclusions regarding the further action it wishes to recommend. These procedures for study and encour-agement of action are therefore to some degree analogous to those established for the application of conventions and recommendations.

62. Another innovation of the Declaration as updated in 1981 was the inclusion of a detailed programma of assistance to those affected by apartheid, through States neighbouring South Africa, national liberation movements and independent trade unions in South Africa (where Black workers have recently been granted trade union rights, although these are strictly controlled by various police and security measures). A broad range of technical co-opeation activities in this connection have been undertaken by the ILO in order to palliate the effects of apartheid and to lend support to those seeking to put an end to that system. A special Tripartite Conference convened by the Governing Body in Lusaka in May 1984, was requested to review the efforts made and the results achieved since the adoption of the new Declaration in 1981.

63. All these ILO standards and activities aimed at the elimination of discrimination and the promotion of equality in employment have, over the years, gone hand in hand with and supported the considerable change in attitudes which has occurred throughout the world on this subject. Their impact, while not directly measurable, is evident from many revealing signs of their influence based on public discussion, serious technical study and moral authority. [15] The number of ratifications, the effects - both dissuasive and corrective - of the monitoring systems, and the reference instruments which the ILO standards and other publications constitute for employers' and workers' organisations, including the trade unions, are different aspects of this impact. There is, of course, always a gap between the progress of ideas and their translation into practice. The requirement for non-discrimination and equality of opportunity is now a source of increasingly intensive study and increasingly insistent demands. The development of standards and activities on the basis of tripartite discussions and reciprocal verification among governments, exployers and workers at the inter-national level can certainly be regarded as a sound means, not only of expressing these requirements and demands, but also of helping to translate them in national situations.

NOTES

1. Cf. C. Rossillion: **Droit social international à vocation universelle,** (Juris-Classeur droit international, fasc. 574 - A), 1977, avec mise à jour 1984; N. Valticos: **International Labour Law** (Deventer, Kluwer) 1979, **Droit international du travail,** Dalloz, 2nd edition, 1983.

2. 'Discrimination in respect of employment and occupation', Part Three of the report of the Committee of Experts on the Application of Conventions and Recommendations, International Labour Conference, 47th Session, Geneva, 1963, paragraph 23. (Most of the explanatory comments given in sections II, III and IV of the text are reflected in this report).

3. See, for example, the comments on this subject in the Report of the Committee of Experts on the Application of Conventions and Recommendations, 1977, p. 233, and 1981, p. 175, which take note of measures taken by the Governments of Switzerland and Malta further to previous comments of the Committee.

4. **Idem.,** 1972, p. 204.

5. Report of the Committee set up to examine the representation presented by the Norwegian Federation of Trade Unions (LO) concerning the application of Convention No. 111 by the Government of Norway, ILO, Governing Body, 22nd Session (March 1983), document GB.222/18/23 (especially paragraph 29).

6. Report of the Committee set up to consider the representation presented by the ICFTU alleging non-observance of the Convention (No. 111) by Czechoslovakia, ILO, **Official Bulletin,** Supplement, Vol. LXI, 1978, Series A, No. 3 (especially paragraph 21).

7. Report of the Committee set up to consider the representation presented by the WFTU alleging non-observance of the Convention (No. 111) by the Federal Republic of Germany, ILO, **Official Bulletin,** Vol. LXIII, 1980, Series A, No. 1 (especially paragraph 40).

8. Report of the Committee appointed under Article 26 of the Constitution of the International Labour Organisation to examine the observance by Chile of ... the Discrimination (Employment and Occupation) Convention, 1958 (No. 111), ILO, 1975, (especially paragraphs 174 and 175).

9. **Equality in respect of Employment under Legislation and Other National Standards,** ILO, 1967, p. 7 - special national procedures relating to discrimination in employment, ILO, 1981.

10. James E. Jones: 'Reverse discrimination' in employment: Judicial treatment of affirmative action programmes in the United States, **International Labour Review,** Vol. 120, No. 4, July-August 1981.

11. Discrimination in respect of employment and occupation, **op.cit.,** in note 2, paragraph 39 (references to the cases of India, Cyprus and Malaysia).

12. See, for example, **Report of the Committee of Experts on the Application of Conventions and Recommendations,** 1981, Part One: General Report, paragraph 92; idem., 1982, paragraph 92.

13. See C. Rossillion: ILO Examination of Human Rights Situations, New Procedures for Special Surveys on Discrimination, **Review of the International Commissions of Jurists,** No. 12, June 1974;

Les études spéciales de l'OIT sur l'élimination de la discrimination, **Revue des droits de l'homme,** Vol. VII, No. 2-4, 1974. In 1982, the Committee on Discrimination received a request concerning allegations of poltical discrimination in Uruguay, submitted by a workers' organisation in exile from that country. This case was the subject of some discussion by the Committee in 1983, on which occasion the Government supplied explanations and was invited to review its position.

14. **Apartheid and labour,** ILO, 1983.
15. **The impact of international labour Conventions and Recommen-dations,** ILO, 1977.

3. European Communities

J. Egger

INTRODUCTION

I. The term 'discrimination' and the EEC Treaty

1. As to the term 'discrimination' the Treaty founding the European Economic Community of 25 March 1957 provides as follows: The general principle of non-discrimination in European Community law is laid down in Art. 7 of the EEC Treaty and prohibits discrimination on grounds of nationality. This provision is established in the first part of the EEC Treaty and ranks among the principles of the Treaty, thus underlining the importance of the rule of non-discrimination, it is even called the 'Magna Charta' of the Treaty.[1]

A specification of Art. 7 of the EEC Treaty can be found in Art. 48 paragraph 2 of the Treaty by which - as a sub-case of the free movement of workers - prohibition of discrimination in labour law on grounds of nationality has been ordered. Finally, Art. 119 of the EEC Treaty laying down the principle of equal pay for men and women for equal work prohibits sex as a distinctive criterion.

II. Definition of discrimination

2. The term 'discrimination' originated from Anglo-American law. From there it was first incorporated into international law. Through the adoption of ideas deriving from American anti-trust laws it also penetrated national and international commercial law.

The term 'discrimination' derives from the Latin word 'discriminare' and means in its original wording that a differentiation has occurred.[2]

3. Not to discriminate, that is to say not to treat in a different way, means therefore the same as an obligation to treat equally. Hence it follows that a ban on discrimination which prohibits differentiation or differential treatment at the same time commands equal treatment. Consequently, the prohibition of discrimination represents a negatively expressed command of equal treatment.[3]

4. Discrimination in the meaning of an unjustified unequal treatment of persons or groups in an equal or comparable situation[4] may be of different types: Direct or overt discrimination means 'less favourable treatment on forbidden grounds', indirect or covert discrimination covers a situation where special treatment does not directly follow from nationality but nevertheless has essentially the same effect as it had, in fact, been directly connected with nationality,[5] **e.g.** if a provision refers to domicile or origin this may adversely affect foreigners.

PART I. THE EEC TREATY

§ 1. The general principle of non-discrimination

5. The EEC programme is based on the abolition in Member States of obstacles to freedom of movement for goods, persons, services and capital. In order to achieve this end the Treaty provides for a number of different measures. These measures as a whole may be referred to as the EEC non-discrimination principle. In this meaning, the Treaty in its entirety aims at non-discrimination.[6]

6. The primary aim of the rule of non-discrimination is an international division of labour. In a stricter sense the EEC non-discrimination principle has found expression in Art. 7 paragraph 1 of the EEC Treaty which has the following wording: 'Within the scope of application of this Treaty, and without prejudice to any special provisions contained therein, any discrimination on grounds of nationality shall be prohibited.'

7. Art. 7 concretises the general principle of non-discrimination of European Community law and prohibits discrimination on grounds of nationality. Nationality is generally considered to be the same thing as citizenship.[7]

8. The principle of non-discrimination also holds true in arenas where the Member States have limited obligations **e.g.** regarding social policy (Art. 117 of the EEC Treaty).[8]

9. By its wording Art. 7 not only prohibits the Member States from discriminatory treatment of the subjects of another Member State in favour of its own citizens, but also discriminatory treatment of its own nationals in favour of subjects of another Member State (discrimination à rebour), differentiation among nationals of other different Member States, differentiation among subjects of another Member State and subjects of third States and differentiation between subjects of different third States.[9]

10. The ban on discrimination is a general principle that has found expression in many other provisions of the Treaty and as such may be a rule for the interpretation of the Treaty.

11. The special provisions, for example Art. 48 of the EEC Treaty, are subordinate to the general principle of non-discrimination.

12. Art. 7 is immediately applicable law. The addressees of Art. 7 paragraph 1 are the Member States (legislature, administration, courts), the institutions of the Community and private persons.[10]
  Thus the EC Court of Justice[11] pronounced that the prohibition of discrimination on grounds of nationality applies not only to acts of

public authorities but also to rules of any other nature aimed at regulating gainful employment in a collective manner.

13. Art. 7 paragraph 1 not only establishes objective but also subjective rights; therefore a subject of another Member State may claim to be put in the same position as a native.

14. At present, discrimination on grounds of nationality is in question if the Member States, the institutions of the Community or a private person does discriminate on grounds of nationality (subjective theory). Art. 7 does not prohibit all differentiation but only arbitrary differentiation. In such a case discrimination may also be found if objectively differences between foreigners and natives could justify different treatment.

15. Moreover, Art. 7 in principle prohibits any regulation which grants preferential rights to foreigner (overt discrimination). Differentiation is permitted if based on objective grounds not contradictory to the EEC Treaty and its aims. The EC Court of Justice has stated[12] that the general principle of non-discrimination and Art. 7 only prohibit the treatment of comparable situations in a different way in so far as differentiation is not justified objectively.

Indirect (covert, disguised) discrimination - through any regulation which does not expressly refer to the fact of foreign status but primarily or solely concerns foreigners by referring to domicile or origin - is also prohibited by Art. 7 paragraph 1.

16. Differences between subjects of Member States which arise from the heterogeneity of national legal orders do not represent prohibited discrimination in the sense of European Community Law.[13] Such differences cannot be abolished by application of Art. 7 by the EC Court of Justice but only by special Directives.[14]

§ 2. Prohibition of discrimination in labour law according to Art. 48 paragrah 2 of the EEC Treaty

17. In the EEC Treaty prohibition of discrimination in labour law is not regulated as an independent legal rule but as a sub-case of the free movement of workers.

According to Art. 48 paragraph 2 of the EEC Treaty freedom of movement for workers shall entail the abolition of any discrimination based on nationality between workers of the Member States as regards employment, remuneration and other conditions of work and employment. This provision is a central regulation not only of the labour law regulations of the EEC Treaty but of European labour law generally.[15] **Ratio legis** is the establisment of a Common Labour Market free of national impediments.

18. In addition to the general rule of the free movement of workers, Art. 48 paragraph 3 of the EEC Treaty provides that public policy exceptions[16] may be made to limit that right on grounds of public policy, public security and public health. Arising from this, restrictions may also result for the prohibition of discrimination in labour law according to Art. 48 paragraph 2 of the EEC Treaty.[17]

19. In fulfilling Arts. 48 and 49 of the EEC Treaty a number of Regulations and Directives have been issued to abrogate all impediments of the laws of the Member States which are contrary to the free movement of workers within the Community. The central provision establishing absolute freedom of movement for workers within the Member States with regard both to labour market organisation and substantive law is Regulation No. 1612/68 of 15 October 1968[18] in the modified wording of Regulation No. 312/76 of 9 February 1976[19] on the freedom of movement for workers within the Community.

20. As a legal command Art. 48 paragraph 2 demands the abolition of differential treatment of workers by the Member States. It is a specific provision of labour law which as against Art. 7 of the EEC Treaty is considered **lex specialis.**

21. Art. 48 paragraph 2 only concerns unequal treatment on grounds of nationality. Differntiation on other grounds are not covered by these provisions. Thus differential treatment of nationals and foreigners is permitted if made because of less productive capacity or seniority, which can be relevant in the case of redundancy notices caused by circumstances within the enterprise.
    Religion and language may also be considered permitted grounds of differentiation if justified objectively.

22. Nevertheless, according to the jurisprudence of the EC Court of Justice[20] no indirect forms of discrimination are permitted to come into being: If **e.g.** a provision refers to origin or domicile, as a rule foreigners are concerned. Therefore, the fact is only relevant if a provision - singly or in connection with other circumstances - causes discrimination against a foreign national.

23. But Art. 48 paragraph 2 does not cover differences which result from the variety of national legal orders for persons subjected to Community Law.[21]

24. The prohibition of discrimination is immediately applicable. In the first line addressees are the Member States but it is also applicable to subjects of private law (Art. 7 paragraph 4 of Regulation No. 1612/68).[22]

25. Specific rules of equal treatment may also benefit family members. Art. 7 of Regulation No. 1251/70 of 29 June 1970 on the right of workers to remain in the territory of a Member State after having been employed in that state[23] extends the right to equal treatment laid down in Regulation No. 1612/68 to all persons granted the right to stay according to Regulation No. 1251/70.[24]

§ 3. The principle of equal pay

26. Art. 119 paragraph 1 of the EEC Treaty lays down the obligation of the Member States to establish and subsequently to retain the principle of equal pay for men and women for equal work in their legal orders.

Art. 119 paragraph 2 is very explicit in respect of the notion of 'equal pay': for the purposes of this Article, 'pay' means the ordinary basic or minimum wage or salary and other considerations, whether in cash or in kind, which the worker receives, directly of indirectly, in respect of his or her employment from his or her employer.[25]

According to the last paragraph of Art. 119 of the EEC Treaty 'equal pay without discrimination based on sex' means:
(a) that pay for the same work at piece-rates shall be calculated on the basic of the same unit of measurement; and
(b) that pay for work at time rates shall be the same for the same job.

27. Art. 119 of the EEC Treaty is a special provision which only creates conventional obligations between the Member States without granting competence to the organs of the EC themselves. These obligations were considered as conditions for fair competition and for the prevention of dumping within the Common Market. Thus Art. 119 obliges the Member States to apply and to maintain the principle of equal pay for men and women for equal work in accordance with the principle of the rate for the job principle.

28. This obligation, however, has encountered difficulties of the autonomy of the associations of employers and workers in collective bargaining over wages, the Governements of the Member States have no direct influence on the realisation of the pinciple of equal pay. Moreover, there are many industrial branches which employ a preponderance of women (**e.g.** the textile industry). It is true that these female workers are not discriminated against in relation to the few male workers within the same industrial branch; but in relation to other industrial branches it transpires that in such women's occupations branches illegal systems of differential pay rates do exist.

29. Over a long period of time the Commission of the EC has tried to master this problem of equal pay by Recommendations, which have no imperative power. On 30 December 1961, the Ministers for Social Affairs of the Member States agreed a procedure, by which all opportunities for judicial control existing in national law should be used in order to achieve equal pay for men and women in payment conventions. Moreover, collective conventions which do not comply with the principle of equal pay should not be extended to other persons by the administrative authorities if such an extension were possible.

30. These measures succeeded in some Member States. Thus, German as well as Italian jurisdiction derived the obligation of equal pay from constitutional provisions on equality of sex.[26] In Great Britain and in the Republic of Ireland equal pay has been assured by Equal Pay Acts. Nevertheless, in other Member States the respective measures were insufficient.[27] Therefore, on 12 February 1978 the Commission published a report on the application of the principle of equal pay for men and women.

31. Legislative activity has taken place to clarify and to extend this obligation (by way of Art. 100 EEC Treaty) and by the aid of Art. 235 EEC Treaty to lay down further principles of equal treatment of male and female workers beyond the principle of equal pay laid down in Art. 119. Thus Directive No. 75/117 of 10 February 1975 concerns the approximation of the laws of the Member States relating to the application of the principle of equal pay for men and women[28] while Directive No. 76/207 of 9 February 1976 concerns the implementation of the principle of equal treatment of men and women and regards access to occupation, vocational training and promotion and working conditions[29] and Directive No. 79/7 of 19 December 1978 concerns the realisation of equal treatment in the scope of social security step by step.[30]

32. But the question is whether the EC acts within its competence when it develops imperative powers in a field where the EEC Treaty only provides for contractual obligations between the Member States. It is true that Directive No. 75/117 is not based on Art. 119 of the EEC Treaty but on the subsidiary imperative power granted to the organs of the EC by Art. 100 of the EEC Treaty. But as a rule in international law, there exists a presumption in favour of national competences. When the implementation of the principle of equal pay for equal work is restricted to contractual obligations between the Member States by the EEC Treaty, one may doubt whether the organs of the EC may assume further competences in the same field.[31]

PART II. THE PROVISIONS IN DETAIL

33. A distinction must be made between the principle of non-discrimination in the Common Labour Market and the one concerning employment relationship.

§ 1. Equal treatment in the Common Labour Market

34. The main principle of the Common Labour Market is the guaranteed freedom of movement for all subjects of Member States to take up and to practise a dependent occupation in any other Member State under the same conditions as the indigenous population. The purpose and scope of free movement for workers are laid down in Regulation No. 1612/68 of 15 October 1968[32] whose Art. 1 gives all subjects of the Member States the unrestricted right to practise an occupation in paid labour or salary payment in all Member States regardless of their domicile according to the provisions of law and administrative regulations being in force in the host nation. With this is linked a claim to admission to vacant positions equal to the claim that native workers can lay.

This general provision is itemized closely in Arts. 2-6 of Regulation

No. 1612/68 by systematic prohibitions and commands. The right to non-discriminatory treatment concerning workers from other Member States was laid down in an overall and absolute sense by Arts. 7-9 of Regulation No. 1612/68. It covers both individual labour law and collective labour law, including eligibility for the shop committee and the power to practise leading functions in the trade unions but excluding participation in the administration of public corporations or holding public office. In consequence subjects of other Member States have no claim in Common Market law to be nominated as lay judges in the labour court.

35. According to Art. 7 paragraph 4 of Regulation No. 1612/68 provisions in individual labour contracts, work rules and collective agreements contrary to the EC rule of non-discrimination are void. Therefore, the question arises which terms of employement should replace the void provisions.

First of all the wording at Art. 7 paragraph 4 of Regulation No. 1612/68 clarifies the fact that voiding discriminating contractual provisions does not render the whole contract void.

If collective rules of law (collective agreements, factory agreements, schematic terms of employment) include a discriminatory provision, it arises from the purpose of the rule of non-discrimination that discriminatory void provisions are replaced by the provisions in force for native workers. For it is in the nature of collective rules of law that there can only be the two alternatives of prohibited, differentiating or equal treatment.

It is more difficult to answer the question asked in the case of discriminating provisions in individual labour law. This nullity must not bring about an assimilation of terms of employment with terms of employment concluded in the individual labour contract of the native workers. For it is in the nature of terms of employment concluded in the individual labour contract that differentiating treatment of workers must not, at the same time, be discriminatory. Thus native workers may in absolute terms be offered better individual terms of employment on grounds of qualification without regard to nationality.

Differentiation on material grounds, especially on grounds of qualifications, are not prohibited by Regulation No. 1612/68 because it only covers discrimination on grounds of nationality. An automatic assimilation in these cases would conflict with the principle of freedom of contract. No assimilation at all seems promising even if native workers are offered different individual terms of employment. It is uncertain at which level assimiliation should take place to be perfect. Therefore, only the three subsequent guiding principles can bring about a solution harmonising the rule of non-discrimination laid down in Regulation No. 1612/68 with the principle of freedom of contract:

(1) If discrimination against a subject of another Member State is founded on a disadvantageous replacement of written law which can be replaced by free agreement while native workers are not treated in this way, then this replacement is void; instead the respective legal regulation which can be replaced by free agreement is part of the contents of the labour contract.

(2) If a worker, who is a subject of another Member State can prove

that native workers can achieve a certain advantageous level of terms of employment by an individual labour contract without regard to their qualifications, this level takes the place of the void provisions of the contract.

(3) If a worker who is a subject of another Member State can prove that s/he has the same qualifications and when occasion arises the same performance as certain native workers, the terms of employment granted to the comparable native workers replace the void terms of employment.

36. The EC Court of Justice has established the following criteria of interpretation with regard to non-discrimination:

(1) If internal provisions of law which underlie legal claims are motivated by public national interests, it is not permitted to withhold these legal claims from workers who are subjects of other Member States. Thus the EC Court of Justice has stated[33] that an Italian national working in Germany and performing his military service in Italy has the same legal claims which are granted in the case of resumption of the occupation as a German performing his military service in Germany.

(2) The claim on non-discriminatory treatment does not only exist with regard to normative terms of employment but also with regard to **de facto** granted social benefits and advantages, all of which are given by the employer as voluntary benefits or by the state as discretionary benefits.[34] In this context it is of particular importance to observe the rule on non-discrimination even if workers who are subjects of other Member States are occupied in public administration, despite its exclusion from the Common Labour Market as laid down in Art. 48 paragraph 4 of the EEC Treaty. On the contrary the EC Court of Justice advocates the opinion that this exceptional provision only refers to equal admission of workers who are subjects of other Member States to an occupation in the civil service. If in spite of this a Member State employs such workers in its administration, the protective aim of the exceptional provision as laid down in Art. 48 paragraph 4 of the EEC Treaty is no longer appropriate. Weighing the respective interests the balance of the scales favours the individual claims of the worker on the basis of non-discrimination.[35]

(3) On the other hand the principle of non-discrimination only prohibits discrimination on grounds of nationality. Discrimination on other grounds which are justitief by the matter are permitted. Thus the EC Court of Justice has decided that differential allowances for workers domiciled at home and abroad respectively does not infringe the EC rule of non-discrimination if justified by the different purpose of the separation allowance, **e.g.** when the separation allowance is only paid in limited amounts to workers domiciled at home who are obliged to move to the place of employment, whereas it is paid without limit to workers domiciled abroad who do not have such a duty.[36]

A charge of discrimination on grounds of nationality has also arisen in the case of a professional sportsman belonging to an international association which dictates in its articles of association a specific nationality for persons who are to be bound by contract on the occasion of a sporting event, except for the selection of national teams.[37]

§ 2. Equal treatment and employment relationship

37. The organs of the Community have always focused their attention on the equal treatment of male and female workers. Although Art. 119 of the EEC Treaty alrealdy lays down the obligation under international law of the Member States to establish and subsequently to retain the principle of equal pay for men and women for equal work in their legal orders, manifold difficulties still remain in putting this principle into practice. In particular effective wages based on the freedom of contract and the so-called light-wages' categories of predominantly female professions have again and again **de facto** brought about discrimination against women in the wages sector. The organs of the Community saw in this both a distortion of competition, conditioned by the costs of wages which brings discredit upon the functioning of Common Market, and the impeding of social progress. Therefore, in 1975 they obliged the Member States by an initial Directive based on Art. 100 of the EEC Treaty to guarantee the principle of equal pay by intensified measures in the field of legislation. Referring to the fact that equal treatment of men and women is one objective of the Community aiming at an improvement of living and working conditions, the Council enacted a second Directive based on Art. 235 of the EEC Treaty in 1976 by which the Member States are obliged to guarantee equal treatment of men and women also in other fiels of working. These Directives provide for the following in detail:

A. Equal pay

38. Directive No. 75/117 of 10 February 1975 on the approximation of the laws of the Member States relating to the application of the principle of equal pay for men and women[38] leaves the obligation of the Member States on the application of equal pay based on Art. 119 of the EEC Treaty untouched. The EC Court of Justice[39] has stated that the principle of equal pay would be a directly binding right in the Member States according to Art. 119 of the EEC Treaty, that the concerned litigant parties could appeal on the basis of it to domestic courts and that the latter would be obliged to apply it to any range of facts. Within the more narrow area of direct discrimination, the national courts have a duty 'to ensure the protection of the rights which that provision vests in individuals, in particular in the case of those forms of discrimination which have their origin in legislative provisions or collective labour agreements, as well as where men and women receive unequal pay for equal work which is carried out in the some establishment or service, whether private or public'.

The Community Court envisaged a wider area of indirect discrimination. The complete implementation of Art. 119 would be of concern not only to 'individual undertakings but also to entire branches of industries and even the economic system as a whole'. Within this area, the implementation of Art. 119 'to extend to which such implementation is necessary... may be achieved by a combination of Community and national provisions'.[40]

Although Art. 119 of the EEC Treaty in its wording is formulated as a contractual obligation of the Member States under international law, the jurisdiction of the EC has no regard to the different constitutional regulations of transformation of contractual obligations of the Member States under international law into internal law but defines it as 'self-executing' according to Community law.

39. Therefore, the purpose of Directive No. 75/117 is only to realise the principle of equal pay in detail and to make its realisation practicable by additional measures: This is done in the following way:

(1) The principle of equal pay prohibits discrimination on grounds of sex for all elements of remuneration and conditions of remuneration [41] i.e. it has to be laid down in accordance with common criteria for men and women. In particular this principle has to be applied not only to equal work but also to equivalent work of men and women. The latter provision seems to be an attempt to put a stop to indirect discrimination against women by the formation of so-called light-wages' catgeories.

(2) The claim to equal pay must be claimable before the domestic courts.

(3) The internal legal system must provide that all provisions in tariff agreements, in other wage and salary agreements, above all in factory agreements and in individual employment contracts which are incompatible with the principle of equal pay are void or can be declared void.

(4) Notices or dismissals solely on the grounds that the worker raises his or her claim to equal pay out of court or in court are to be declared inadmissible by the national legal system.

(5) With regard to the workers an obligation to publish the applicable provisions on equal pay must be established.

(6) Moreover, the Member States have to take all necessary measures to abrogate internal provisions of law and administrative regulations contradictory to this Directive and to guarantee the realisation of the principle of equal pay. So the EC Court of Justice has stated that the Member States are obliged to institute an office which has the power to judge on the issue of whether one job is equivalent to another.

40. In several recent judgements the EC Court of Justice has dealt with the interpretation of the principle of equal pay for equal work.[42]

41. Regarding the scope of comparison in terms of time and space the following facts were laid before the Court:[43] A stockroom manageress was paid less than the man who had until some four months previously held the same position. She sought to establish a right to equal pay by means of a comparision with the former male employee. The EC Court, in its judgement of 27 March 1980, ruled that the principle of equal pay for equal work is not confined to situations in which man and women are contemporaneously doing equal work for the same employer.

42. As to equal pay and part-time work the EC Court of Justice has ruled[44] that a difference in rates of pay between full and part-time workers did not amount **per se** to discrimination prohibited by Art. 119: Such a difference could however amount to prohibited discrimination if it could be established that it was in reality only an indirect way of reducing the level of pay of part-time workers because they as a group consisted exclusively or predominantly of women.

43. It has to be called into question whether Directive No. 75/117 is in a position to resolve the various problems of equal pay for men and women.

Unresolved is the problem of establishing which criteria are to be used in deciding the equivalence of typical women's work to men's work. Questionable too is the problem of the relation of the obligation to equal pay as against freedom of contract in the area according to extra tariff and according to supratariff. Does this obligation restrict itself to an equalisation of men and women in industrial remuneration schemes in principle or does it supplant freedom of contract such that it is not permitted to make an agreement with individual women on special occasions about a more disadvantageous remuneration in the contract? The latter alternative does not seem justified by the matter because the employer may reach an agreement about individual differences of remuneration with individual male workers, too. Thus why not also among women or among individual women and men?

44. Nonetheless it is certain that such different individual agreements of remuneration are not allowed to be arbitrary because they would act contrary to faith and trust. Moreover, the special provisions in labour law concerning womens' safety are not a relevant motive for diminishing their remuneration.

B. Other equal treatment of men and women in working life

45. The EC Court of Justice has stated[45] that Art. 119 of the EEC Treaty may not be applied beyond the principle of equal pay analogously to other questions of equal treatment of men and women in working life: In the case Defrenne III the Court refused to accept that a contractual term requiring female employees to retire at the age of 40 amounted to discrimination in relation to pay, even though this term had pecuniary consequences in relation to the allowance on termination of service and the retirement pension.[46]

This gap was filled by Directive No. 76/207 of 9 February 1976 regarding the implementation of the principle of equal treatment of men and women as regards access to occupation, vocational training and promotion and working conditions[47] which is based on Art. 235 of the EEC Treaty. The contents of this long-winded Directive which tends to repetition can be summed up as follows:

(1) The Member States are obliged to abolish or respectively to hinder any direct or indirect discrimination on grounds of sex in working life. The different treatment of men and women on grounds of marital status or family status is also considered as prohibited

discrimination. The Directive explicitly prohibits the different treatment of sexes concerning access[48] to occupations or places of employment, regardless of whether it deals with public labour exchange or criteria of engagement under civil law, concerning preferments within the enterprise, vocational guidance, vocational education, vocational development of knowledge and retraining and concerning terms of employment belonging to collective law and individual labour law including the right of notice.

(2) The Directive exhaustively enumerates the cases of unequal treatment which are not considered as discrimination on grounds of sex: the proviso of occupations for the practice of which gender is an inevitable precondition; the special provisions for the protection of women, especially the protection of motherhood; and measures for the promotion of equality of opportunities for women.

(3) Regarding equal treatment the Directive orders the Member States to provide for similar supplementary measures as exist on equal pay based on Directive No. 75/117, i.e. judical suitability of the claim to equal treatment, legal nullity or the possibility of the annulment of discriminating measures, the prohibition of notice or dismissal because of the enforcement of the claim to equal treatment and the obligation of promulgation of the provisions relevant to the workers.

NOTES

1. See H.P. Ipsen, **Europäisches Gemeinschaftsrecht,** 2nd ed., Tübingen 1982, p. 592.
2. Cf. I. Bode, **Die Diskriminierungsverbote im EWG-Vertrag,** Göttingen 1968, p. 4.
3. R. Blanpain, 'Equality and Prohibition of Discrimination in Employment' in R. Blanpain (ed). **Comparative Labour Law and Industrial Relations,** Deventer 1982, p. 33 speaks of 'two sides of the same coin'.
4. Justitied unequal treatment is called differentiation.
5. Cf. B. Sundberg-Weitman, **Discrimination on Groups of Nationality,** Amsterdam 1977, p. 107.
6. Cf. B. Sundberg-Weitman, **op.cit.,** p. 10.
7. See B. Sundberg-Weitman, **op.cit.,** p. 93.
8. An objective understanding of Art. 117 of the EEC Treaty means that the Member States have a contractual obligation to co-operate in achieving the Community purpose of social progress; Cf. G. Schnorr and J. Egger, 'European Communities', in R. Blanpain (ed), **International Encyclopaedia for Labour Law and Industrial Relations,** Deventer 1980, p. 24.
9. Cf. A. Bleckmann, in von der Groeben, **Kommentar zum EWG-Vertrag,** 3rd ed., Baden-Baden 1983, p. 131.
10. Cf. A. Bleckmann, **Europarecht,** 3rd ed., Münster 1980, p. 336; EC Court of Justice No. 13/76, **Collection** 1976, p. 1333.
11. Case No. 36/74, **Collection** 1974, p. 1405.
12. Case 147/49, **Collection** 1980, p. 3005.
13. EC Court of Justice No. 126/82, **Collection** 1983, p. 73.

14. Cf. A. Bleckmann, in von der Groeben, **op.cit.**, p. 140.
15. Cf. G. Schnorr, 'Das arbeitsrechtliche Diskriminierungsverbot nach Art. 48 Abs. 2 EWG-Vertrag', **Arbeit und Recht** 1960, p. 161.
16. For details see D. O'Keeffe, 'Practical Difficulties in the Application of Art. 48 of the EEC Treaty', **Common Market Law Review** 1982, p. 35.
17. Cf. P. Karpenstein, in von der Groeben, **op.cit.**, p. 492.
18. OJ 1968, L 257.
19. OJ 1976, L 39.
20. Case No. 152/73, **Collection** 1974, p. 153.
21. EC Court of Justice No. 1/78, **Collection** 1978, p. 1489.
22. EC Court of Justice No. 32/75, **Collection** 1975, p. 1085.
23. OJ 1970, L 142.
24. Cf. EC Court of Justice No. 321/75, **Collection** 1975, p. 1085.
25. Therefore supra-tariff remuneration, premiums, commissions and gratifications etc. are covered by this provision.
26. Art. 3 paras 2 and 3 of the German Basic Law; Art. 37 of the Italian Constitution; see also the Preamble to the French Constitution and Art. 22 of the Greece Constitution.
27. In 1976 Denmark issued an Equal Pay Act; Equal Treatment Acts followed in 1977 (Italy) and in 1980 (Germany and Netherlands).
28. OJ 1975, L 45.
29. OJ 1976, L 39.
30. OJ 1979, L 6.
31. See G. Schnorr and J. Egger, **op.cit.**, p. 27.
32. OJ 1968, L 257.
33. EC Court of Justice No. 15/69, **Collection** XV, p. 363.
34. EC Court of Justice No. 9/74, **Collection** 1974, p. 773; No. 68/74, **Collection** 1975, p. 109 (claim on public training furtherance); No. 32/75, **Collection** 1975, p. 1085 (claim of widow of an alien railwayman on the same fare reductions which are conceded to native railwaymen and their family members); No. 65/81, **Collection** 1982, p. 33 (rent-free loans on the occasion of birth).
35. EC Court of Justice No. 152/73, **Collection** 1974, p. 153.
36. EC Court of Justice No. 152/73, **Collection** 1974, p. 153.
37. EC Court of Justice No. 36/74, **Collection** 1974, p. 1405; similar No. 13/76, **Collection** 1976, p. 1333.
38. OJ 1975, L 45.
39. Case No. 43/75, **Collection** 1976, p. 455.
40. See F. Schmidt, **Discrimination in Employment**, Stockholm 1978, p. 141.
41. If an employer rants in the case of retirement - without contractual obligation - special benefits in tourist traffic to male ex-workers without giving female ex-workers the same benefits this is considered as discrimination according to Art. 119 of the EEC Treaty: Judgement of the EC Court of Justice No. 12/81, **Collection** 1982, p. 359.
42. Cf. C.A. Crisham, 'The Equal Pay Principle: Some Recent Decisions of the European Court of Justice', **Common Market Law Review** 1981, p. 601.
43. EC Court of Justice No. 129/79, **Collection** 1980, p. 1275.
44. Case No. 96/80, **Collection** 1981, p. 911.

45. EC Court of Justice No. 149/77, **Collection** 1978, p. 1365.
46. In case No. 19/81, **Collection** 1982, p. 555 the Court stated that the regulation of a minimum age of retirement different for men and women is not considered as discrimination prohibited by Community law.
47. OJ 1976, L 39.
48. Regarding access to occupation, recently the EC Court of Justice has stated in its judgement of 10 April 1984 (cases No. 79/83 and 14/83) that in cases of discrimination on grounds of sex the employer is not obliged to conclude an employment contract with the discriminated applicant. Directive No. 76/207 does not order a definite sanction but the Member States are left freedom of choice among several solutions. To guarantee efficiency and exemplary effect a special sanction laid down by a Member State has to be adequate to the damage suffered and has to go beyond symbolic damages such as the compensation of the costs of application.

4. Belgium

J. Walgrave

I. HISTORICAL INTRODUCTION

Important legal sources

'Discrimination' is a concept which has very recently appeared in Belgian law and jurisdiction. It is above all the equal treatment of men and women and thus the prohibition of discrimination that has clearly been defined in social legislation. Since Collective Labour Agreement No. 38, concluded on 6 December 1983 at the National Labour Council, an employer may no longer discriminate on the basis of age, sex, civil status, nationality, personal life, religious or political opinion when recruiting or selecting. Another legal source operating against discrimination is the law of 30 July 1981[1] which forbids discrimination on the basis of race and colour. However, this law covers other areas besides discrimination at work. Let us also remember that Belgians according to Article 6 of the Constitutional law are, with respect to each other, equal before the law. Since in this contribution the accent is laid on inequalities in working life, it is mainly equal treatment between men and women that constitutes our subject.

International Organisations such as the United Nations, the ILO and the European Communities encourage their respective Member States to banish discrimination based on sex. In the United Nations the ratification procedure of the Convention on the elimination of all forms of discriminations against women[2] has nearly been completed. In the ILO Belgium has not yet ratified Convention No. 111 which forbids all differentiation based on sex[3] at social and professional level. But it is above all the political determination and the impact of the European Communities (the European Commission, the European Council of Ministers and the European Parliament) which have produced tangible results in Belgian social legislation.

This started with the Treaty of Rome (1957) where Article 119 imposed: equal pay for equal work. Two EEC Directives[4] one on equal pay for equal or equivalent work[5] and the other on equal treatment at the workplace[6] have already been integrated into Belgian national legislation. A third Directive (19 December 1978) on equal treatment in social security will come into effect in Belgium before 22 December 1984.

How have the Directives been translated into Belgian law?

Collective Labour Agreement No. 25[7] was approved on 15 October 1975 at the National Labour Council.[8] This Collective Labour Agreement regulates equal pay for men and women in private industry. In the law of 4 August 1978 on economic reorientation Title V was inserted on equal treatment of men and women with respect to working conditions, access to employment, vocational training, promotion and access to an independant profession.[9] The most important legal sources for prosecution of discrimination at work based on sex are Collective Labour Agreement No. 25 and the different Joint Collective Agreements in execution of it as well as the law of 4 August 1978 with its executory Royal Decree.

The current situation

The participation of women in the labour force is an irreversible phenomenon in the social context of Belgium. It is no secret to anyone that women have been (or are?) treated in a discriminatory manner and that they had (or have?) to work for lesser wages than men. For a long time this was possible without legal intervention. This social fact made it necessary for the legislature to step in.

As early as the end of the 19th and the beginning of the 20th centuries, regulations were passed to protect women and children against hard labour such as was the case in mines or night work. After the phase of protection it became imperative to provide equal pay for equal or equivalent work. Equal pay, however, did not guarantee equal work with equal opportunities. The acquisition of equality is an 'obstacle-race' in which Belgium needed several European nudges. Without the Directives mentioned above, without Convention No. 100 of the ILO[10] and without the law of 4 August 1978 (rushed through Parliament) we would not have come so far, at least so far as a legal framework is concerned.

Why all the bother?

The facts speak for themselves and facts are best substantiated by figures. Working women are nothing new, since 1830[11] there has always been at least 25 per cent of the female population at work. Although the active population (employed and registered unemployed) increased between 1961 and 1981 by 18.5 per cent, this was mainly caused by an increase in the number of women workers. If women only constituted 26.6 per cent of the total active population in 1961, their numbers increased so as to represent 37.8 per cent in 1981. Nevertheless between 1975 and 1982 the number of employed men decreased by 19.1 per cent and that of the employed women by 29.7 per cent. This increase was mainly due to younger women and married women entering the labour market. The number of married women, for example, increased between 1970 and 1977 by 200,000. Nearly 70.8 per cent of married women between 20 and 24 years are professionally active. When examining the category of unmarried young people we find that there are nearly the same number of boys and girls professionally active. Moreover the starting of a family has less and less influence on the participation of women in the work process.

Where do women work?

There are more non-manual women workers (61.2 per cent) and helpers (5 per cent) than manual women workers (22.3 per cent); the remaining 11.5 per cent are self-employed or employers. They are mainly to be found in the service industries (79.8 per cent); only 20.1 per cent work in manufacturing industry. Some 90.7 per cent of women non-manual workers and 57.8 per cent manual workers belong to the service sector.

The labour market itself continues to be divided at industry level as well as at professional level into a labour market for men and a labour market for women workers. The labour market for men has a wide variety of opportunities, the other labour market is limited to certain professions and certein industries: 64.5 per cent of women workers are in manufacturing industry and work in textiles, food, the clothing industry and the electro-technical industry[12]; they are stickers, packers etc. In the service sector we find them in education, public health, food, catering and hotel services where they work as teachers, nurses, typists, secretaries and waitresses. In general they perform menial tasks and they find themselves at the low end of the job classification scale.

Specific working conditions

Women's wages were and remain lower than men's wages. The average daily wage of a manual woman worker in industry is 70 per cent of her male colleague's pay; in commerce and service industry it is 80 per cent. Women non-manual workers in commerce and service industries receive 89 per cent and in manufacturing industry 85 per cent of the average male remuneration. These figures are produced by the Social Security Institution (RSZ) and refer to average daily and monthly salaries without taking into account the number of actual hours/days worked. The differences in per cent are therefore slightly biased because part-time workers - mainly women workers - count as full-time workers. Differences can also result from other factors: men do more overtime, do more night and shift work and these account for higher wages for men because of wage supplement. In 1979 19,000 men and 185,000 women worked part-time. The average work time is higher for men workers because of their higher overtime. Women workers are less eager to do overtime because at home their domestic tasks must still be done. This is certainly not the case for all men... 14.6 per cent of male workers also work at night compared to 4 per cent of women workers. A further reason for the difference in wages lies of course elsewhere than a mere interpretation of statistics allows or because of differences in working conditions.

For equal work it is normal that equal pay follows. Difficulties how-ever emerge with the interpretation of equivalent work. After classification of jobs we notice that women are often put into lower categories because apparently job evaluations are in most cases based on norms where average male characteristics prevail over average female characteristics. Moreover there are senior jobs in management which for a number of reasons are difficult for women to obtain, but that is a somewhat different subject.

II. DEFINITION OF DISCRIMINATION[13]

Article 118 §1 of the law of 4 August 1978 declares: 'The principle of equal treatment as meant by Title V of this law is the exclusion of all types of discrimination based on sex be it direct or indirect through reference to marital status or family situation'. This principle is applicable of course to both men and women. Direct as well as indirect discrimination is forbidden. Direct discrimination is immediately perceptible in definition and practices. Indirect discrimination is more difficult to discern. The European Commission[14] in its Report on the third Directive concerning social security[15] gave a more precise description. The Commission believes that: 'there is a presumption of indirect discrimination as soon as an apparent neutral regulation in fact preponderately touches the workers of one of the sexes and this without the need to indicate the intention to discriminate'.

One cannot speak of indirect discrimination when there are objective justified reasons, qualitatively necessary for a certain job. The reference to marital status or family situation are in themselves not forbidden unless by this reference more discriminating results would follow for one particular sex than for the other. For example, the concept 'head of the household' has disappeared in civil law but re-appears more and more in social law. This concept however refers to a relation of subordination or of economic dependancy (breadwinner) of one partner towards the other. The concept 'head of the household' as it is used in Belgium is to be found in the unemployment regulation[16] as follows:
(a) a married worker who lives with a spouse who has no professional income nor other source of income;
(b) a worker who lives with a person of the other sex who has no professional income nor other source of income;
(c) a worker who is exclusively responsible under certain conditions for one or several dependants.
The fact there is a significant difference in the number of men who find themselves in this situation as compared with women. Thus one sex is disproportionately affected by these regulations. The person who is 'head of the household' continues to receive after the first year of unemployment 60 per cent of basic salary while the other unemployed see their benefits continuously decreased. A sample taken by the Social Security Institution (RVA) in 1982 indicates that out of 100 'heads of households' 18.6 per cent are women and 81.4 per cent are men.

Royal Decree No. 255 to promote employmet in the non-commercial sector allows priority to be given in the 'Third Employment Cycle' to 'heads of households' older than 45 years.[17] Not only of 100 'heads of households' are there 18.6 women but moreover 82.1 per cent of these women are under the age of 40. The European Commission [18] believes that it is impossible to define the concept 'head of household' neutrally since this concept always refers to some order of dependancy between the partners, and this is forbidden by the Directives as well as by Article 118 of the Belgian law of 4 August 1978.

III.

A. Basis and field of application

The most important grounds on which discrimination at work is forbidden, is sex. Equal pay as well as equal treatment may be claimed by man or woman alike when he or she feels discriminated against on basis of his or her gender. This prohibition was recently tightened up by National Labour Agreement No. 38 of the National Labour Council of 6 December 1983 concerning the recruitment and selection of workers. Art. 10[19] declares: 'the recruiting employer may not treat the applicant in a discriminatory manner'. The comment on that article not only forbids discrimination on the basis of sex whereby reference is made to the law of 4 August 1978 but neither may an employer differentiate on the basis of personal factors such as age, sex, marital status, nationality, political or philosophical convictions or membership of a trade union or other organisation.

B. Fiel of application

National Labour Agreement No. 38, Art. 10 applies to all workers in private industry who work for an employer who is a member of an employers' organisation which has co-signed the Collective Agreement. The Law of 4 August 1978 applies to all workers and employers in the private as well as the public sector as follows:
(1) All employers and workers, as well as the apprentices from private industry, are covered by it (Article 117). Outworkers, however, according to the Parliamentary debates are excluded.[20] Third parties, in particular those woking on the circulation of advertising also fall under this law. Some of its provisions apply to 'all those who circulate offers of employment or advertisements of employment and promotion possibilities' (Art. 120). We refer here to the Employment Office (RVA), and to Belgian radio and television, newspapers and advertising agencies.
(2) The field of application covers all possible provisions (Royal Decrees, Collective Agreements, individual contracts of employment, work regulations) and practices. Practices refer to 'every independent or repetitious fact of a public or private institution of an employer or a person with regard to a person or group of persons who are related to the matters as indicated by Title V of this law' (Art. 117, 4). Here we refer to factual discrimination. The law covers provisions and practices relating to access to work, promotion possiblities, job selection and information, vocational guidance, continued vocational training, additional and conversion training, conditions of work and access to an indepedent profession (Art. 116, §1). Legal[21] and extra legal[22][23] social security benefits

- with the exception of the annual holiday - are not covered by the law.

But all advantages connected to work which are advantages for the workers at the expense of the employers are considered as an element of wages; therefore they should be equal for men and women alike for equal or equivalent work. The difference between extra-legal social security which are not covered by this law and therefore need not (yet) be equal for both sexes and the bilateral agreements providing advantages and/or benefits which must be equal for all workers is very difficult to determine. The interpretations gap is wide.

IV. EXCEPTIONS

1. Bona fide occupational qualifications (BFOQ)

This exception is foreseen in Belgium by the law of 4 August 1978. BFOQ applies to a job for which only one of the sexes can be considered because of the necessary inherent qualities for that particular job **e.g.** as a soprano, one can hardly recruit a male candidate.

The general rule remains all jobs must be open to men and women. The possible legal exceptions must be interpreted with extreme caution. According to Article 122 of the law of 4 August 1978 it is possible by Royal Decree decided upon by the Council of Ministers to indicate professions for which it is permitted to mention the gender of a worker as a decisive element due to the particular nature of those professions. It is only the conditions of access which are restrictive, not the activities themselves nor training for them.

At the Council of Ministers of 2 February 1979[24] the Royal Decree was approved on 'the determining of cases in which reference can be made to the sex of the worker for the conditions of access to a job or a professional activity'. A list was drawn up including actors, singers, dancers, artists who can be called upon to perform a male or female role and models for artists and fashion models. Moreover, other jobs or professional activities are considered when they are to be performed in countries which are not members of the European Communities and where according to local laws and practice the performance of these jobs are restricted to a particular sex.

The recommendation of the Committee of Women at Work[25] and the National Labour Council is required to determine exceptions on the basis of Article 122 by way of Royal Decree elaborated by the Council of Ministers.

Several authorities (**e.g.** Institutions for youth care) can introduce a petition for exception to the law on equal treatment on the basis of Article 122. There seems to be general confusion on the application of Article 122 of the law and Articles 118, 123 and 129 of the same law. Only Article 122 refers to jobs and professions where the sex of the worker is of a decisive nature. Articles 118, 123 and 129 refer to protective laws which either prevent access to a profession (**e.g.** the mining Arts. 118-123) or if not preventing access, they foresee other working conditions for women **e.g.** a ban on night work (Article 129).

2. Security of state

The Belgian Government voiced certain reservations concerning the UN Convention[26] on the political rights of women. 'Royal Authority can according to Constitutional Law only be exercised by men'. As to the exercising of the official position of Regent, Article 3 of the above Convention cannot derogate from the application of the Constitutional rules such as they are interpreted by the Belgian State.

One year after the coming into force of the law of 4 August 1978 and in the absence of explicit mention all positions in the Public sector are in principle open to men and women. There is one exception though: a few years ago the Council of Ministers voiced reservations about male wardens in women prisons and **vice versa**. In an experiment some mixed groups of wardens were allowed. This one-year experiment was not renewed; the conclusions of the experiments were not made public and therefore nothing changed.

In the army, State police and local police, important changes also came about. Women as well as men could apply as candidate for officers in the armed forces (land force, air force, navy, state police etc.). The physical prerequisites are sometimes such that in the present social configuration women have fewer opportunities **e.g.** one requirement of the municipal police staff is the ability to run a 100 meters in x seconds.

It also happens that positions in the public sector can hardly be filled by women because of the additional protective regulations (**e.g.** night work) for women due to the degree of danger involved. For example, in regard to civil servants of Military Security[27], 'The assignments of these civil servants are such that they are exposed to acts of violence and therefore specific prerequisites are required in particularly tiring and alternating circumstances needed at all hours of the day and even at night.' Similarly administration of the land registry specifies that 'These positions correspond to duties which produce serious physical tiredness and of which moreover a number require night work and are exposed to acts of violence.'

3. Special protective measures

The law of 4 August 1978 explicitly mentions exceptions which are or are not connected in time and which because of the penal characteristic of the law must be interpreted in a narrow sense.

a. Maternity protection

By maternity protection is understood the legal prescribed 14 weeks' rest which are compulsory for the women at the birth of a child: six weeks before or after confinement and eight weeks after confinement. The Minister of Labour himself indicated during debates in the Senate that a clear distinction must be made between motherhood and the education of children. By this latter is meant leave of absence for family reasons, parental leave, additional post-confinement leave or interruption of career; it is forbidden by European as well as Belgian law not to grant that leave also to men.

By Royal Decree[28] a list was drawn up of jobs which are considered dangerous for mother and/or child. Women may not work with certain chemical and physical elements. The works' rules of the company are of great importance here. The local works' docter may also impose a specific personal prohibition. The employer must in that case do everything possible to provide a replacement job. The woman's income is assured during the 14 weeks of rest, partly paid by the employer and partly by the social security.

From the moment at which the employer is informed of the pregnancy of a woman worker she enjoys protection against unilateral termination of the employment contract for reasons of pregnancy. If the employer does so, she receives damages. This prohibition period lasts until one month after the end of the post-confinement rest period. The woman worker is thus protected from the moment the employer was informed of the pregnancy and the employer can end her contract only for reasons unrelated to the pregnancy **e.g.** for urgent reasons or for technical and economic reasons. The employer must justify the dismissal to prove that such reasons exist.

b. Access to jobs

Article 123 of the law of 4 August 1978 declares: 'At present the provisions of Title V of this law are not considered as contrary to the provisions of Article 8 paragraph 1 of the Labour Law of 16 March 1971 and to the provisions taken in application to Article 10 of this same law which prevent access to the work process as well as the possibility of promotion.'

Having proceeded to consultation, as required by Article 122, the King may abolish the provisions foreseen by the first paragraph. This was recently done by Royal Decree of 26 July 1984. Article 8 of the Labour Act of 1971 prohibits women working in mines and quarries and Article 10 allows the King to forbid the performing of dangerous or unhealthy work to women workers or to impose certain protective measures. It is however still forbidden to employ women workers in the following jobs:
- manual work, groundwork, excavations and digging works;
- manual work in compression caissons.

The law therefore allows these measures either to be abolished or to remain.

The Committee of Women at Work tries to give circumstantial recommendations on these matters to the Minister of Labour. In order to examine whether these measures only work discriminatorily or whether they are mere protective measures it is necessary to examine them scientifically. One must examine whether it is possible to modify these measures in the light of changing working conditions and the developing knowledge of new toxic products. Another question which must be examined is whether these activities are not hazardous to health for both sexes.

Up to the present no steps have been taken to abolish any of

these protective measures. Only one woman mining engineer received authorisation a few years ago to descend into a mine to perform scientific research. Some contradictions in the law itself must be underlined:
- why may women archeologists do digging work?
- why may nurses work in compression caissons? Is it because they perfom only intellectual work? Is it therefore suddenly no longer unhealthy?

c. Protective measures

Article 129 of the law of 4 August 1978 declares: 'For the present are not considered contrary to the provisions of this section:
1. the provisions on night work of Articles 35 and 36 of the Labour Law of 16 March 1971 and its execution provisions;
2. the provisions determined by the King concerning health and safety of the workers as well as the salubrity of the work and of the work-places and which specifically protect women.'
After having proceeded to the consultations prescribed for by Article 122 the King can abolish the provisions foreseen by this article. The difference in regard to the remaining protective measures lies in the fact that night work or other conditions do not prohibit women from performing a particular job; she is merely obliged to perform the work under specific conditions. The most important point here is that night work is organised according to the Royal Decree of 24 December 1968.

The Labour Law in principle generally prohibits night work for every worker. Some exceptions are written into the Labour Law itself.

The King may also foresee exceptions. For men these exceptions are much more extensive than for women. 'L'hygiene, la morale, l'humanité et jusqu'à des considerations de police font desirer la suppression du travail de nuit en ce qui concerne les femmes, les enfants et les adolescents.'[29]

The upholders of labour regulations for women and among others the prohibition of night work not only invoked health and morality but also stressed the role of women in the family. The imposed rest period for women is longer than that for their male colleagues. Specific measures also exist on hygiene at work, separate cafeterias, washing places etc. The recommendations on protective provisions in general are divergent, not only in the case of different committees (Committee on women at work - National Labour Council) but also as far as the social partners are concerned. The differences are fundamental.

The trade union organisations are distrustful of every unilateral modification of protective measures for women in the directionof greater flexibility. This would mean social regression for the sake of equality. The employers' organisation wants equality pure and simple, for example, with regard to night work.

The general conclusion might be that Belgian law has not evolved with modifications on the social, economic and mainly on the medical - biological level. Too little attention is given to the evolution of the production process, of industrial technology and most of all of the use of new toxic elements.

V. AFFIRMATIVE ACTIONS AND REVERSE DISCRIMINATION

Article 119 of the Law of 4 August 1978 permits measures which aim to promote equal opportunities especially by abolishing the factual inequalities which negatively influence the possibilities for women envisaged in Article 116, paragraph 1. We refer here to recruitment, promotion, vocational training and working conditions, as well as to access to an independant profession. The King may take measures to end a discriminatory situation or in order to reinstate the balance in favour of women. Up to now no such measures have been taken. We could for example allow priority for women for some types of vocational training to which they have not previously had access. In October 1984 the Committee of Women at Work organised a colloquium on this subject. Legislation abroad for example in America and Sweden as well as experiments held in some French companies were closely examined. The few Belgian experiments held in the private sector were scrutinised in order to allow a draft recommendation with proposals to make the carrying out of the law in this area possible.

VI. EXCEPTIONS

Special protective measures - New evolution in this field

In Belgium more and more frequently experiments are conducted on the introduction of flexible worktime[30] with the double objective of offering employment to more workers and of terminating the employment of as few workers as possible in this period of crisis. In most cases shiftwork is extended and the opportunity is offered to work for example for 24 hours at weekends whereby this work schedule is considered as a full-time job. This means nevertheless that one must work late in the evening, do night work and start early in the morning. Recruiting women in this context becomes very difficult. Royal Decree No. 179 however provides for the posibility to rescind certain articles of the Labour Law such as those relevant to night work.

ILO Convention No. 89 on night work which Belgium ratified and which has not yet been renounced is invoked in order not to abrogate night work for women. The employers also believe that the prohibition on night work is an important obstacle to the recruitment of women for flexible worktime schedules. Only one company (out of 25 involved up to now in these experiments) solved this problem by allowing women on dayshifts only and the men on day and night shifts but this in turn is discriminatory for male workers.

A collective agreement[31] in the textile sector also provides for the introduction and organisation of week-end shifts as well as for an extension of shiftwork. As a result, at the end of 1983, 18 companies operated in this way; 320 men and 30 women were additionally employed. Besides the above experiments a number of other companies have also introduced worktime flexibility by means of company agreements.

One could ask whether with the introduction of new technology and the persisting uncertainties inherent in a period of crisis, night work prohibition is not detrimental to the employment of women. Night work as such is basically against human nature and should be restricted to a strict minimum for both sexes. Because of new unintentional but insuperable factors one cannot remain passive and allow women workers to become isolated and dispossessed of equal opportunities. At the request of the Minister of Labour, the Committee of Women at Work examined in autumn 1984 the question of the derogation of night work for women in several specific companies. If this prohibition on night work cannot be abolished, many women will be out of a job.

VII. ENFORCEMENT

The Control is exercised by civil servants appointed by Royal Decree of 27 November 1978[32] from the inspection services of certain Ministries. Penal sanctions, administrative fines and damages are provided for by law for persons subjected to prejudice. As the law is one of public order, it makes all provisions and practices contrary to the principle of equal treatment void. This is an absolute nullity 'ex tunc'. The judge can invoke ex officio this nullity. The proof of discrimination must be given by the person subject to prejudice. The different law courts are competent according to the nature of the prejudice and the procedures. For inequalities in the Civil Service (Public Sector) a complaint may be lodged with the State Council. The tribunal of first instance is competent because the law provides for penal sanctions. Administrative fines are determined by the competent department of the Ministry of Labour. The Labour Courts are of course competent for labour questions.

The Committee of Women at Work has, contrary to other examples abroad, the competence to give certain advice but according to the law of 4 August 1978 it has no investigative right nor the right to lodge a complaint with a Court of Justice. The right to act in the name of a member is and remains within the competence of the Trade Union. Nevertheless women's organisations can lodge a complaint with the European Commission when the Public Authorities infringe the Directive on equal treatment. The European Commission can then call the Member State to order according to a procedure which could lead to condemnation by the European Court in Luxemburg.

The law of 4 August 1978 enlarged the competence of the Labour Courts. Besides declaring the nullity of an act a labour judge can decide on damages for an individual whose claim is well-founded and proven and can also order an end to the discriminatory situation. In matters of vocational training working conditions and dismissals the labour judge can, for the first time in Belgian social legislation, demand for example a change within a fixed period of time of the situation in a company, in a department of the Public Sector, or at a Ministerial Cabinet.

This might seem to grant very broad powers but the reality is different and much less evident. Very few decisions have thus far been taken by the Courts of Justice. What are the reasons for this?

1. It is rather difficult to summon an employer before the Labour Court for unequal pay for the same work or because of unequal treatment in general working conditions while an individual labour contract still exists between this employer and the woman worker in question.

An employer in Belgium can dismiss a worker without reason and at any time provided a period of notice is observed or serverance payment is made. Exceptions to this general rule are provided for protected workers such as pregnant women, members of the works' council and plaintiffs to a court case. To take your current employer to Court is therefore not a good idea, especially at a time of economic crisis.

2. Trade Unions can defend the rights of the worker. But it is not clear that workers prejudiced against always have the courage to inform systematically their Trade Union of infringements of the law. In the case of equal treatment there is always one person favoured above another (the worker appointed, promoted or not dismissed and the worker prejudiced against). The problem is that probably both are members of the same Trade Union.

One should not in this context forget the following rule in Belgian Labour Law: Article 14 of the Law on Labour Contracts of 1978 stipulates that the nullity of the contract cannot be invoked relative to the right of workers which result from the application of the Law on Labour Contracts when work is executed in accordance to a contract 'nullity through infringement of the stipulations which have as object the regulation of labour relations'. The other worker therefore remains appointed and/or promoted unless naturally bad faith on his or her side can be proven.

3. The third reason is one of procedure, namely the burden of evidence which lies with the worker discriminated against. The employer remains totally free to recruit and alone can determine the person s/he considers the most competent. In private industry there are no public examinations, no obligation to make publicly known the results of interviews or psychological and other tests, no quotas etc.

How can one prove - one has indeed the right to do so with all possible means - that one was discriminated against after an interview between the personnel manager and oneself! How can one prove that a person was recruited for reasons forbidden by the law on equal treatment?

Even written proof was recently rejected by the Court of Appeal of Liège because Constitutional law in Belgium guarantees freedom of opinion (see below).

4. Finally of course there is the fear of the unknown whereby costs and time are involved and the possibility of remaining labelled with a bad name as regard to potential subsequent employers.

Examples of sentences on basis of the law of 4 Augst 1978

1. Tribunal of First Instance, Verviers 19 May 1981 and Court of Appeal of Liège 17 November 1981

A candidate women teacher was informed in writing by two members of the council of aldermen of the town that they preferred the male candidate because they preferred a man as teacher. The claimant put the case that these letters were clearly proof of an infringement on the law of 4 August 1978 which states that no one may be excluded from recruitment because of his/her sex.

The tribunal of first instance as well as the Court of Appeal however found that Article 145 of the Belgian Constitution guaranteeing freedom of opinion supersedes Article 121 of the law of 4 August 1978 which forbids access to the workprocess for implicit or explicit reasons which pertain directly or indirectly to the gender of the worker.

The Constitution limits this freedom to 'except for punishment of offences committed during the exercising of this freedom'. This freedom is therefore not absolute. The Tribunal unjustly, in this case did not take into consideration the fact that the law of 4 August 1978 is a law of Public order to which penal sanctions are attached. It was the intention of the legislature to punish also factual discrimination. The judiciary interprets the law more restrictively than the legislature intended.

The Committee of Women at Work has requested the Minister of Justice to examine the possibility of proceeding immediately to a reversal of the judgement. The second Chamber of the Court of Cassation ruled on 11 May 1983. The Court reversed the judgement of the Court of Appeal of Liège. According to the Court of Cassation, Article 14 of the Constitutional law allows imposing sanctions to curb offences committed during the execution of this fundamental freedom. Article 141 of the law is violated by the judgement which acquits suspects on the basis of freedom of opinion, after it has been established that on the occasion of discussions prior to the appointment of the municipal teacher they had indicated their reasons for preferring a male teacher.[33]

2. Another well-known example is the case of the dismissal after long weeks of strike of 13 women in a Belgian company because they refused to change their full-time job to a part-time job in order to leave full-time jobs to their male colleagues. The case is still under debate before the Labour Tribunal of Charleroi as well as at the European Commission. These judgements are of extreme importance because in the absence of jurisprudence, for the first time, judgement must be passed on types of direct (among others regarding wages) as well as indirect discrimination (essentially women in part-time work).

General remarks by way of conclusion

1. The law obliges one to examine certain provisions of labour law, among others the question of abolishing or not specific protective measures for women with the exception of cause for maternity protection. The investigation must decide if in the present labour constellation some provisions are not discriminatory rather than protective.

This examination must be speeded up because of the phenomena of economic crisis such as unemployment and because of the expansion of new technologies. Opportunities decrease for women to find work as well as for those already employed in a company. The unemployment rate of women which stagnated for a while is again increasing more rapidly than is male unemployment.

Besides all possible types of flexible worktime it appears that a difference exists between full-time and part-time work. The Public

Authority promotes this distinction. This is however an unequal redistribution of work whereby the only advantage is more time off (**e.g.** women and their family duty ...). All possible disadvantages arise for part-time work: reduced income, less interesting work (except research work), fewer promotion possibilities, less involvement with colleagues and social organisations and less protection against dismissal.

If these work schedules become compulsory this would result in unequal treatment of the part-time worker. This will mainly be the case when one can only choose between dismissal or part-time unemployment (short-time) and part-time work. Moreover a great majority of those who find themselves in the situation of part-time work are women. Men are according to Belgian norms the protected heads of household.

2. The law of 4 August 1978 is not well known and the automatic correct application of it is not evident. Concretely, despite incessant discussions which must change those steeped in prejudice, the change is limited to spoken and written advertising adressed to 'M/W' (man-woman) and to equal starting opportunities for girls in vocational training. As far as advertising for recruitment is concerned, the progress made is questionable. Regular surveys show a worsening of the situation. In 1981, 44 per cent of the advertisements compiled in private industry conformed to the law and in 1983 only 31 per cent.

Finally, the individual right to work is still, as far as women are concerned, under the influence of two factors which are present in what is vaguely called 'public opinion'
- more rights for women in times of economic prosperity than in an economic depression;
- the rights apply first to male colleagues and then to women.
This should not arouse aggression. On the contrary as the Chairman of the Committee of Women at Work once declared: 'the dreadful conception that the other sex does not belong to one's own world but is a stranger, an intruder against whom one must be protected, goes against the reality of life itself and against society as a whole'.

NOTES

1. Belgian Governement Gazette, 8 August 1981.
2. The General Assembly of the United Nations approved by Resolution 34/180 on 19 December 1978 the Convention.
3. See also J. Walgrave, 'Vrouwenarbeid in de Internationale Wetgeving', **Kultuurleven,** 1975, p. 695.
4. A Directive is a binding instrument unanimously adopted by the European Council of Ministers.
5. Directive 75/117 of 10 February 1975 on the approximation of the legislation of Member States on the application of the principle of equal pay for men and women. Published L 45/19 19 February 1975.
6. Directive 76/207 of 9 February 1976 on the execution of the principle of equal treatment of men and women workers with respect to access to employment, to vocational training, to promotion and as regards to working conditions. Published L 39/40 14 February 1976.

7. Collective Labour Agreement No. 25 was made generally binding by Royal Decree on 9 December 1975 (**B.S.**, 25 December 1975). As a result, the Collective Labour Agreement is now binding for the entire private sector.
8. The National Labour Council is a national body where workers's and employers' representatives sit jointly to make recommendations on social matters as well as to negotiate binding agreements for specific employers and their workers.
9. Belgian Government Gazette BS, 17 August 1978.
10. ILO Convention No. 100 (1951) concerning Equal Remuneration for men and women workers for work of Equal Value.
11. Most of this information was collected in a statistical survey which the work group 'Women and Society' (Vrouw en Maatschappij) drew up and which was published in the Autumn of 1984.
12. Social Security Institution (RSZ), Annual Report 1981, p. 171-172.
13. See also R. Blanpain and J. Walgrave, **The equal treatment of men and women according to European and Belgian law,** Series Social Law, Kluwer, Antwerp, p. 708.
14. Intermediate report on the application of Directive 79/7 Com(83) 793 def 6 January 1984.
15. Directive of 9 December 1978 79/7 takes the same definition of equal treatment.
16. Royal Decree of 24 December 1980 modified by Royal Decree of 20 December 1983 on employment provisions and unemployment.
17. Third Employment Circuit (TEC): Associations which are engaged, **de facto** or **de jure**, in non-profit making activities or without intention of gain, may apply to the TEC, an institution in which the Government undertakes to pay the remuneration of the workers engaged, who must however be 'hard core' unemployed living in the Department of Employment subregion which covers the place where the association operates. The employer concerned cannot reduce staff to take on such workers. The workers must be recruited in a certain order of priority and the activities must be in a non-commercial sector.
18. Interim report (supra).
19. Strangely enough only Articles 1, 2 and 6 and Article 19 were made generally binding by Royal Decree of 11 July 1984 (**B.S.,** 28 July 1984).
20. Parliament Document Kamer No. 470 §1977-1978) No. 9, p. 67.
21. Regulated in the European Directive 79/7 of December 1978.
22. A draft Directive regulates these matters but has not yet been approved by the Council of Ministers.
23. Additional social security is also excluded from the scope of application of the Collective Agreement No. 25 of 15 February 1975 on equal opportunities.
24. Royal Decree of 9 February 1979, **B.S.,** 16 February 1979.
25. Committee of Women at Work (Commissie Vrouwenarbeid) is a consultative institution where trade union organisations and employers are jointly represented and where delegates of important Ministries are present as observers. The CWW operates under the auspices of the Minister of Labour.
26. New York signed on 31 March 1953.

27. These motives are also to be found in the RD's which preceded the law of 4 August 1978 and which still continue to influence the facts.
28. Royal Decree of 27 December 1968 concerning women at work in execution of Royal Decree No. 40 of March 1967 on child and women's work which was replaced by the Labour Law of 16 March 1971, **B.S.**, December 1968.
29. Report van Mr. Van Cleemputte for the central section of the Chamber session 1888-1889, part. No. 193, p. 192.
30. Royal Decree No. 179 of 30 December 1982 (**B.S.**, 20 January 1983) is named after the Minister of Labour: the Hansenne experiments provides for negotiation procedures between the Public Authorities and the social partners to allow in certain companies the introduction of temporary experiments on worktime organisation.
31. National framework agreement of 25 March 1983 on the introduction and organisation of supplementary shifts in the textile industry and knitting sector. The national framework agreement of 25 March 1983 on the introduction and organisation of a five shift system in the textile and knitting industry.
32. **B.S.**, of 1 December 1978.
33. Sociaalrechtelijke Kronieken year 1983 No. 8, p. 493.

5. Canada

H.C. Jain

Employment discrimination against minority groups and women has become a matter of serious social and political concern. The concern for equality of opportunity has been dramatised in recent decades because of the variety and number of immigrants, especially from the third world, who arrived in Canada in the late 1960's and after. As a result, Canadian society is multi-cultural, multi-lingual, and multi-religous.[1]

The existence of human rights statutes across Canada is an attempt to ensure equal employment opportunity for minorities and women. Canada has also enacted the Constitution Act, 1982 which contains a Canadian Charter of Rights and Freedoms. The equal rights provision of the Charter (section 15) prohibits discrimination based on race, national or ethnic origin, colour, religion, sex, age and mental and physical handicap.

The Charter and its provisions have become the supreme law of the country. However, the equality provision does not become law until April 1985. In the meantime, Federal and Provincial human rights laws cover discrimination in employment. Under the British North America Act of 1867, Federal and Provincial Governments are allocated very specific areas of responsibility. In the equal employment area, approximately 10 per cent of the labour force in Canada falls under Federal jurisdiction and the remaining 90 per cent under the jurisdiction of 10 provinces. Thus, all governments have human rights responsibilities. As of now, there is no one supreme law of the country in the equal employment area; instead there are at least 11 human rights statutes in this area.

Despite the existence of anti-discrimination legislation across Canada, minority groups and women continue to face discrimination in employment. For instance, third-world immigrants, relative to other immigrants, experience higher rates of unemployment, earn less money and are more frequently unable to find work in their chosen fields.[2] Moreover, recent recession has affected them far more adversely than others.[3] Similarly, women face occupational segregation and earn lower income than men.[4] Native people have a substantially lower labour force participation rate than the national average. Their average wages and incomes are also well below national levels and their unemployment rate is abnormally high.[5]

One of the most important reasons for the continued inequality faced by women and minorities is the existence of both entry-level and post-employment job barriers. These include narrow recruitment channels, credentialism, employment tests and interviews, seniority provisions, discriminatory promotion and layoffs and the like.[6] Human rights laws across Canada are intended to remove these job barriers.

Legal definition of employment discrimination

Direct or intentional discrimination involves searching for a motive or an intention to discriminate on any of the prohibited grounds of discrimination above by an employer. It means having to prove prejudicial treatment namely harmful acts motivated by personal antipathy towards the group of which the target group was a member. Thus, intent to discriminate must be proved.

Increasingly, however, there has been a realisation that employment discrimination in most cases does not result from isolated, individual acts of bigotry but rather from historical assumptions and traditions which have become embedded in the normal operations of employment and industrial relations systems.

Systemic or indirect or unintentional or constructive discrimination

The Canadian Human Rights Act as well as numerous decisions by boards of inquiry in several provinces have borrowed the legal definition of discrimination from the US case law and the relevant British legislation. In the US the concept of indirect or systemic discrimination was articulated by the Supreme Court in Griggs v. Duke Power Co. case in 1971. The Court unanimously endorsed a results-oriented definition of what constitutes employment discrimination. The Court indicated that intent does not matter; it is the consequence of an employer's actions that determine whether he may have discriminated under Title VII of the Civil Rights Act. In this case, the Court struck down educational requirements and employment tests on two grounds. (a) These requirements could not be justified on the grounds of business necessity since they were not valid or related to job performance. Moreover, (b) they had adverse impact since they screened out a greater proportion of blacks than whites. However, if business necessity could be proved i.e. if the educational and testing requirements that had disproportionate or adverse impact on minorities were in fact related to job performance, then the practice was not prohibited. Thus, disproportionate impact is not sufficient to outlaw credentialism, tests and other hiring standards. Business necessity is the prime criterion in hiring and promotion decisions.

The approach adopted in the Griggs case has been adopted in Canada in both equal pay and equal employment cases. In the employment area, for example, one of the leading cases which changed the intent to discriminate situation involved a member of the Sikh faith. He complained to the Ontario Human Rights Commission, after he was refused a job as a security guard. The dress and grooming regulations of the firm to which he had applied required employees to be clean-shaven and to have their hair trimmed. The Sikh applicant wore a turban and had a beard as required by his religion and therefore was unable to comply with the firm's regulation. In this case, Ishar Singh v. Security and Investigation 1977, the Ontario board of inquiry found that the 'employer bore no ill will toward Sikh people ... had no intention to insult or act with malice ... and did not have the intention or motive of discrimination'. The board, however, found that the effect of the employer's policy which required that their security quards be clean-shaven and wear caps, was to deny employment to Sikhs. It ruled that intention was not necessary to establish a contravention of human rights legislation.

A similar concern is reflected in a January 1979 board of inquiry case. In the case of Ann Colfer against Ottawa Police Commission the board decided that the Commission's minimum height requirement of 5 feet, 10 inches 'virtually eliminated women as police constables', as only 5 per cent of females in Canada are that height or taller. This height and weight (160 pounds) requirement, the board declared, had a disproportionate effect upon female gender relative to the male gender.

The systemic approach is also evident in a variety of other board cases involving such diverse organisations as the BC College of Physicians, a BC mining company, a Saskatchewan food company, a branch of Royal Canadian Legion in New Brunswick, and a variety of organisations in Ontaria including a taxi-cab Co., The Liquour Control Board of Ontario, Hamilton Tiger Cats and an investigation security company.[7]

Until early 1982, the concept of unintentional discrimination, that is, impact instead of intent, was becoming the prevailing view and the principle in Canada even in those jurisdictions without express indirect discrimination clauses in their human rights codes. However, the Ontario Court of Appeal in O'Malley on 12 August 1982 and the Federal Court of Appeal in the Canadian National Railway Company v. Canadian Human Rights Commission and K.S. Bhinder in 13 April 1983 have decided that intent must be proved to establish a human rights violation. The ruling in O'Malley will have no impart in Ontario since constructive or indirect discrimination has been written into the new Ontario Human Rights Code, which became effective in June 1982; the O'Malley case was decided under the old Ontario code. Both the O'Malley and the Bhinder cases are at present on appeal to the Supreme Court of Canada. The Supreme Court is being asked to decide whether discrimination can be unintentional or systemic. In the meantime, in two recent (1984) cases, the Manitoba Court of Queen's Bench has ruled that intention to discriminate is not a necessary element of a contravention of the Manitoba Human Rights Act and that the Act contains results - oriented or impact language. The two cases are Wayne Osborne v. Inco Ltd. and Canada Safeway v. Manitoba Food and Commercial Workers union. The final resolution of impact vs. intent definition of discrimination is unlikely to occur prior to the Supreme Court of Canada's decisions in the O'Malley and the Bhinder cases, since several provincial statutes either contain language similar to the old Ontario code, or have no specific indirect discrimination provision.[8] The recent human rights legislation, Bill 11, in British Columbia which Received Royal Assent on 16 May 1984, is the only statute that provides for direct discrimination. The 'reasonable cause' provision of the previous BC legislation has been dropped from Bill 11.

Prohibited grounds and coverage under the laws

The prohibited grounds for discrimination in employment include race, religion, colour, national or ethnic origin, marital status, and age; age groups protected vary among jurisdictions, with the most common being between the ages of 18 and 65 and 45 to 65. Physical and mental disability is proscribed in several jurisdictions. Other prohibited grounds include sexual orientation in Quebec and pardoned offences in the Federal and the Ontario jurisdictions.

Generally, the relevant statutes apply to employers, employment agencies, and trade unions and, in some jurisdictions, to self-governing professions. Dicrimination is prohibited with respect to advertising, terms and conditions of employment, including promotion, transfer, and training.

Enforcement

Almost all jurisdictions have Human Rights Commissions which enforce human rights laws.[9] Enforcement in all jurisdictions relies primarily upon the processing of individual complaints. However, in some jurisdictions, Human Rights Commissions may file a complaint or commence an investigation on their own initiative.

All the Acts provide for the settlement of complaints, if possible, by conciliation and persuasion. They provide for an initial informal investigation into a complaint by an officer who is directed to endeavour to affect a settlement. If conciliation fails, a broad of inquiry may be appointed in most jurisdictions.[10] Such a board may issue orders for compliance, compensation etc. This order may be appealed to the Supreme Court of the province on questions of law or fact or both. The Federal jurisdiction allows an appeal by either the complainant or person complained against, to a Review Tribunal, where the original Tribunal had fewer than three members.

In actual practice, the emphasis has been to 'concentrate rather less on the issues of legal guilt than on the issue of effectuating a satisfactory settlement', according to Dr. Hill, the former chairman of the Ontario Human Rights Commission.[11] This is also true in Canada as a whole, where the Ontario legislation has been the prototype of statutes in most other jurisdictions.

LEGAL DECISIONS AND CONCILIATED SETTLEMENTS PERTAINING TO VARIOUS GROUNDS OF DISCRIMINATION

Race, colour, ancestry, place of origin, national of ethnic origin, nationality or citizenship

These characteristics have not been defined with any precision by either the legislators or boards of inquiry or courts. The latter have done so for limited purposes and generally only when necessary to decide a specific issue. These characteristics form the basis of the largest number of employment discrimination complaints and cases that have come before Human Rights Commissions, boards of inquiry and courts.[12]

In F.W. Woolworth Company Ltd. v. Dhillon (1982, an Ontario board of inquiry decided that providing a proper working environment was a condition of employment. Dhillon, who had worked for 2 years as a warehouseman for the Company was of East Indian ancestry. He was subjected to racial insults and was subsequently dismissed. While management was aware of racial tension in the warehouse, they were ineffective or indifferent to the situation.[13]

In the case of Dr. M.A. Rajput v. Dr. Donald Watkins and Algoma University College and its Agents, 1976 an Ontario board of inquiry found that Dr. Rajput was not offered re-employment on the basis of 'nationality' of 'place of origin'.

In another case, Export Plastics Co. Ltd. v. Williams, (1981) Ms. Williams, a black Canadian woman of Jamaican origin, complained that she had been demoted and therefore discriminated against by the company due to her race, colour, nationality, ancestry and place of origin. She had obtained sick leave without pay from her superiors. When she returned to her employment, her supervisory position had been filled. She alleged that she was offered a lower position with lower pay and was told to either accept it or quit. A board of inquiry found that the complainant by being demoted was in effect dismissed and the company failed to give any valid reasons for this action. The board concluded that Ms. Williams dismissal was discriminatory.

In Mears etal. and Ontaria Hydro, 1983, a board of inquiry decided that discrimination against blacks was an aspect of assessment of the four complainants at the time of the layoffs by Ontario Hydro's foremen, even though the layoff of 23 employees was motivated by financial circumstances. That was because the foreman's previous actions towards these four employees indicated a discriminatory attitude towards black persons. Evidence indicated that the foremen kept no written records about the productivity or quality of work of their crew members, and did not use objective, standardised criteria to assess their members on a day-to-day basis.

The board also concluded that Ontario Hydro was directly responsible for the discrimination against the complainants since the company 'must assume responsibility for the actions of its foremen ... because of both the authority it vested in these employees and the ineffective personnel policies that were in force in South Pickering'.

Sex

Employment practices which differentiate between men and women without justificable business necessity have been declared illegal. For instance, several boards of inquiry have held that stereotypes and misconceptions held by employers about male and female jobs have no bearing upon ability to perform the job. In Stairs v. Maritime Cooperative Services Ltd. 1975 in New Brunswick, Mrs. Stairs had applied for a position as a cost Accountant Trainee. She was told by the interviewer that she would lose her 'feminity' if hired. In a second interview she was told that 'I was the best qualified for the job, but he could not see having a woman in his department'. In Francis Perry v. Robert Simpsons Ltd. in 1976 in Nova Scotia, Mr. Perry applied for the position of a copywriter with the company. When visiting the employment office at the company to apply for the position he was told it would be a waste of his time, since the company only hired women for the position. Subsequently, a woman was offered the job. In Betty-Ann Shack v. London Drive-Ur-Self Ltd. in 1974 in Ontario, the rental truck agency refused to hire an inexperienced woman as a rental clerk because the employer thought the work was 'too ardous' for a woman, and that she would occasionally be alone in the office at night. The chairman of the board held that 'this is merely one of the "stereotyped" characterizations of the sexes ... this factor would have no bearing whatsoever upon her ability to perform the job in question'.

Similarly, women cannot be denied a job because of heavy duty janitorial work according to an order of a BC board of inquiry. In two private settlements, the Federal Human Rights Commission has decided that women cannot be refused work because of night work or shift work.

Another aspect of sex discrimination is the disparate impact of minimum height and weight requirementa. For instance, height and weight requirements for a police constable's job in the Ottawa Police Force (1979), weight requirement for a labouring job in Sechelt Building Supplies Ltd. (1971), in BC (1979) and height requirement for an entry level labouring job in a sawmill, BC Forest Products Ltd. (1979) were declared illegal by boards of inquiry in Ontario and BC. These requirements were held to have an adverse impact on females as a group. In the BC Forest Products Ltd. case, the BC Supreme Court upheld the decision of the board of inquiry. The Canadian Human Rights Commission reports that the CNR and the Greyhound Lines of Canada have agreed to abolish height requirement for the job of a trainman and for a job as a bus driver respectively; in both cases, a woman had complained to the Commission that height requirement discriminated against females.[14]

Marital status

Marital status is defined in Ontario as the status of 'being married, single, widowed, divorced or separated' and expressly includes 'living with a person of the opposite sex in a conjugal relationship outside marriage'.

In Kerry Segrave v. Zeller's Ltd., 1975 the complainant alleged that he was refused employment and refused training because of his sex and marital status by Zellers Ltd. The applicant arranged for an interview with Zellers in response to and advertisement in the Hamilton Spectator for personnel manager trainees and credit management trainees positions. He was interviewed by a female personnel manager trainee who told him that there were only women in the position of personnel management trainees in the Zellers Company and that the wage scale was too low for the complainant to consider. She also told him that they did not hire men because women would not go to them with their problems. The applicant then expressed interest in the credit manager trainee position. He was given a preliminary interview for the position, bus was not processed further because of 'undesirable' martial status. He had been divorced three months ago and Zellers took this as 'a sign of instability in his background which could cross over into his business life as well'. The board of inquiry found that Zellers had discriminated against Segrave on both sex as well as martial status grounds.

Religion or creed

Judicial and board of inquiry decisions have given no clear indication whether religion and creed include only beliefs in a supreme being or a broader spectrum including a personal philosophy, political beliefs, agnosticism, atheism, and others. Rather, legal decisions have thus far addressed a narrow range of issues such as dress and safety requirements as in Ishar Singh, and Bhinder referred to before, and sabbath observance and staffing requirements as in O'Malley above.

Age

Canadian laws set varying protected age groups: 45 to 65, 40 to 65, 18 to 64, 19 and over, and 19 to 64. Pension and benefit entitlement based on acturial computations and related to an individual's age are uniformly exempted from prohibited discriminatory practices. The Supreme Court of Canada has (1982) ruled that in order for employers to deny employment on the basis of age, two standards must be met. One is based on production and economic reasons and the other is related to the concern for public safety. In either case, more than impression and belief must justify the employer's practices. There must be some objective evidence relating to safe, efficient performance in order to claim exemption as a bonafide occupational requirement.[15]

Bona-fide occupational qualification (BFOQ)

All jurisdictions have a 'bona-fide' occupational qualification exemption in respect of several prohibited grounds of discrimination. This exemption has generally been narrowly construed. The burden of proof in seeking to declare the existence of a BFOQ rests with the employer in most jurisdictions.

On 9 February 1982, the Supreme Court of Canada in a unanimous award established a subjective and an objective standard for a BFOQ, as noted earlier. First, the Supreme Court declared, a BFOQ must be imposed honestly, in good faith, and in the sincerely held belief that such limitation is imposed in the interests of the adequate performance of the work involved with all reasonable dispatch, safety and economy and not for ulterior or extraneous reasons aimed at objectives which could defeat the purpose of the code.

Second, in addition, the Court held, it must be related in an objective sense to the performance of the employment concerned, in that it is reasonably necessary to assure the efficient and economical performance of the job without endangering the employee, his fellow employees and the general public. This judgement was rendered in the Borough of Etobicoke and the Ontario Human Rights Commission and Dunlop, Hall, Gray.[16]

The issue under appeal was whether the Borough discriminated against firefighters Hall and Gray in imposing mandatory retirement at age 60. The Court found that while the requirement was honestly imposed, there was not sufficient evidence that it was objectively based.

As noted above, in Shack v. London Drive-Ur-Self Ltd. in 1974 the employer had claimed that a truck rental clerk's position was too strenuous for a woman and that she would occasionally be alone in the office at night. The board held that neither of these considerations constituted a bona-fide occupational qualification. Similarly, in the Via Rail case, 1980, the tribunal held that Via's acuity standards were not based on a bona-fide occupational requirement since Via had failed to justify the standards.

Several other boards of inquiry have also held that a defense based on BFOQ because of sex will probably only be successful where there is convincing evidence that considerations of public decency eliminate one sex from consideration as in Lindsay v. Provincial Protection and Security Agency Ltd., 1975 in Saskatchewan.

However, other considerations such as (1) an employer's customer preference for service from one or the other sex which might result in economic loss for the employer if that preference is not catered to; (2) a desire to create a particular restaurant atmosphere by having all-female waitresses; or (3) the fact that work site is remote and male dominated; or (4) a lack of female washroom facilities in a plant, are all insufficient grounds for claiming an exemption on the basis of BFOQ.[17]

Affirmative Action

One of the important features of most of the Canadian Human Rights statutes is their provision of special programmes known as affirmative-action programmes. The rationale for such programmes is that because of the effects of pre and post employment job barriers discussed above, the minority groups have not had and do not currently have the opportunity to obtain training and experience in order to qualify for better jobs. Affirmative-action programmes are designed to correct the consequences of past and continuing discrimination.

Affirmative-action is a deliberate, structured approach to improving work opportunities for minority groups and women. This approach involves a series of positive steps undertaken by employers to remove barriers to employment and achieve measurable improvement in recruiting, hiring, training, and promoting qualified worker groups who have in the past been denied access to certain jobs.

Voluntary affirmative programmes are legal in 10 jurisdictions - nine provinces and at the Federal level. In Alberta, the cabinet can approve such a programme. Such programmes are also legal under Section 15 (2) of the Canadian Charter of Rights and Freedoms to come into force in April 1985. In Saskatchewan and at the Federal levels, boards of inquiry can order affirmative-action programmes, if discrimination is found.

A tribunal under the CHRA has recently (22 August 1984) ordered the Canadian National Railways to undertake a mandatory affirmative-action programme. The tribunal, after three years of hearings and deliberations, found that the company had discriminated against women in its hiring practices in the St. Lawrence region. In a landmark decision, the tribunal has ruled that the company is required to hire women for one in four non-traditional (blue collar) jobs in the region until they hold 13 per cent of such jobs. The CN is also required to implement a series of other measures, ranging from abandoning certain mechanical aptitude tests to modifying the way it publicises available jobs.

It is an important decision in several respects. It arose from a complaint laid against CN in 1979 by a Montreal women's lobby group, Action Travail des Femmes. It is the first time that goals have been specified; the goal of 13 per cent roughly corresponds to the proportion of women in blue-collar work in industry generally. The CN has decided to appeal the tribunal ruling to the Federal Court of Appeal.

Affirmative-action programmes have also been ordered by boards of inquiry in other jurisdictions in previous years. For instance, in 1980 in Betty Hendry v. Liquor Control Board of Ontario (LCBO), a similar programme was ordered by an Ontario board in a ruling against the LCBO. However, no goals were specified. The LCBO was required to collaborate with the provincial women's bureau to design a programme which could reduce imbalance in employment opportunities for women. In Shirley Naugler v. The New Brunswick Liquor Corporation in 1976, the New Brunswick board's order on afffirmative-action was appealed to the New Brunswick Supreme Court where it was not upheld. The Hendry ruling was not appealed by the LCBO.

The Saskatchewan Human Rights Commission has published a proposed set of regulations. It has employed these regulations in approving 16 affirmative-action plans. The regulations entail: (1) a systematic analysis of an employer's current workforce, (2) a comparison of the make-up of that workforce with that of the larger surrounding community, (3) establishment of management policies which will move in the direction of overcoming those imbalances which have been identified, within a certain time frame, and (4) a monitoring system to ensure that goals and timetables are being adhered to. In Quebec a 1978 state legislated affirmative-action for the handicapped in the area of education, employment, accessibility, transportation and telecommunications; this statute requires that employers of over 50 persons file plans with the government showing how, over a reasonable period of time, they will alter buildings and facilities to accommodate the handicapped and incorporate handicapped persons into their employment systems. This legislation, while limited to the disabled, is one of the most extensive mandatory 'affirmative-action' in any jurisdication in Canada.

Voluntary affirmative-action programmes have been adopted by some business organisations at the Federal level, in Nova Scotia, Saskatchewan and Ontario. However, a majority of organisations in Canada do not have such programmes. The existing programmes have resulted in very limited progress for minorities and women. It is also true of affirmative-action programmes in the Federal and the Ontario Public Service. [18]

Mandatory affirmative-action or contract compliance programmes

Under these programmes, private contractors are required to have mandatory affirmative-action programmes as a condition of doing business with a government agency. This involves the setting of goals and timetables for minority employment in job categories where such minorities have been under-utilised in proportion to their representation in the labour force. Failure to develop and implement numerical goals which are significant, measurable, attainable and specific could result in the cancellation or termination of existing contracts, and disbarment from competing for futher government contracts.

A provision for mandatory compliance programme exists in the Federal Oil and Gas Production and Conservation Act of March 1982. Similarly, large resource developers such as Amok and Eldorado Nuclear in Saskatchewan and Syncrude in Alberta and the James Bay Project in Quebec have also recruited, employed and trained native people as part of contract compliance programmes.[19]

A study by the author of 74 decisions of boards of inquiry including some court cases from 1975 to 1980 in Alberta, British Columbia, New Brunswick, Nova Scotia, Ontario and Saskatchewan revealed that (a) discrimination was found in 73 per cent or every 7 out of 10 cases that went before a board; (b) a majority (76 per cent) of cases in which discrimination was found pertained to sex discrimination; (c) systemic discrimination was becoming the prevailing view in Canada in an increasing number of cases; (d) a majority (40 per cent) of the cases analysed pertained to employers in the community, business and personal services industrial sector including such enterprises as hospitals, universities, school boards etc. One-fifth of the cases pertained to trade as well as manufacturing sectors; (e) most of the complainants (more than 7 out of 10) were white-collar workers; (f) in the white-collar occupational category, more than half were in the secretarial and service occupations, one-quarter were professionals and one-fifth were in technical occupations.[20]

Remedies

In most cases that went before a board of inquiry, in which discrimination was found, more than one remedy was ordered. The most frequent remedy was compensation for lost wages. The other remedies in order of frequency were an order to employers to (a) display the relevant human rights code in predominant places in employer premises, (b) stop their unlawful conduct, (c) compensate for general damages, (d) compensate for expenses incurred by the complainant, (e) compensate for pain and humiliation suffered by the complainant, (f) reinstate the complainant, (g) write a letter of apology to the complainant, (h) offer employment or opportunity for employment or interview etc. at the next available job opening, (i) allow the relevant human rights commission to conduct human rights workshop for company executives, (j) amend application form and/or other selection tools, (k) write a letter of apology to the relevant human rights commission, and (l) to provide separate facilities for women.[21]

Conclusions

If equal opportunities and affirmative programmes are to work, they have to be effective. However, the little empirical evidence that does exists points to only a limited impact of such legislation.

Critics have suggested changes in both the scope and enforcement of such legislation in Canada in order to improve its effectiveness. Instead of the case-by-case approach adopted by most human rights commissions, class action suits, routine investigation of firms,[22] and contract compliance have been advocated.[23]

Given the multiplicity of factors operating in the labour market, equal opportunity legislation may be a necessary but not sufficient condition for the elimination of inequality between majority and minority groups within the labour force. Legal approaches are limited because they operate only on the demand side of the problem (**i.e.** employer side) and do little to change supply, (**i.e.** education and training of minorities).

Education and training of minorities and women for professional and managerial jobs require lead time. Thus, the lowering of racial and sex barriers does not in itself ensure a supply of qualified people to take advantage of new opportunities. While employers, unions and other institutions can be compelled to stop discrimination against minorities and women, they cannot be compelled to recruit them actively or train them. This suggests the need for supportive policies such as improvements in education and training, affirmative-action programmes, the achievement of sustained levels of employment, and a more equal division of labour in the household.

NOTES

1. **Equality Now!,** Report of the Canadian Parliamentary Committee on Visible Minorities, Ottawa, House of Commons, March 1984.
2. **Ibid.**
3. H.C. Jain and P.J. Sloane, 'The impact of recession on equal opportunities for minorities and women in the United States, Canada and Britain', **The Columbia Journal of World Business,** Summer, 1983.
4. H.C. Jain and P.J. Sloane, **Equal Employment Issues: Race and Sex Discrimination in the Unites States, Canada and Britain,** New York Praiger, 1981.
5. H.C. Jain, 'Discrimination against Indians: Issues and Policies', in K. Lundy and B. Warme (editors), **Work in the Canadian Context: Continuity despite change,** Toronto: Butterworths, 1981.
6. For a detailed discussion of these job barriers, see H.C. Jain, 'Employment and Pay Discrimination in Canada: Theories, evidence and policies', in J. Anderson and M. Gunderson (editors), **Union-Management Relations in Canada,** Don Mills, Ontario: Addison-Wessley, 1982. Also see, H.C. Jain, **Disadvantaged Groups on the Labour Market and Measures to Assist Them,** Paris: OECD, 1979.
7. The cases mentioned here have not been published and hence the lack of documentation. The author collected these cases from the relevant Human Rights Commission.

8. In the **O'Mallay** case, Mrs. O'Malley had worked full-time for Simpsons Sears for seven years as a sales clerk in the ladies wear section. She accepted working on two out of three Saturdays as a normal part of her job until she joined the Seventh Day Adventist Church. Because of the religious requirement, of observing Sabbath from the sunset on Friday evening to sunset on Saturday, she informed the store that she was unwilling to work on Friday evenings or Saturdays. The Personnel Manager explained that the Saturday work requirement applied to all sales people. She was asked to resign but she refused to quit. She was, therefore, transferred to part-time employee status. She filed a complaint with the Ontario Human Rights Commission (OHRC) on the basis of religious discrimination.

Since the OHRC could not affect a settlement between the parties, a board of inquiry was appointed. The board concluded that the Saturday work condition amounted to unintentional discrimination. Therefore, the board decided, the Simpsons Sears store had a duty to offer her reasonable accommodation.

The Ontario Divisional Court and the Ontario Court of Appeal both decided that intention was essential to employment discrimination as defined by the old Ontario code; in addition, they decided that the old code did not have an indirect discrimination provision and that the Saturday requirement was a bona-fide occupational requirement. In the **Bhinder** case, the complainant before the court was a practising Sikh, who after four-and-a-half years as a railway electrician was required to wear a hard hat when his work area was designated a hard hat area persuant to the **Canada Labour Code** dress code regulations. Since Bhinder's religion required him to wear a turban and he decided to abide by the tenets of his faith, his employment was terminated by the employer. He filed a complaint with the CHRC claiming employment discrimination on the basis of religion.

Since no settlement could be reached by conciliation, the Commission appointed a tribunal. The tribunal found that wearing a turban had safety implications for no one except the electrician himself, and that wearing a hard hat was not a bona-fide occupational qualification, even though the CNR had innocently imposed this requirement resulting in the adverse impace. The tribunal ordered the railway to reinstate Bhinder with no loss of seniority and $14,500 in lost wages.

The Federal Court of Appeal overturned the tribunal decision. The Court ruled that (1) indirect discrimination does not exist in the language of the Canadian Human Rights Act, (2) employers are under no duty to make reasonable accommodation, and (3) the hard hat policy was a bona-fide requirement.
9. Except for British Columbia, all jurisdictions have Human Rights Commissions.
10. The Province of Quebec is the only exception to this rule.
11. D.G. Hill, 'The role of the human rights commission: The Ontario experience', **University of Toronto Law Journal**, 19, 1979.
12. H.C. Jain and P.J. Sloane, 'The impact of recession ...' **op.cit.** Also see **Equality Now! op.cit.**

13. **Annual Report,** Ontario Human Rights Commission, Toronto: OHRC, 1983.
14. **Summary of decisions taken by the Canadian Human Rights Commission at its meetings of 17 and 18 November 1980,** (Nov. 1980) and **Summary of decisions taken by the Canadian Human Rights Commission at its meetings of 15 and 16 September 1980,** September 1980).
15. **The Ontario Human Rights Commission et al v. The Borough of Etobicoke,** Supreme Court of Canada, judgement delivered 9 February 1982.
16. **Ibid.**
17. H.C. Jain, 'Race and sex discrimination in Canada', **Relations Industrielles,** 37, 1982.
18. H.C. Jain, 'Visible Minorities and Affirmative Action', an unpublished report, August 1984.
19. **Ibid.**
20. H.C. Jain, 'Race and sex discrimination in Canada', **op.cit.**
21. **Ibid.**
22. Apparently, routine investigation of firms does bring increased back pay settlements. For instance, 157 investigations and routine audits under Ontario's equal pay regulations resulted in $284,000.00 of salary increases and back pay settlements for women employees over a 10 month period, April 1980 to January 1981. Thirty-six employers were found to be in violation of the law in cases involving 134 women. The beefed-up inspection procedures by the Ministry of Labour were made possible by the hiring of 11 new officials who were added to the Ministry's equal pay monitoring team in Spring 1980. See, **Globe and Mail, 27 February 1981, B-8.** A comparison of previous statistics highlights the role of routine audits in increasing back pay settlements. In 1979/80, nine employers were found in violation of the law involving 44 employers and $56,212.00 in settlement; in 1978/79, eight employers involving 29 employees were found to be in violation and the settlement was $8,311.00; in 1977/78, nine employers involving 20 employees were found to be in violation and the settlement was $6,672.67. The exception to the rule was the year 1976/77 when 29 employers and 452 employees were involved and the settlement was $535,966.02. In 1975/76, however, the settlement sum of $31,248.88 was in line with other years and involved 17 employers and 76 employees. These figures were provided by the Women's Bureau in the Ontario Ministry of Labour.
23. **Equality now! op.cit.**

6. France

J. Rojot

I. INTRODUCTION

A. International sources

In France the main relevant international source derived from the ILO is now Convention 111 adopted by the International Labour Organisation on 25 June 1958 and ratified by the French Parliament by an Act of 15 April 1981 (Act No. 81-357). Nevertheless the Migration for Employment Convention (97), the Right to Organise and Collective Bargaining Convention (98) and the Equal Remuneration Convention (100) are also applicable, having been ratified by the French Parliament on 31 June 1953 (Act No. 53-1290), 7 September 1951 (Act No. 51-1072) and 10 December 1952 (Act No. 52-1309) respectively. These three conventions deal with specific aspects of discrimination in employment in less general terms than Convention 111, but apply to equal treatment for migrant workers, discrimination on grounds of union membership and the equality of male and female wages.[1]

However, it should be noted that Convention No. 117 which was adopted by the ILO on 19 June 1962 and assigns to national social policies the goal of suppressing dicrimination against employees on the basis of race, colour, sex, beliefs, tribal associations or trade union affiliation, has not been ratified by the French Parliament and thus has no consequences in France.

The main International Sources derived from European Law[2] include the Treaty of Rome and EEC Directives. Section 48 of the Treaty of Rome lays down the principle of the Free Movement of Workers from Member States within the Community and specifies that this provision implies the abolition of discrimination based on nationality (against workers from Members States only, of course). In addition, Section 119 of the EEC Treaty obliges the Member States to implement the principle of equal pay for equal work for men and women.

These provisions of the EEC Treaty were later completed as follows: Sections 7-9 of Regulation No. 1612/68 prohibits in the widest sense discrimination on grounds of nationality. Again this applies only to nationals of Member States and also only for reasons of nationality. Contrary provisions are automatically void. Regulation 312/76 provides for equal treatment for EEC nationals in terms of access to positions of administration or leadership of a labour union.

Directive No. 75-117 of 10 February 1975 provides for equal pay for men and women and Directive 76-207 of 9 February 1976 provides for equal treatment of men and women in occupational life, whilst allowing for positive discrimination to remedy inequalities presently affecting women.

The 1948 Declaration on Human Rights, not being a convention, has no imperative consequences under French Law. Nevertheless, the European Convention of Human Rights elaborated in 1950 embodies the universal declaration principles for European countries. France ratified it by an Act of 31 December 1973 and a Decree of 3 May 1974. Its Section 11 on Trade Union freedom covers aspects of discrimination because of union activities not falling under Convention 111. Finally, the European Social Charter, signed in 1961, was ratified by France by an Act of December 1972 and a Decree of October 1974. Section 4 provides for equal wages for men and women and Section 5 for union freedom.

It should be noted that under French law once an international convention has been ratified by parliament it supercedes national law and theoretically in a case of conflict with national law the convention should be applied directly by the courts.

B. National Sources [3]

National sources of a general nature are twofold: The 1789 Declaration of Rights of Man and Citizen and the Constitution of 1946. Section I deems less men to have been born and remain free and with equal rights, thus social differences may only be rooted in common utility. Section VI of the Declaration further establishes that all citizens have equal access to all honours, positions and public employment according to their capacities without any difference other than 'their virtues and their talents'.

The preamble of the Constitution of 27 October 1946 reiterates that all human beings possess sacred and inalienable rights, without distinction of race, religion or beliefs. It also specifies that the law guarantees women rights in all domains equal to those of men. It further provides that no-one can be victimized in his or her work or employment for reasons of origin, opinion or belief.

For a long period these national sources were the only available basis of judicial protection against discrimination of all kinds. Individuals who felt discriminated against had to sue for redress in the civil courts if they were in private employment or in the administrative courts if they were civil servants or public employees of certain categories. The highest courts of the judicial and administrative order, the Cour de Cassation and the Conseil d'Etat[4] elaborated jurisprudence on this basis as well as on the basis of the public order nature of some generally acknowledged rights, which therefore could not be ignored or contradicted by individual contracts, such as for instance, the right to matrimony. Also many decisions had the consequence of repressing discriminatory measures by employers on the grounds that it constituted unwarranted interference with the private life of the employee who enjoyed a general right to protection.

More recently, a large number of legal texts covering different kinds of discrimination have appeared. Some cover general aspects, some cover employment only. Some are aimed at protecting several categories of people, other at only one; some cover a broad range of discriminatory practices in employment other than dismissal or hiring. Thus the concepts such as the definition of discrimination, the Acts/sources etc. ... vary.

The situation is therefore rather complex and the best and clearest way to deal with it is perhaps to take in chronological order Acts of a somewhat general character, then move to categories of individuals who are specially protected and who may or may not fall under the texts of a general nature. These new provisions are embedded in the Penal or the Labour Code[5], thus providing for criminal penalties in cases of proven discriminatory practices, in contrast with the civil or administrative remedies which were the only ones available heretofore.

This being noted we shall review discrimination in employment case by case.

II. DISCRIMINATION FOR REASONS OF ORIGIN, NATIONALITY, ETHNIC, RACE OR RELIGION

Firstly a difference should be underlined. According to Convention 111 the provisions to be discussed do not mention specifically 'colour' or 'social origin'. Nevertheless it can be held that the term 'origin' applies also to social origins, and that 'ethnic' covers discrimination for reasons of colour. Sex and political opinion will be treated separately below.

A. Provisions of the Penal Code

Section 416-1 and 2 aims at 'general Acts of discrimination: Refusal of selling, a good or a service etc...' It was introduced by an Act of 1 July 1972, whose purpose was to fight racism and to make it easier to prosecute or allow victims to sue for acts of racism in everyday life. But sub-section 3 of section 416 is specifically aimed at employers or persons responsible for hiring who, without legitimate reason, decline to hire or decide to dismiss a person because of his or her origin, his belonging or not belonging to an ethnic group, a nation, a race or a religion, or who has submitted a job offer to a condition on these grounds. Later, as will be discussed below, an Act of 11 July 1975 added sex and family situations to these discriminatory motives.

The penalties incurred by such discrimination are a prison sentence of between two months and one year and a fine of from 2,000 to 20,000 francs. The court may also order posting of the decision and its publication in newspapers to a cost of up to 20,000 FF. Two other provisions of the Penal Code should be mentioned:

Sections 187-1 of the Penal Code, instituted by the same Act of 1972, punishes any public servant or person in charge of a public service who knowingly denies the benefit of a right to a person because of his or her origin, his belonging or non-belonging to an ethnic group, a nation or a religion.

Section 187-2 punishes the same persons who by their actions, whether omissions or commissions, have contributed to rendering more difficult the exercise of any economic activity in normal conditions

85

for reasons of national origin, ethnicity, nationality, race or religion.

Obviously sections 187-1 and 187-2 do not fall exactly within our field of analysis because their scope of application is restricted to public employees. Nevertheless, their existence should be noted.

Reasons of sex and family situation have also been added to section 187-1 by the Act of 11 July 1975, but not to section 187-2, enacted later in 1977. The penalties are a prison term of from six months to two years and a fine of from 3,000 to 40,000 FF.

Section 416-3, the provision of a more general nature, was given facilities for its application by the legislature. Not only 'the employer' was responsible but also anyone having the right to hire or fire in the enterprise. This provision avoided complex issues which could have voided the provision because of the legal status of allocation of responsibility for fault between the employer and an employee acting within or outside his or her job prerogatives. Although it could certainly have been held that an employee engaged in discriminatory activities was rightly dismissed for a serious offense, that solution was not automatic and carried no penal consequences.

Also the legislature held that some Associations constituted in order to fight racism were given the right to bring a victim's suit to court for discriminatory activities, without the agreement of the victim. The goal of this provision was to avoid intimidation of people discriminated against in order that they should take no legal action. This would be particularly easy in the case of an employment relationship.

Nevertheless, as a whole the results of section 416 were particularly disappointing. First, only direct discrimination was mentioned. Indirect discrimination was forgotten. Second, some discriminatory motives were omitted and therefore not liable to punishment; these include motives rooted in political views, membership of a political party or a sect, and the like. Thirdly, only denial of hiring and dismissal were covered. Transfer, demotion and denial of promotion remained free of punishment. Fourthly, and even more importantly, the resulting number of suits on grounds of discrimination, including but not limited to employment, was very small.[6] Thus section 416 has been relatively ineffective. This can be attributed to two reasons:[7] the inclusion of a legitimate reason as a justification for discrimination and the difficulties of proof of discrimination.

The first cannot be easily altogether avoided, for it may have to apply for reasons not linked to racism but to public policy, as for instance in the case of foreign workers in illegal situations. The second is hard to avoid, especially in matters of hiring where it is easy and legally acceptable for the employer to claim any reason, or no reason at all, for not hiring an employee. It is more difficult but still possible to hide an illegitimate racist reason for dismissal but such cases are probably rarer, except for change of employer.

No statistics are available on the application of section 187-1 and 187-2 of the Penal Code, but it can safely be assumed that the results are unlikely to be better since it is no easier to bring proof against a civil servant than against an employer.

It should be noted that the opportunity of suing on behalf of a victim given to associations was one reason for what little efficacy section 416 achieved. But of 18 cases introduced, leading to the ten convictions registered,[8] 13 were introduced by the public prosecutor on complaint by the victim and five by associations.

Within this framework a different, but related, point should be made here. An Act of 17 October 1981 gives Trade Unions the possibility of bringing suit by exercising the employee's right to sue in cases where a migrant worker who is in a fraudulent situation (**i.e.** an illegal immigrant), is owed wages or severance pay by an employee. The union does not need the explicit consent of the employee; it suffices that s/he does not oppose the suit. This provision, of course, aims to avoid undue advantage taken by unscrupulous employers of the illegal situation of the employee, unlikely to sue for what is due to him or her because of the threat of expulsion.

New Provisions in the Labour Law

The new majority which gained access to power in May 1981 carried out a wide range of reforms, including important changes in Labour Law.[9] One-third of the Labour Code was changed. Some of the new provisions directly affected discrimination in employment for reasons of sex and will be discussed below. Other provisions deal with discrimination in a much more general way and will be described here.

An Act of 4 August 1982 dealt with individual freedom of employees within the enterprise. Two provisions are directly aimed at discrimination in employment:

The shop rules (réglement intérieur) govern behavior at the work place and complement labour law, collective agreements, and individual contracts of employment as far as the reciprocal rights and duties of employer and employee are concerned. They were previously freely unilaterally elaborated by the employer after non-binding advice from the entreprise committee and controle for conformity to the letter of the law by the labour inspector. They are still not negotiated and are unilaterally decided, but the provisions they may now legally include have been limited by the new act.

Notably, the new section L 122-35 of the Labour Code provides that shop rules cannot contain provisions harming employees for reasons of their origin, sex, family situation, ethnicity, nationality, race, political opinion, faith or handicap when they have equal capacities. The new act also confirms that the employer retains disciplinary powers but it further provides in the new section L 122-45 that 'No employee can be punished or dismissed because of origin, (sex, family situation), ethnicity, nationality or race, (political opinions, union activities) or religious convictions'.

The new provisions are too recent to have been subject to court interpretation; therefore their harmonisation with other existing provisions, and their clarification and interpretation by the Supreme Court are as yet unknown. It should nevertheless be observed that section 122-45 covers cases of discrimination in employment in a slightly different manner than section 416-3 of the Penal Code. It does not deal with the denial of hiring, probably because of its location within the section of the code dealing with shop rules and disciplinary procedures, **i.e.** with existing employees. Nevertheless it forbids dismissal and all minor disciplinary sanctions. However, it does not apply to transfer, demotion or refusal of promotion for non-disciplinary reasons but strictly and openly based on origin or ethnicity, race, nationality or religion. Curiously enough, discrimination here remains free of sanctions. Also religious convictions are wider than religions and cover religious beliefs, without membership of a cult, which was unprotected by section 416-3 of the Penal Code.

Finally, an Act of 6 October 1982 covers grounds which is at the limits of discrimination for reasons of nationality and union activity. Formerly, French Labour Law allowed some discriminatory provisions against foreign nationals in terms of union rights. They have been progressively dismantled but this act now cancels the last vestiges of such discrimination.

The new section L 411-5 of the Labour Code spells out the freedom of any individual to join a trade union 'whatever sex, age, nationality'. Foreign nationals may now hold leadership postitions of responsibility within a union without fulfilling a condition of five years' prior residence in France and without being limited in number to one-third of such positions, as was the case previously (New section L 411-4 of the Labour Code). It had also been necessary to be able to express oneself in French in order to be elected as an employee's delegate or a member of the enterprise committee. (A former condition of French nationality had been abolished earlier.) The Act (section L 420-9 and L 433-4 of the Labour Code) abolishes that final barrier.

III. DISCRIMINATION FOR REASONS OF GENDER

Gender

This topic deserves particular attention. Previously it was generally treated like other types of discrimination and was also often mentioned alongside them within legal texts dealing with the subject. However, it has recently been the focus of governmental scrutiny and the object of specific wide-ranging legislative provisions, some of which are of an innovative character:

Several previous governments had demonstrated an interest in the condition of women in society, and the present one is no exception to that new concern. A minister in charge of womens' rights, attached to the Prime Minister, has again been appointed.

In the wake of a report calling attention to discrimination and disparities in female work,[10] the ministry issued a new report dated 26 August 1982 and titled 'Women in France, within a Society of Inequalities'. The ministry's analysis and work did not limit itself to the employment aspect of women's condition in France but gave a general view of the subject. The aspect which specifically concerns us gives rise to new important legal provisions regarding innovations in employment.

Previous Existing General Provisions

Nevertheless provisions existing before the new Act of 1983 should be first recalled in order to bring about a better understanding of the change of perspective, and also because most of them still stand in their own right independently of the new act and usefully supplement it, beyond the civil action outlined in the introduction in terms of civil rights.

An Act of 13 July 1965 modified section 223 of the Civil Code which provided that the husband could, in the interest of the family, forbid the exercise of professional activity by his wife and it cancelled that provision.

An Act of 4 July 1975 modified section 416-3 of the Penal Code discussed above, including sex among the discriminatory conditions. Employers were forbidden to make a job offer, employment or dismissal under penalties outlined above, unless there were legitimate reasons for so doing.[11]

The same act forbade the employer to take into account the state of pregnancy of a woman to deny her hiring, to dismiss her during her probationary period, or to transfer her to another job.[12] Het outright dismissal was already forbidden by an Act of 30 December 1966, which also granted paid confinement leave before and after childbirth.

Section 187-1 of the Penal Code, discussed above, also applies since the same Act of 1975 for reasons of gender and this covers a case where any public servant or person in charge of a public service has knowingly denied benefits issuing from a right because of sex. Nevertheless, section 187-2 does not cover gender and thus excludes the activity of a public servant who has contributed to making more difficult the exercise of an economic activity in normal conditions for a woman (or a man), whereas it applies to other cases of discrimination.

Specific Provisions

In the domain of wages a Decree of July 1946 abolished the concept of a 'female wage', that is the application of an automatic legal discount applied to womens' wages. The Act of 11 February 1950 established a new system of collective bargaining making compulsory the inclusion of provisions mandating equal wages for equal work in collective agreements if they were to be extendable industry-wide by decree of the ministry. The Act of 22 December 1972 introduced new sections, L 140-2 to L 140-8, into the Labour Code. Its goal was to make it compulsory for employers to ensure that for the same work or for work of equal value, men and women were paid equal compensation. However, relatively little use was made in practice of that legal provision and it was of little effect. In particular, the term 'equal value', retained by the act without a definition being given of what was to be 'value' and how it was to be estimated opened the doors to some discrimination allowed by the courts.[13]

Besides, economic studies clearly demonstrated that a remaining wage gap existed between male and female workers. In 1975 the wage differential measured in terms of comparison of hourly wage for workers in industry was 3.6 per cent. But in terms of yearly comparisons for the same year, individual compensation received by women was on average 31.6 per cent below that received by men (a 29.5 per cent differential for workers, increasing to 36.0 per cent for managerial employees). The reason for this differential was not so much that wages were different for identical jobs held by men and women but that the structure of the female labour force compared to the male labour force embraced lower paid jobs in terms of type of industry, seniority, skill, grade, etc... The author noted that the legal provision against sex discrimination was mostly aimed at that first area whereas the second was probably most pertinent for explaining the largest part of the differential.[14]

Women were also the object of 'positive discrimination' consisting of measures aimed at protecting the 'weaker sex'. This trend has also been reversed to take into account the realities of modern employment and the increased proportion of women in the labour force. It gave rise to a new kind of provision of positive discrimination aiming to facilitate the access of women to employment and no longer solely to protect them. The following provisions are illustrative of that trend.[15] The hird pact for employment of 10 July 1979 partially exonerated from paying wage-related social contributions employers hiring unemployed women who had been for more than 10 years widowed, divorced, legally separated or single and raising at least one child. Concurrent provisions were aimed at facilitating their professional training. An Act of 1 July 1980 included women who had raised one or more children to members of the labour force in order to benefit from provisions granting easier access to higher education.

Besides, women can apply for state and local government . jobs without age limit if they are obliged to work after the death of their husband (since 1975) or if they are mothers of three or more children, or of one child and widowed, divorced, legally separated or single.

Also, some previous legal barriers to the employment of women have been removed. Since an Act of 10 July 1975, no disctinction can be made between men and women for the recruitment of civil servants, except for specific jobs listed by decree (Decree of 25 March 1977).

Besides, several provisions of the Labour Code regulate for reasons of safety and hygiene the jobs and conditions of work applicable to women and young workers below 18 years.[16] These provisions were updated by a Decree of 5 August 1975. Later the prohibitions of work at night was lifted for women with managerial or technical positions.

Forerunners of the New Act

The texts we reviewed were separate texts aimed at specific and narrowly defined discriminatory practices.

The new sections (Act of 4 August 1982 and Act of 28 October 1982) L 122-35 and L 122-45 of the Labour Code were made in the wake of the new legislation and discussed above with racial discrimination. Section 122-35 includes sex among the reasons which cannot be written into the shop rules by the employer as justifying discriminatory treatment. Section 122-45 includes gender among the reasons which cannot legally justify discipline or dismissal by the employer. However, the qualification of the action of the employer as being discriminatory will be the key to the application of this text. Already the Supreme Court in 1976 decided that no discrimination had taken place in the following circumstances: A married couple were hired as joint watchmen in a building. Without a global loss of the couple's salary, the husband's wage was raised and the wife's wage was reduced by 2/3 and she was demoted to assistant watchman with all lighter workload, on the grounds that the constant presence of two employees as watchmen was unnecessary. The Supreme Court accepted that reasoning, denying discrimination for reasons of sex in that case.[17]

The wave of new acts in 1982 also opened the way for certain methods of information on discrimination and the implementation of equality of treatment, which were forthcoming with the new Act of 1983.[18]

Section L 432-4, introduced by an Act of 28 October 1982, and dealing with the powers of the enterprise committee, provides that the employer must submit to the committee information on the pattern of evolution of hourly and monthly wages, sorted out notably by sex (Sub-section 3), with the evolution of employment analysed also by sex (Sub-section 8).

The Act of 13 November 1982 introduces changes into the regulation of collective bargaining in France, including a 'duty to bargain' heretofore unknown to French law. It also contains two provisions of interest here: Section L 132-28 of the Labour Code now provides that the annual round of negotiations at company level, which compulsorily bears on current wages and the actual duration and organisation of work, begins with information provided by the employer 'which must allow a comparative analysis of the situation of men and women regarding employment and their qualifications, wages paid, time worked and organisation of work'.

In addition, section L 132-12 and L 133-15 concern bargaining at industry level, which remains the most favoured level for collective agreements in France. It is now compulsory to bargain annually over wages and every five years over job scales. The parties are to examine them by sex. Also collective agreements, in order to be liable to be extended industry-wide to all enterprises, even where they are not party to the collective agreement through the employers' association, must now contain provisions explicity applying the principle of 'equal wage for equal work' (L 133-5-4°-d) as well as the principle of equality of treatment in employment[19] and measures aimed at correcting existing inequalities (L 133-5-9°). A new section, 136-2, gives to the National Commission of Collective Bargaining (formerly known as the Superior Commission of Collective Agreements) the power to monitor that situation at national level. The commission also has competence to make proposals to the Minister of Labour and Social Affairs to remedy situations of inequality.

The Act of 13 July 1983 - New Regulation

The new provisions contained the germs of the new act, but were still without a coherent legal framework:

91

The Act of 13 July 1983 modifies in depth chapter III of Title II of Book I of the Labour Code where it introduces new sections L 123-1 to L 123-7. It has the effect of adducing a general principle of equality between women and men in all aspects of life at work, called 'occupational equality' (égalité professionnelle). Even though the act refrains from expressly formulating such a principle in explicit terms, the wording of its contents has the same results.[20] In particular this is because section L 123-1 mentions that no one can take into account gender in any measure, notably in the field of payment, etc. This has the result that the list of areas that follows is not inclusive. This means indirectly that equality of the sexes in all aspects of life at work is now established. Nevertheless the meaning of this new principle of 'occupational equality' is nowhere defined.[21]

In any case the new principle of occupational equality goes further than a formal affirmation of the principle of equality of rights between men and women. It aims at **'de facto'** actual and genuine equality in employment: equality of rights, equality of treatment, in fact equality of opportunity, including the possibility of remedial action.

Then the act proceeds to spell out specific provisions.

A new section, L 123-1-a, forbids 'mentioning or having someone mention, in an employment offer, whatever the characteristic of the contract of employment may be, or in any form of advertisement related to hiring, the gender of the candidate'. Clearly this section covers part of the ground already covered by section 416-3°, striking out the possibility of claiming a 'legitimate reason' for discrimination by the employer, thus answering some criticisms of section 416-3. Besides, section 416-3 now carries an appendix providing that its provisions regarding discrimination for reasons of sex apply 'according to the conditions listed in section 123-1 of the Labour Code'. Penalites are thus identical in both cases and apply to both the employer and the advertising media.

If legitimate reason is no longer valid to justify discrimination, section 123-1 nevertheless applies only 'within the limits of the provisions of the present code and except if belonging to one or the other sex is a determinant condition to fill a position or carry out occupational activities'. First, women cannot be employed for work presenting some special hardships, as discussed above; thus a job offer for such work could legally discriminate. Second, it is of the nature of certain activities that they can only be carried out by a man or a woman, as in the case of a model for instance. Nevertheless, the interpretation of this point will not be left freely to the parties or even the courts. A list of such activities and occupations will be established by decree and periodically revised. They will be the only ones where sex can be admitted as a determinant condition to fulfil a position. The first list is expected shortly.

Section 123-1-b forbids refusals of hiring, job transfers, termination or non-renewal of employment contracts based on the sex of the individual concerned, or decided on criteria which are different according to sex. It is combined with section 416-3 of the Penal Code in the same terms as above, but it is to be noted that is goes further. Heretofore, discriminatory transfers were not covered by the law, other than for the relatively difficult civil actions discussed in the introduction.

The limits to application are the same as for section 123-1-a. They apply also to section 123-1-c, which forbids taking into consideration the sex of an employee notably for matters of pay, training, posting, job classification, qualification, promotion or transfer.

Section 123-2 extends to collective agreements the provisions of section 123-1-c which are aimed at the behaviour of the employer. In other words, a collective agreement can no longer contain a provision granting special benefit to one or several employees for reasons of their sex, whether male or female. This applies also to provisions which would have been beneficial to women. The penalty is that the whole collective agreement, not only the wrongful provision, becomes void. Nevertheless, such acquired rights, for reasons of custom, individual contracts of employment or existing collective agreements valid at the time the acts were passed remain in force and the collective agreements remain valid; but the parties are invited by the law to re-negotiate them.

Of course section 123-2 does not mean that the existing protective provisions for women, whether or not in the code, are also void. The law having a value superior to that of collective agreements, such protective provisions which apply can validly be written into collective agreements,[22] although they probably cannot be improved upon and must respect the wording of the law. Section L 123-2 also explicitly expects from its scope a series of dispositions protective of women and spelled out at various places in the code. They all deal with maternity, pregnancy or motherhood. Clearly it is the spirit of the new act to grant specific advantages to women for reasons of child bearing only and not because of their sex. Specific advantages to men are of course also condemned by the terms of the law; thus both sexes are to be treated equally, in terms of advantages as well as in terms of hardships, except for inescapable reasons.

Finally a new section, L 900-4, of the Labour Code included in the Book of the Code dealing with continuous occupational training within the framework of permanent education provides that 'for the application of the present book no distinction can be made between men and women except in cases where belonging to one or the other sex is the determinant condition for filling the position or carrying out the occupational activity which is related to the purpose of the training'.

Section L 152-1-1° provides for the penalties of a fine of from 2,000 to 20,000 FF and/or imprisonment of between two months and one year, but the sentence may be suspended or decreased by the court for conviction of infringement of the provisions of section 123-1. Besides, the court may order at the expense of the convicted defendant the posting of the court decision and its publication in newspapers, within a cost limit of 20,000 FF. Nevertheless, the goal of the law being to remedy a state of affairs rather than to punish, the court may adjourn its sentencing and enjoin the employer to take within the enterprise the measures necessary to re-establish occupational equality between men and women, after consultation with the enterprise committee and within a given time period. The court may further in its decision to adjourn sentencing enjoin the employer to implement the provisions thus defined. Then at a session after the delay has elapsed the judge, after appreciation of the provisions decided and implemented by the employer, may or not decide to impose penalties.

Section 140-2 of the Code has also been amended. We noted above that the absence of definition of 'equal value' hampered the application by the employer of equal pay for men and women. A new section, 140-2-3, remedies that state of affairs by spelling out criteria allowing concrete appreciation of the value of work to be taken into account to decide on equal value: To be considered as of equal value, work demands of the employee a comparable set of:

- Occupational knowledge demonstrated by a title, diploma, or occuaptional acquired practice
- Capacities flowing from acquired experience
- Responsibilities
- Physical or nervous capabilities.

A new section, 140-2-4, also provides that 'disparities in pay between establishments of the same enterprise cannot, for similar work or for work of equal value, be based on the belonging of the employee of these establishments to a particular sex. This last provision was added to cover a situation which was recently the subject of a court decision.[23] A company operating a plant in a given city employing mostly men opened another plant more than 100 Km away in a region with a high percentage of available unemployed female manpower, and for manufacturing the same product hired almost entirely women, who were paid less. The courts denied sexual discrimination on the grounds of freedom of the separate plant managers to manage and the absence of discrimination within any given single plant. However, it seems unlikely that the new text would result in a different decision in a similar case.[24] Nonetheless it would be easy for the employer to claim convincingly that the difference in wages was based on other considerations than sex, such as labour market conditions. Evidence that the wage differential is exclusively due to sex would be in such a case very difficult to adduce.

Failure to observe the prescriptions of section L 140-2 is liable to the same penalties that apply to section L 123 as discussed above. The penalties apply as many times as there are employees discriminated against. The same possibilities for agreement of positive action and adjournment of the sentence apply.

To render the application of section 140-2 easier the legislature has introduced a provision relatively new in French law but already introduced and used to some extent for cases of dismissal for unjust or unreal causes and which applies fully to restrictions of individual rights and freedom of employees within the enterprise. It deals with the way in which proof has to be brought. Without going to the extreme of reverting the burden of proof (the employer would then have to prove that he does not discriminate) section L 140-8 nevertheless provides that the judge, who has knowledge of the elements of proof of discrimination claimed by the plaintiff will also have the employer furnish elements of proof justifying the absence of discrimination in the alleged wage differential. The judge may order all provisions deemed necessary (experts, etc.) before reaching a decision. If a doubt remains, it should benefit the employee according to the Act of 13 July 1983 - Implementation and Positive Discrimination.

In the first place, the legislature forecasts that many female employees might hesitate to sue their employer for discrimination, fearing for their job security. Thus unions have been allowed to take on all law suits issuing from sections L 123-1 and L 140-2 to 140-4 in favour of an employee of the enterprise without being empowered to do so by the employee, but only provided that the employee has been warned and has not opposed the suit within a period of 15 days. The employee retains the right to join the suit later.

Secondly, if an employee is dismissed after having brought suit against his/her employer, directly or after having not opposed a union suit, and if there is no real or serious cause for dismissal whose only reason is the suit, then Section L 123-5 provides that the dismissal is void and of no effect and the employee is to be reinstated, or by his/her choice to consider him/her self wrongly dismissed and be compensated by the severance pay provided by law, [25] the applicable collective agreement and contract of employment plus a sum equal to a minimum of six months' wages. This provision is extremely strong. Mandatory reinstatement was previously ordered by courts only in the case of wrongful dismissal for no genuine and serious cause of employee representatives or union delegates. The burden of the proof of discriminatory intention is here too placed equally on both parties and assessed independently by the judge.

Thirdly, the text of sections 123-1 to 123-7 must be posted at the work place and within and at the door of places of hiring.

Fourthly the provisions regarding the information of the enterprise committee have been enhanced. In addition to the existing provisions, in all enterprises over 50 employees, the employer must now give the committee[26] and the union section 'a written report on the compared situation on the general conditions of employment and training of women and men within the enterprise'. This report must include 'a quantitative analysis' evidencing, for all categories of employers the respective situation of men and women as far as are concerned 'hiring, training, promotion, qualifications, classification, conditions of work and actual pay'. Besides the report must enumerate all provisions taken during the past year in view of insuring occupational equality, objectives for the following year, and it must define quantitatively and qualitatively specific actions to that goal and an evaluation of their cost. If actions asked for by the committee or forecasted by the report of the precedent year did not take place, the report should also explain why. Also the enterprise committee has, in French law, the right to give its advice on the plan for employer training established by the employer, which must compulsorily amount to a minimum of 1.2 per cent of the wage bill. Before deliberating the committee has to be given, three weeks in advance, a set of documents to which are now added the 'provisions to be taken to ensure occupational equality between women and men within the enterprise.'

This set of five provisions clearly demonstrates that the legislature intends the law to be enforced as much as possible. Besides, the Act of 1983 also provides for positive descrimination and measures aimed at 'catching up' on the actual **de facto** situation where past discrimination has caused inequality to the disadvantage of women. There also exists the possibility already discussed for the court to adjourn sentencing in exchange for positive action by the employer.

Two provisions have been introduced. Section L 123-3 of the Labour Code provides that with the exception of sections L 123-1 and L 123-2 discussed above, temporary measures to the benefit of women, in order to re-establish the equality of opportunity between men and women, and particularly to remedy the current **de facto** inequalities, are allowed. They may result from regulatory governmental action, from extended collective agreements or from enterprise plans for professional equality, which constitute the second provision.

Section 123-4 provides that such plans are negotiated within the enterprise by the employer and unions, unless there is opposition, written and motivated, by the Departmental Director of Labour. Without union agreement on the plan, the employer can implement it unilaterally. These plans can benefit from governmental subsidies[27] up to 35 per cent of the capital investment needed and 50 per cent of other expenses, if they constitute exemplary actions to realise occupational equality between men and women and if they concern notably training, promotion or organisation of work. The subsidy is the subject of a convention with the Minister in charge of womens' rights upon the advice of a commission created for that purpose. Finally, a superior council for occupational equality is to be created shortly with the task of participating in the definition, implementation and application of policy in that domain.

IV. OTHER GROUNDS OF DISCRIMINATION

The main grounds for discrimination under the French Law have already been covered: we dealt with race, colour, ethnicity, national or social origin and religion in section II. Sex discrimination was also discussed in section III. However, certain of the legal texts we reviewed also apply in part to discrimination on other grounds, such as marital status, handicap and political opinions. Besides, French law also covers other grounds of discrimination and specifically prohibits discrimination for reasons of union membership or union activities. The relevant provisions will be briefly reviewed for each case.

A. Marital Status

Sections 416 and 187-1 of the Penal Code and L 122-35 and L 122-45 of the Labour Code already discussed also use the term 'family situation' which includes but is not limited to marital status. Currently most of the problems raised under the heading of the family situation related to marital status. It is not necessary to come back to the meaning of these new provisions. They have already been dealt with. There is of course as yet no case law, no cases having reached the Supreme Court on the basis of sections 122-5 and 122-45 which were introduced in 1982. Nevertheless, case law established before on general principles was already restricting discrimination because of marital status. In the case of 'provisions of celibacy' in employment contracts these were voided by the courts because the 'right to marriage' was an individual right protected by public order which could not be limited or alienated, but the possibility that 'evident reasons' might justify it was left open. Pure and simple dismissal of a female employee for reasons of marriage [29] was deemed unlawful as were shop rules forbidding marriage between employees of hiring a spouse from an employee[30] (still with a reference to exceptional cases where the necessities of the position could justify it).

Nevertheless, dismissal of an employee whose husband was hired by a competitor was deemed justified.[30] Most of the cases where dismissal is held valid seem to apply to situations of that kind when business or commercial interests are at play. Typically the employer sees the spouse of an employee join a competitor's firm or marry someone hired by a competitor, while the employee is in a position of responsibility or has access to confidential information. Unable to prevent the change of family situation, the employer fears that marital ties will be stronger than ties of company loyalty. Many such dismissals have been held valid. It is questionable now whether they will remain so under section L 122-45, which protects against dismissal and discipline for reasons among others of marital status, although it is still too early to tell. Nevertheless there is now no doubt that where commercial interest is not involved, dismissal because of a change in family status is definitely discriminatory and not acceptable 'as cause' as it was often before held to be. Besides, the penalties of section 416-3 apply. Although there is no doubt that now under section L 122-35 shop rules imposing celibacy or forbidding marriage between employees, or providing that the company cannot have two spouses in its employment are invalid. They can be now justified only by the 'nature of the task to be carried out' or must be 'proportional to the goal for which they were imposed'. Again, the courts will have to define these terms. Before the application of the law the dismissal by a Catholic school of a divorced female teacher who remarried had been held valid. It would be interesting to know if it still would be.

B. Private Life

Discrimination in employment for reasons related to an employee's private life are not covered by any text and therefore fall under the civil remedies described in the introduction. The same type of general principles which applied to marital status before sections L 122-35 and L 122-45 were written into the law would apply here. However, it should be underlined that in addition section 9 of the Civil Code provides that all persons should enjoy the right to the protection of their private lives. Thus, enquiries before hiring as well as job applications must respect the private life of a candidate. We already know that questions relating to a condition of pregnancy are forbidden. Such would also be the case for questions asking about political opinions and political or union affiliations.[31] Further, court decisions held that an employer has no right to meddle into the private life of an employee;

[32] with no right, for example, to investigate whether a candidate was a priest/worker.

But if, as in the case of the family situation, a negative business or commercial consequence may stem from private life, dismissal is justified. This was the case with a manager having an affair with a subordinate 'which was unduly publicised', whereas his position demanded that he get 'respect and obedience from his subordinates'. Also justified was the dismissal of a journalist whose private life was 'of such a nature as to bring discredit to the newspaper employing him'.

C. Age

Only one provision applies to age to our knowledge. The new section 311-40-5 of the Labour Code provides that job offers cannot include an upper age limit. Discrimination because of age is difficult in the case of dismissal because of seniority rights. However, it is widespread in the case of denial of hiring where it is general knowledge that it is extremely difficult for an unemployed person above a certain age to find a new job. Nevertheless, there is no specific protection against discrimination because of age. Age may even be a justified cause in cases of collective lay-offs for economic reasons, where workers above a certain age are forced into early retirement.

D. Handicap

Section 122-35, already discussed, includes handicaps among the causes of discrimination which cannot be included in shop rules. It should also be noted that handicapped persons benefit from positive discrimination. An Act of 23 November 1957 amended an Act of 30 June 1915 and imposes a quota of 3 per cent of the work force to be compulsorily hired in enterprises of over 10 employees, but this is subject to various qualifications.

E. Union activities

Finally, even though it is beyond the scope of Convention 111 and the scope of the collective report, the subject of this issue of the journal, section L 412-2, forbids discrimination for reasons of joining a union or for union activities under the penalties of section L 461-3 of the Labour Code. That is, a fine of from 2,000 to 8,000 FF for a first offence and 4,000 to 16,000 FF plus a prison sentence of from two months to one year in the case of a second offence. The terms of section 412-2 are very comprehensive. It forbids discrimination in hiring, allocation of work, training, promotion, pay and benefits, discipline and dismissal.

Here again the problem of proof is determinant. In hiring, the only cases where discrimination has been considered proven by the courts was in the case of application forms asking for union affiliation. The simple existence of that question on the form was held by the Supreme

Court to be proof of discrimination.[33] Cases relating to dismissal were numerous because the Supreme Court took the position that the alleged reason for dismissal by employees to be justified as discriminatory for reason of union activities had to be totally foreign to union membership or activities.

NOTES

1. On this point see N. Valticos, 'International Labour Law' in **The International Encyclopedia for Labour Law and Industrial Relations**, Kluwer, Deventer, the Netherlands, 1979.
2. On this point see G. Schnorr 'European Communities' in **Ibid.**
3. See **liaisons Sociales**, legislation Sociale, 14 October 1982, No. 5235.
4. The division of French Courts between the two systems and their respective competences is a specific feature of French Law and too complex to be dealt with, even briefly, here.
5. It is also specific to French Law that many provisions of Labour Law provide for criminal penalties, usually against the employer, for non-respect of these provisions. However, when a penalty including a prison term is incurred, the sentence is usually, in most cases, suspended.
6. There is no breakdown of cases by type of discrimination; 10 sentences had been passed in 1977, five years after the provisions were enacted. cf. J.P. Brill, '20 années de lutte contre la discrimination sociale dans le code de l'article 416 au Code Penal'. **Revue de Sciences Criminelle,** 1977, p. 35 ff.
7. **Ibid.**
8. Cf. Brill, **op. cit.** and J. Costa Lacoux, 'La loi du 1er juillet 1982 et la protection penale des immigrés contre la discrimination sociale', **Droit Social,** 1976, No. 5, p. 181.
9. See M. Despax and J. Rojot, 'France' in R. Blanpain, Ed. **The International Encyclopedia,** Revised edition (forthcoming).
10. Rapport Baudouin, 25 February 1980.
11. Section 416 of the Penal Code is discussed above when dealing with social discrimination.
12. The new section L 122-25 of the Labour Code generally provides also that a candidate for a job who is pregnant is not under obligation to mention that fact to the recruiting employer. Generally under French law, false information given at the time of hiring constitutes legitimate grounds for ulterior dismissal.
13. See C. de Marguerye, 'Les juges français et la discrimination sexuelle', **Droit Social,** 1983, p. 119 as well as for an earlier analysis M. Choisez and A. Benoit Eck, 'La discrimination dans l'emploi', **Droit Social,** January 1979, No. 1, p. 29.
14. P. Hernu, 'Inégalités de salaires entre hommes et femmes', **Revue Française des Affaires Sociales,** No. 4, October-December 1981.
15. See N. Catala, 'Activité Professionnelle des femmes et évolution de Droit', **Revue Française des Affaires Sociales,** No. 4, December 1981, pp. 167.
16. Work at night, outside in freezing temperatures, or certain jobs

involving handling of mercury, free silicon etc. (for women), driving tractors, cleaning mobile parts of heavy machinery etc. (for young females). Many more cases are covered, especially for young workers. See section R 239-1 to R 239-23 of the Labour Code.

17. See C. de Marguerye, **op. cit.**, 'L'Egalité Professionnelle dans les Droits Nouveaux', **Droit Social**, No. 12, December 1983.

18. For a more detailed comment on these Acts see Sutter, **op. cit.**

19. See Sutter, **op. cit.**, on these points. These specific provisions spell out explicitly the principle of equality of treatment for employment. According to the author the principle goes further than the general principle of 'occupational equality', motivating the Act of 1983. M.T. Lanqueting (**op. cit.**) refers to a principle of 'equality of chances'.

20. See **Liaisons Sociale**, 'Legislation Sociale No. 5382', 12 August 1983.

21. M.T. Lanquentin, 'De l'Egalité Professionnelle entre les Femmes et les Hommes a propos d'un Profil de Loi', **Droit Social**, No. 4, April 1983.

22. It is customary for Collective Agreements in France to repeat some provisions spelled out by the law, aside from the new provision or provisions specific to the industry or enterprise or improving on the legal dispositions.

23. Cass. Soc., 9 June 1982. Essilor C, Mme Scheffler, Mme Noziere **et. al.**, C/Essilor Bull No. 380 Ch 381 p. 282.

24. See Sutter **op. cit.**

25. Sections 122-9 of the Labour Code.

26. In enterprises above 50 employees where there is no enterprise committee, the personnel delegates should receive the report. In enterprises over 300 employees a specific commission of the enterprise committee on training receives it. It is possible that above 50 employees an enterprise has notwithstanding no committee. See Despax and Rojot **op. cit.**

27. Section 18 of the Act of 13 July 1983 and Decree 84-69 of 30 January 1984.

28. Cass. Soc., 17 March 1971 Bill (co4 or-216).

29. Cass. Soc., 10 June 1982 see C. Sutter **op. cit.**

30. Cass. Soc., 9 October 1959 D 1960, 8.

31. Javillier, **Traité de Droit de Travail**, Paris 1983, p. 271.

32. Cass. Soc., 18 April 1963.

33. Cass. Soc., 13 May 1969.

7. Federal Republic of Germany

R. Birk

I. INTRODUCTION

Based on the recent constitution of 1949 the general principle of equal treatment binding for every employer has been developed in Germany with reference to labour law and exceeds the state-citizen relationship. Consequently, the Federal Republic of Germany contrasts with many states in which a prohibition on discrimination exists only in very particular cases.

Primarily, the decisions of the Labour Court of the German Reich (as of 1928) and of the Federal Labour Court[1] (since 1954) have been relevant for this development. It has not been clear, though, whether courts refer the general principle of equal treatment under labour law directly to the constitution (**e.g.** art. 3), or whether it is only influenced by the constitution and is exclusively and deeply rooted in the labour law and therefore in the private law.

As to German Law, the result of this sixty years of continuous development are the problems of equal treatment which may be outlined under two aspects, namely:
(1) the general principle of equal treatment, and the
(2) absolute prohibition of discrimination.

1. The general principle of equal treatment

The essential meaning (contents) of the general principle of equal treatment of the labour law[2] is the prohibition for the employer to treat his employees arbitrarily. He is not allowed to differentiate acoording to irrelevant criterion between his employees: equal is equal, unequal is to be treated unequally. The general principle of equal treatment consequently has a collective tendency; it continually presumes that the employer recruits several employees. Its legal basis is the law of the employment relationship in other words the individual labour law, however, it reaches beyond the individual employment relationship.

The general principle of equal treatment in particular develops its effectiveness in the existing employment relationship. The radius of its application however is controversial with regards to the constitution and termination of the employment relationship. As topics of the general principle of equal treatment the following have crystallised in the labour law: the application of the employer's right to give instructions in order to reinforce the obligation of the employee to work,[3] the unilateral determination of uniform working conditions by the employer as well as the granting of fringe benefits to the staff.[4]

In this case the courts have especially elaborated in detail the limits of admissible differentiation and developed relative prohibitions of discrimination.

2. Absolute prohibitions of discrimination

It is necessary to distinguish between the general principle of equal treatment of all employees by their employer, in other words the prohibition of irrelevant unequal treatment, and the absolute prohibitions of discrimination. They each prohibit unequal treatment in the cases covered by them. Such absolute prohibitions of discrimination refer to the prohibition of each discrimination resulting from birth, origin, religion, sex, the admissible political activity and activities in the trade union. They are legally based on art. 3 subsect. 2 and 3 (Basic Law).

This provision is not only binding as provided in art. 1 subsect. 3 (Basic Law) for the legislation, administration and the courts but also, according to general opinion, for the collective bargaining parties.[5] The Federal Labour Court also applies them to the individual employer and consequently considers the employer as the addressee of art. 3 subsect. 2 en 3 (Basic Law).[6]

As far as the absolute prohibitions of discrimination are applicable the employer is consequently not allowed any discrimination concerning age, sex, etc. Hence, the general principle of equal treatment is replaced by the absolute prohibitions of discrimination.

With reference to sex discrimination, it is by means of interpretation of the EC-directive 76/207 explicitly prohibited to the employer under § 611 a subsect. 1 of the Civil Code.

In addition, some more prohibitions of discrimination are embodied in labour statutes such as §§ 75, 78 of the Works Constitution Act and others.

The Federal Republic of Germany and partly also the employers are obliged to take care of equal treatment within the different spheres of working life according to the supranational and international laws[7] such as art. 48 subsect. 2, 119 EEC Treaty Regulation No. 1612/68, the EC-Directives 75/117 and 76/207, art. 23 No. 2 of the UN-Universal Declaration of Human Rights, the UN-Convention about the elimination of any discriminatory practices concerning women dated 18 December 1979 (not yet ratified), and art. 4 of the European Social Charter.

II. DIRECT AND INDIRECT DISCRIMINATION

Discrimination as unequal treatment of employees by their employer is possible in various ways and also occurs in practice.

The obvious, direct unequal treatment may be ascertained without great difficulties where it relates to details. In most cases, unequal treatment means a less favourable treatment of the employee with regard to his fellow employees but not his preferential treatment. Discrimination may be put on the same level with less favourable treatment which directly refers to special characteristics of the employee.

The concealed, indirect less favourable treatment specially reveals the fact that the concerned employee encounters more difficulties in complying with a condition or a requirement (height, weight) than other employees. Consequently, this affects him in a discriminating way. The existence of an indirect discrimination may be proved under much more difficult conditions than a direct one. But direct discrimination is of less actual significance in the Federal Republic of Germany than the indirect less favourable treatment of an employee.[8] Due to general political and social development the employer avoids treating a person less favourably in an open and direct way.

Consequently, one essential and actual question arises in the sphere of discrimination when starting or carrying on a business. How may and should the borderline be drawn in a convincing way between admissible differentation and inadmissible discrimination.

The employer who makes voluntary additional payments has to fix the relevant presuppositions in such a way that some of the employees are not excluded arbitrarily and without any good reason. Such characteristic differentiations are illegal differentiations when, in establishing groups of employees they violate the principle of equal treatment of art. 3 subsect. 2 (Basic Law) or the prohibition of unequal treatment of art. 3 subsect. 3 as well as the prohibition of discrimination of § 75 subsect. 1 of the Works Constitution Act. If only the male employees receive additional payment and not the female employees and if the reasons for preferential treatment only concern a part of the employees the exclusion of the female employees as a rule is not justified.[9]

III. THE ESSENTIAL SPHERES OF THE PROHIBITION OF DISCRIMINATION

Hardly one essential and factual sphere of working life and working conditions and no phase of the employment relationship may evade the principle of equal treatment under labour law and the prohibition of discrimination. They are more or less always comprehensive and present. In the following they are to be explained in detail and reinforced by means of the essential spheres.

1. Race - colour - national and social origin

a. Race and colour

Art. 3 subsect. 3 (Basic Law) prohibits each discrimination or preferential treatment because of race and consequently because of colour. Being addressed to the public authority § 75 subsect. 1 phrase 2 of Works Constitution Act provides this absolute prohibition of discrimination for the Law of Works Constitution. It is addressed to the employers and to the works council. This provision, which contains a comprehensive prohibition of discrimination, is also called the Magna Carta of the law of works constitution.[10] Where it is not applicable because a works council does not exist, art. 3 subsect. 3 (Basic Law) is directly applied to labour law.[11]

Nowadays discrimination on racial grounds is of no great importance in the Federal Republic of Germany. Cases from the court are unknown.

b. National and social origin

Of much greater importance is the discrimination of employees because of their nationality rather than their social origin. Art. 3 subsect. 3 (Basic Law) does not prohibit the state favouring Germans to aliens. Therefore the state is entitled to exclude or limit, in the home country, the admission of aliens to employment so long as citizens from EC-member states are not affected. With reference to them the special prohibitions of discrimination under European law are applied which are laid down in art. 48 EEC-Treaty and in the VO 1612/68. They are not only binding for the respective member state but also for the individual employer.[12]

In addition § 75 subsect. 1 phrase 1 (Works Constitution Act) places a general prohibition on the Works Constitution against differentiation of employees on nationality. With regard to its contents it is applied for the individual labour relationship too.[13] Above all the provisions have significance if foreign employees from countries which are not EC-member states are concerned such as Yugoslavia, Portugal, Spain and Turkey as the EC-Law does not apply to them. The general problems of immigrant workers (employment permit, residence permit authorisation) are indeed part of the area of responsibilities of the state and not of the employer.

In the Federal Republic of Germany foreign employees have the same rights and obligations as German employees. This applies in a similar way to the Social Security Law. However, an employer may be obliged in case of comprehension problems to draw the foreign employees' attention to the importance of a requested legal instrument.[14]

2. Sex [15]

Of greatest importance today, without any doubt, is the prohibition of unequal treatment of men and women. With regard to the state this fact results directly from art. 3 subsect. 2 (Basic Law). As to labour law a series of legal sources are referred to. Concerning individual labour law, § 611 a subsect. 1 as well as § 612 subsect. 3 of the Civil Code which refer tot the EEC-directive 76/207, require a comprehensive prohibition of discrimination as to hiring, practicing a profession (job), termination of employment and remuneration. § 75 subsect. 1 phrase 1 (Works Constitution Act) applies the same to the Works Constitution Law. In the remaining spheres of labour law (e.g. Law of Collective Agreements, Labour Protection Law) art. 3 subsect. 2 (Basic Law) applies which according to general opinion is not only binding for the state but also for the collective bargaining parties.

Sensitive points on the equal treatment of men and women in working life today are above all; access to employment, equal chances for all concerning promotion, the discrimination of female labour by means of lower remuneration as well as the practice in dismissals of firing women before men in cases of conflict.

The application of the individual and the collective prohibition of discrimination does not depend, in contrast to the US-American Civil Rights Act of 1964, on a definite number of employees being engaged by the same employer. The total severity of the prohibition of discrimination also affects that employer who wants to hire only one male employee when the question is about a neutral selection from several applicants of different sex.

The existence of special protective regulations in favour of women such as the Maternity Act or special regulations about working hours does not violate, according to general opinion, the prohibition of discrimination as they only have to compensate certain sexual disadvantages.[16]

a. Access to employement (work)[17]

According to § 611 a subsect. 1 phrase 1 of the Civil Code the recruitment of an applicant is not allowed to depend on sex: women are not te be discriminated against, men are not to be favoured. Of course, this applies in reverse bu such an example is an exception.[18]

Recruitment regulations as well as the concrete recruitment of a paticular applicant must not discriminate with regard to women. The employer should, according to § 611 b of the Civil Code, advertise a vacancy as neutral in terms of sex.

If a woman succeeds in proving that she had not been recruited because of her sex, the German law does not provide for the redress of recruitment towards the discriminating employer.[19] Under § 611 a subsect. 2 phrase 1 of the Civil Code, the employer is only obliged to pay the financial damage the employee suffered. In other words a female applicant could put forward only the costs of her application, in most cases an unimportant amount. The European Court of Justice however, defined in two decisions dated 10 April 1984 that this provision of the German law represents an insufficient translation of the EC-directive 76/207. Actually which conclusion the legislator and the Labour Courts of the Federal Republic of Germany will draw is still unsettled.[20]

b. Equal opportunities in promotion

Within the scope of an existing employment relationship women are often withheld from promotion to better paid positions despite equal qualification. Through legal steps this fact may only be influenced in a limited way. If the promotion is considered as a contractual action, in other words an amendment of the actual contract of employment, it is not possible simply to introduce a third contract with regard to § 611 a subsect. 2 phrase 1 of the Civil Code which explicitly puts 'the promotion' under its protection and to declare its existence up till then as being null and void. On the other hand there is no general opinion as to what is to be done in such a case.[21]

c. *Remuneration*

According to § 612 subsect. 3 phrase 1 of the Civil Code no difference in remuneration for equal or equivalent work on the basis of sex may be stipulated. Even before entry into force of the EC-adjustment statute, dated 13 August 1980, inserting § 612 subsect. 3 the Federal Labour Court derived the equal remuneration of men and women directly from art. 3 subsect. 2 (Basic Law).[23]

Direct and obvious discrimination in the remuneration of women is hardly to be observed, neither in collective labour agreements nor in workshop practice. Discrimination in remuneration however, results from the fact that certain work being from a practical point of view performed only by women from the beginning is paid in a very humble way. However, under collective labour agreements special low wage groups (Leichtlohngruppen) are disappearing.

The Federal Labour Court is obliged to realise the principle of equal payment of men and women with regard to remuneration and to additional payment. The principle of equality in remuneration excludes the fact that the work of a woman is less well paid under the protection regulations by which she is covered.[24] A clause of a collective agreement violates the equality of remuneration if it grants female employees in general, and systematically, only a certain percentage of the collective remuneration as minimum wage.[25] These regulations are applied too when additional payment is higher than the wage settled by the collective agreement.[26] If male employees are granted an additional payment because they are not ready to work for the same wage as the female employees working at the identical work place and under the same conditions, illegal discrimination against the women is the result of such an additional payment.[27]

But one should not have the illusion that it is only up to the legislator and the courts to abolish the inferior remuneration of women. Social consciousness, lack of trainingand so on need changing as well in order to guarantee women in general equal opportunities of remuneration vis-à-vis men.

d. *Dismissal*

Whether women rather than men are dismissed may not be proved definitely. But it is obvious that the courts tend towards the view that the decision of an employer does not represent inadmissible discrimination against the married women if he terminates the employment contract of a married woman and not of a married man where she is in a secure economic position due to her husband's job and consequently not dependent on her employment relationship.[28] The problem of the 'married double wage earner' is increasing more and more with the continuing unemployment; on the one hand the question is about how to prevent the discrimination of women at work, yet on the other hand this principle affects other persons who possibly need special economical protection.

3. Personal status

In general the personal status, in other words the question whether an employee is single or married, is of no importance. As a social criterion it is of considerable significance. This is not only applied in relation to recruitment but also to the termination of employment.

Art. 3 (Basic Law) however is not violated in so far as in a double wage marriage only the employee who always makes the financial contribution to the household is granted an additional budget allocation which is paid on an assessement of the income.[29] But a collective agreement violates art. 6 (Basic Law) if it excludes married female employees in contrast to single ones when granting additional payments.[30] When granting children's supplements it is also inadmissible to differentiate between mothers of legitimate and illegitimate children.[31]

Is it legally justifiable to prohibit the employer such a social consideration with reference to discrimination? This question may not simply be affirmed.[32]

According to general opinion so-called 'celibacy clauses', in which a female or male employee binds herself/himself, by the labour contract, not to get married within a definite period of time in order to be at the disposition of the employer at any time and irrespective of any family obligations are illegal.[33]

4. Age

Differential treatment due to age may result in preferential treatment as well as in discrimination. § 75 subsect. 2 phrase 2 (Works Constitution Act) prohibits any discrimination of the basis of age. § 80 subsect. 1 No. 6 (Works Constitution Act) even imposes an obligation on the works council to promote the recruitment of older workers.

It is contrary to § 75 subsect. 1 phrase 2 (Works Constitutions Act) if the employer and the works council stipulate in a works agreement that the employment relationschip automatically terminates upon completion of the 65th year.[34] On the other hand senior systems do not generally infringe the prohibition of discrimination.[35]

5. Private life

The modern employment relationship is especially characterised by its functional reference to work performance. The activities of an employee which do not establish any direct connection to its functions provided by contract are in general not subject to any restrictions through the employer. The employer is not entitled to interfere in the private life of his employee.[36]

This rule however contains certain exceptions if work and private life are not to be permanently separated, and the interests of the employer are to be considered as needing protection. Such constellations are relevant for: jobs requiring a certain religious[37] and moral obligation in order to carry them out in a satisfactory way; and the position of executive employees because they hold a special position of trust, and consequently have to take into consideration the interests of their employer in a stronger way, such as restraining from free expression of opinion.[38]

6. Religious activities

§ 75 subsect. 1 phrase 1 (Works Constitution Act) as clearly mentioned above prohibits the employer from discriminating against the employee on religious grounds. On the other hand, the reference to free religious practice of the employee does not entitle him not to perform the obligations of his contract. This is relevant in a special way for the claim for freedom of conscience. Consequently, an employee is only entitled to refuse in extreme cases the work assigned to him because of reasons of conscience or religious motives.[39]

7. The classification of employees into blue-collar workers and white-collar workers [40]

A series of rules and statutes of labour law only concerns either white-collar workers or blue-collar workers, or both groups are treated differently concerning an identical question. The reason is based on the different but today hardly perceptible function of both groups: white-collar workers perform essentially mental work and blue-collar workers merely manual work. The right to give notice contains different terms of notice for white-collar workers and blue-collar workers.[41] Pension plans discriminate in part against the blue-collar workers. The payment of remuneration in case of illness is different on some points. [42] Furthermore, blue-collar workers and white-collar workers belong to their own social pension insurance schemes.

The legislator differentiates again between white-collar workers and executives. The Works Council Act does not affect the latter,[43] they enjoy also a certain preferential status as to Co-determination Law.[44]

The general illegality of differentiation between blue-collar workers and white-collar workers as well as the resulting unequal treatment in various spheres of the labour and social law has not been pleaded till now. However, the Federal Constitutional Court considers the discriminating assessment of the terms of notice as substantial and not being justified as to § 2 (Termination of Employment Act for white-collar workers) and to § 622 subsect. 2 of the Civil Code for blue-collar workers.[45]

8. Union activity - the right to be a non-unionist

The activity for a certain union which contains also the question of membership is protected by the constitution. Art. 9 subsect. 3 phrase 2 (Basic Law) provides explicitly that agreements and measures which interfere or restrict them are null and void. This is the only constitutional provision which is directed at third persons and therefore also at the employer (direct binding effect of the constitutional rights on a third party). By § 75 subsect. 1 of the Works Constitution Act the employer and the works council are prohibited in general from any discrimination of persons because of their union activity or pro-union attitude.

Membership of a certain union is not sufficient reason to refuse an applicant. Nor is it further justified to restrict the lock-out exclusively to union members.[46] On the other hand special benefits are conceded to the union members as was the case in collective bargaining agreements by so-called distinguishing clauses.[47]

According to German Law the non-membership may not be subsequently disadvantaged. Nobody may be forced directly to join a union. This would be a violation of the constitutionally protected right to be a non-unionist.[48] The closed shop is therefore not consistent with the German Law.[49]

IV. RESTRICTIONS ON THE PRINCIPLE OF EQUAL TREATMENT AND OF THE PROHIBITION OF DISCRIMINATION

Restrictions on the general principle of equal treatment mean admissible differentiation: unequal should be treated unequally. To limit the individual prohibitions of discrimination to those based on specified occasions means not to convert them into relative ones. Each principle and each prohibition has to admit certain exceptions in order to be sensibly applied.

A general declaration as to at what point a state of affairs is to be estimated unequal compared with another one may not be abstractly laid down. Consequently, it makes little sense to look for general restrictions on the general principle of equal treatment.

It is here only possible to elaborate in detail some restriction on the absolute prohibitions of discrimination which are adapted to specified questions.

1. Enterprises serving ideological purposes

If the employee works in a workshop whose owner is concerned above all, in its management, with political and publishing purposes the regulations of § 118 subsect. 1 (Works Constitution Act) are applied only in so far as the character of the workshop or enterprise does not conflict with the provisions of this Act. The Works Constitution Act is not applied at all to religious communities and their instituations (§ 118 subsect. 2).

As to the individual labour law an equivalent explicit regulation does not exist, but according to court decisions and doctrine it is upheld that the employees are obliged to extend their loyalty,[50] even to the promotion of the tendency pursued by the employer[51] which

109

may affect not only attitudes at work but also in private.

This has been noticed frequently by the courts with regard to the employees being involved in religious communities and their institutions.[52] Somebody who participates in the missionary evangelism of the church has to respect it also in his private life; if he does not do so, his contract of employment can be terminated.[53] The catholic employee of a catholic parish kindergarten who marries and lives with a divorced man incurs due notice depending on the personal and actual circumstances.[54]

2. Extremists in public service

Employees in general are subject to the same requirements as civil servants if they enter the public services. They are expected to have that positive attitude towards the constitution as is required in the case of an enterprise serving ideological purposes.[55] If they fail in attitude they are not recruited; if they change their attitude later they are to be removed from the public service. This is valid irrespective of the duties they have to perform.

3. Special protective measures for specified groups of employees

The legislator has embodied a series of additional protective measures for women, juveniles and severely disabled persons, such as the Maternity Act, Children and Young Persons Protection Act and Severely Disabled Persons Act. These groups of employees are consequently specially protected. The additional protection however is not illegal favourable treatment because according to the general understanding it mainly aims at a compensation of structural deficits of the individual groups of employees.[56]

The special protection against dismissal by § 9 Maternity Act in the form of a prohibition of dismissal does not violate art. 3 (Basic Law). [57] Legal favourable treatments of women are only considered to be contrary to the constitution if they have been adopted obviously without knowledge of the facts and arbitrarily. The special protection of the pregnant mother, however, should also take into account an eventual decrease in efficiency, or a disability, resulting from the pregnancy and preserve the job. This corresponds to the spirit of art. 6 subsect. 4 (Basic Law) according to which each mother is entitled to the protection and assistance of the community.

Constitutional doubts on the special protective regulations in favour of juveniles and disabled persons have not yet been expressed, in contrast to female work protection.[58]

V. REVERSE DISCRIMINATION[59]

Affirmative action or reverse discrimination may be of some importance in the Federal Republic of Germany only in the sphere of sex discrimination. It aims at the preferential treatment of male to female applicants in order to compensate a former discrimination. In contrast to the protective regulation in favour of women the reverse discrimination proceeds from the equalisation of women and aims at its realisation in working life.[60] Indirectly it is also directed against the members of the other groups. The equalisation of the woman in working life ought to be realised by an unequal treatment of the man[61] in other words in an individual unequal treatment of the applicants in order to obtain collective equalisation.

Quotas providing that women of equal performance or qualifications are to be granted preferential treatment up to a definite quantitative limit are, according to German law, constitutionally problematic.[62] The absolutely necessary determination of specified quotas or aims of working and training places which have to be filled with women exceeds the promotional measures to establish the equal opportunities between female and male applicants. It transforms sex into a central criterion, this should however not be the case at all. The employer should take his decision neutrally regarding the applicants' sex and not use it as a kind of compensation.[63]

VI. ENFORCEMENT OF THE PRINCIPLE OF EQUAL TREATMENT AND OF THE PROHIBITION OF DISCRIMINATION

The enforceability of equal treatment and of the prohibition of discrimination does not only depend on legal but also on social factors which may hardly be influenced. But as far as legal aspects are concerned especially the guarantee of the efficiency of the absolute prohibition of discrimination, the problems the Federal Republic of Germany is involved in are mainly of procedural and substantive law.

1. Questions of evidence

The most difficult practical problem of an effective enforcement of the different prohibitions of discrimination is to prove that the employer or other addressees have discriminated. The different sanctions may be imposed only if this is possible.

En explicit regulation diverging from the general strong regulations of the burden of proof is only provided in § 611 a subsect. 1 phrase 3 of the Civil Code in the case of sex discrimination. In contrast to the normal case in which the burden of proof is on the plaintiff for the facts which create a right, the burden of proof lies here with the employer that he has not decided because of the sex, but because of other material reasons, if the employee can satisfactorily show that there is a presumption of sex discrimination by the employer. This legal regulation is not quite clear and therefore controversial in its consequences,[64] it does not give any real reverse of the burden of proof but only a certain lightening for the discriminated employee.

To the other cases of the prohibition of discrimination the general rule of the burden of proof is applied. Some modifications in favour of the discriminated employee are possible by the principles of **prima facie** evidence.

2. Sanctions of the private law

In contrast to other states the law of the Federal Republic of Germany provides only private law sanctions against violations of the different prohibitions of discriminations. As far as the violations are concerned, legal transactions are null and void according to § 134 of the Civil Code because they infringe a legal prohibition. If an applicant was repudiated in a discriminating manner because of his sex, religion or union membership then he has no right to be engaged by the discriminating employer.[65]

In case of a sex discrimination he is actually only entitled to assert the damage he had suffered because he relied on the fact that the constitution of the employment relationship would be realised irrespective of such a violation. The so-called damage because of reliance on a declaration covers in general just the costs for the application and no more.

In two identical decisions, dated 10 April 1984 the European Court of Justice has characterised this sanction of the German Law as not being satisfactory and has claimed to find other remedies in order to guarantee a more effective enforcement of the EC-Directive 76/207. [66] How this will look cannot be said - as yet.[67]

If prohibitions of discrimination are violated the general sanctions are applied and damage is paid according to the general regulations which, however, may not be specified in detail here. It may be possible to consider the prohibition of discrimination of § 75 (Works Constitution Act) as a protective law as defined by § 823 subsect. 2 of the Civil Code;[68] in this case the violated employee could claim the resulting damages caused by the discrimination. A claim for compensation for moral damage, however, is excluded (§ 847 subsect. 1 of the Civil Code).

3. Special control bodies

The idea of special commissions concerned with equal treatment, or of similar institutions, was not successful in the Federal Republic of Germany in contrast to other states. It is mainly up to the individual employee to enforce his rights. Nor can trade unions or other classes of employee claim a right of action on their own.

The works council merely represents an independent control body. According to § 80 subsect. 1 No. 1 (Works Constitution Act) it has the task to control the enforcement of the applicable laws in favour of the employees. This is explicitly emphasised in § 75 subsect. 1 (Works Constitution Act) as to the prohibitions of discrimination mentioned there. The works council disposes of the corresponding means provided in the Works Constitution Act.

NOTES

1. Cf. G. Hueck, **Der Grundsatz der gleichmässigen Behandlung im Privatrecht**, 1958, p. 58.

2. Cf. Mayer-Maly, **Arbeitsrechts-Blattei: Gleichbehandlung im Arbeitsverhältnis** I, 1975; Zöllner, **Arbeitsrecht**, 3rd ed., 1983, p. 177; Hunold, **Gleichbehandlungsgrundsatz, Gleibehandlungsgesetz und Gleichberechtigungssatz im Betrieb,** Der Betrieb, 1984, Beilage, No. 5.
3. Birk, **Die arbeitsrechtliche Leitungsmacht,** 1973, p. 309.
4. Mayer-Maly, op. cit.; Zöllner, **Arbeitsrecht,** p. 180.
5. Bundesarbeitsgericht (BAG), **Arbeitsrechtliche Praxis** (AP) Art. 3, Constitution No. 4, 7, 16, 87; Zöllner, **Arbeitsrecht,** p. 91.
6. **E.g.** BAG AP § 242, Civil Code, Gleichbehandlung, No. 53.
7. Cf. in general Mc Kean, **Equality and Discrimination under International Law,** 1983, especially p. 166.
8. Gamillscheg, 'Die mittelbare Benachteiligung der Frau im Arbeitsleben', in: **Festschrift für Hans Florett,** 1983, p. 171.
9. BAG AP § 242 Civil Code, Gleichbehandlung, No. 39, annotated by Birk.
10. Dietz/Richardi, **Betriebsverfassungsgesetz,** 6th ed., 1983, § 75, N. 1.
11. Cf. BAG AP Art. 3 Constitution, No. 4, 7, 16 and further decisions.
12. There can be no detailed discussion here of this question.
13. Dietz/Richardi, § 75 N. 16.
14. Landesarbeitsgericht Düsseldorf Arbeitsrechts-Blattei: Ausgleichsquittung, Entscheidung, No. 1.
15. The literature on this topic is enormous. Only some dissertations can be quoted here: Löwisch, 'Welche rechtlichen Massnahmen sind vordringlich, um die tatsächliche Gleichstellung der Frauen mit den Männern im Arbeitsleben zu gewährleisten?', in: **Verhandlungen des fünfzigsten deutschen Juristentages,** vol. I, 1984, p. D 11; Säcker, vol. II, 1974, p. L 9; Köbl, **Meine Rechte und Pflichten als berufstätige Frau,** 2nd ed., 1983; Zöllner, Gleichberechtigung und Gleichstellung der Geschlechter, in: **Festschrift für Rudolf Strasser,** 1983, p. 223.
16. Cf. Gitter, 'Frauenarbeitsschutz und Gleichberechtigungsgebot', in: **Festschrift für Gerhard Müller,** 1981, p. 161; Mayer-Maly, 'Die Frauengleichbehandlung' als Thema der arbeitsrechtlichen Gesetzgebung in Deutschland und Österreich, in: **Festschrift für Wilhelm Herschel,** 1983, p. 257.
17. Cf. Hanau, 'Der gleiche Zugang zur Beschäftigung in der Privatwirtschaft nach deutschem Recht', in: **In memoriam Otto Kahn-Freund,** 1980, p. 457.
18. Such an exception is the so-called 'Hausarbeitstagsgesetz' of the Land Nordrhein-Westfalen (Statute on the housework day for women) which was applicable only to women. The Federal Constitutional Court declared this statute unconstitutional (BVerfGE 52, 269); see further BAG, **Der Betrieb,** 1982, p. 1014.
19. Zöllner, **Arbeitsrech,** p. 186; Birk, **Neue Zeitschrift für Arbeits- und Sozialrecht,** 1984 (forthcoming); for the opposite position Bertelsmann/Pfarr, **Der Betrieb,** 1984, p. 1297.
20. Cf. Bertelsmann/Pfarr, **Der Betrieb,** 1984, p. 1297; Birk, **Neue Zeitschrift für Arbeits- und Socialrecht,** 1984 (forthcoming).
21. Cf. Schleicher, **Arbeitsrechts-Blattei: Gleichbehandlung im Arbeitsverhältnis,** II, 1982, D VIII 2; Jauernig/Schlechtriem, **Bürgerliches Gesetzbuch,** 3rd ed., 1984, § 611 a/b N. 3e.

22. Langkau, 'Lohn- und Gehaltsdiskriminierung von Arbeitnehmerinnen in der Bundesrepublik Deutschland', 1979; Pfarr/Bertelsmann, Lohngleichheit' 1981.
23. BAG AP Art. 3 Constitution, No. 4, 6, 7, 16 and many other decisions.
24. BAG AP Art. 3 Constitution, No. 7.
25. BAG AP Art. 3 Constitution, No. 4.
26. BAG **Arbeitsrechts-Blattei**: 'Gleichbehandlung im Arbeitsverhältnis Entscheidung', No. 64.
27. BAG AP § 242 Civil Code Gleichbehandlung No. 53.
28. BAG AP § 1 KSchG 1951, No. 26.
29. BAG AP Art. 3 Constitution, No. 111.
30. BAG **Arbeitsrechts-Blattei**: 'Gleichbehandlung im Arbeitsverhältnis Entscheidung', No. 15.
31. BAG **Arbeitsrechts-Blattei**: 'Gleichbehandlung im Arbeitsverhältnis Entscheidung', No. 21.
32. Cf. BAG AP § 1 KSchG 1951, No. 26.
33. BAG AP Art. 6 Abs. 1 Constitution, Ehe und Familie, No. 1 and 3.
34. BAG AP § 57 BetrVG. 1952,No. 5; AP § 99 BetrVG. 1972, No. 9.
35. Cf. Hueck, 'Kündigungsschutzgesetz', 10th ed., 1980, § 1 N. 117.
36. Birk, 'Die arbeitsrechtliche Leitungmacht', p. 345.
37. Cf. Richardi, 'Arbeitsrecht in der Kirche', 1984, p. 42.
38. Cf. Buchner, 'Zeitschrift für Arbeidsrecht', 1979, 335 (351).
39. Birk, 'Die arbeitsrechtliche Leitungsmacht', p. 314; Otto, 'Personale Freiheit und soziale Bindung', 1978, p. 127.
40. Trieschmann, 'Ungleichbehandlung im gesetzlichen Arbeitsvertragsrecht', in: **Festschrift für Wilhelm Herschel**, 1982, p. 421; Farthmann, 'Gleichbehandlung aller Arbeitnehmer', in: **Festschrift für Marie-Luise Hilger/Herbert Stumpf**, 1983, p. 177.
41. § 622 subsect. 1 and 2 BGB.
42. **Blue-collar worker:** Gesetz über die Fortzahlung des Arbeitsentgelts im Krankheitsfalle (Lohnfortzahlungsgesetz); **white-collar worker:** § 616 subsect. 2 BGB, § 63 Handelsgesetzbuch, § 133 c Gewerbeordnung.
43. § 5 subsect. 3 BetrVG.
44. Cf. § 15 subsect. 2 and 4 Mitbestimmungsgesetz.
45. BVerfG Der Betrieb 1983, 450.
46. BAG AP Art. 9 GG Arbeitskampf No. 66.
47. BAG AP Art. 9 GG No. 13; Gamillscheg, 'Die Differenzierung nach der Gewerkschaftszugehörigkeit', 1966; Zöllner, 'Tarifvertragliche Differenzierungsklauseln', 1967; Leventis, 'Differenzierungsklauseln nach dem Grundgesetz und dem Tarifvertragsgesetz', 1974.
48. Scholz, Koalitionsfreiheit als Verfassungsproblem', 1971, p. 41, 267.
49. Scholz, **op. cit.**, p. 279.
50. Buchner, 'Zeitschrift für Arbeitsrecht', 1979, p. 335.
51. Buchner, **loc. cit.**, p. 346.
52. Cf. Richardi, 'Arbeitsrecht in der Kirche', p. 42.
53. Richardi, 'Arbeitsrecht in der Kirche', p. 54.
54. BAG AP Art. 140 GG No. 2.
55. Cf. § 8 subsect. 1 Bundesangestelltentarifvertrag.
56. Zöllner, **Arbeitsrecht**, p. 289.

57. BAG **Arbeitsrechts-Blattei:** 'Gleichbehandlung im Arbeitsverhältnis Entscheidung', No. 57.
58. Cf. Gamillscheg, 'Frauenarbeitsschutz, Gleichbehandlung, Begünstigung der Frau', in: **Festschrift für Rudolf Strasser,** 1983, p. 209.
59. Hanau, 'Die umgekehrte Geschlechtsdiskriminierung im Arbeitsleben', in: **Festschrift für Wilhelm Herschel,** 1982, p. 191.
60. Hanau, 'Die umgekehrte Geschlechtsdiskriminierung', p. 194.
61. Hanau, (N. 59), p. 215.
62. Löwisch, **op. cit.,** p. 68; Hanau, (N. 59), p. 212; contra: Hohmann-Dennhardt, **Zeitschrift für Rechtspolitik,** 1979, 241 (247).
63. Hanau, (N. 59), p. 215.
64. Cf. Prütting, 'Gegenwartsprobleme der Beweislast', 1983, p. 334.
65. Zöllner, **Arbeitsrecht,** p. 186; Birk, **Neue Zeitschrift für Arbeits- und Soziaalrecht,** 1984 (forthcoming); contra: Bertelsmann/Pfarr, **Der Betrieb,** 1984, 1298.
66. **Der Betrieb,** 1984, 1042.
67. Some suggestions by Bertelsmann/Pfarr, **Der Betrieb,** 1984, 1297; Birk, **Neue Zeitschrift für Arbeits- und Sozialrecht,** 1984 forthcoming.
68. Fitting/Auffarth/Kaiser, **Betriebsverfassungsgesetz,** 14th ed. 1984, § 75 N. 24; contra: Dietz/Richardi, § 75 N. 46.

8. Great Britain

B. Hepple

HISTORICAL INTRODUCTION

The conscious model for legal measures against racial and sex discrimination in Geat Britain has been anti-discrimination legislation in the United States and Canada. The common law of England, Wales and Scotland imposed no restrictions on the power of employers to discriminate on grounds of race, sex or for other arbitrary reasons. Legislation was therefore required to impose standards of equal opportunity on hitherto private decisions. The present legislative sources are: (1) the Equal Pay Act 1970, which came into force on 31 December 1975 and which has been amended on a number of occasions, most recently by new regulations on equal pay for work of equal value, in force from 1 January 1984. This Act requires equal treatment for men and women in the same employment in regard to their terms and conditions of employment. (2) The Sex Discrimination Act 1975 which outlaws discrimination on grounds of sex and against married persons on grounds of marital status in respect of matters not covered by the contract of employment, such as recruitment, training, promotion and other benefits. The Act also applies to termination of employment and to this extent supplements the general law on unfair dismissal because it applies to all workers, including those with less than the fifty-two week qualifying period required for protection against unfair dismissal. (3) The Race Relations Act 1976 which outlaws discrimination on grounds of colour, race, ethnic or national origins, or nationality. (4) Certain EEC legislation which is directly applicable in the United Kingdom and other member states. In particular, Art. 119 of the Treaty of Rome, setting forth the principle 'that men and women should receive equal pay for equal work', as clarified by the Equal Pay Directive 75/117/EEC, has been the basis for a number of test cases brought before the European Court of Justice which found that Art. 119 and Art. 1 of the Equal Pay Directive apply to several situations not coverd by the British Equal Pay Act and Sex Discrimination Act. Moreover, the EEC Commission brought two infringement proceedings against the United Kingdom in both of which the ECJ held that the UK had failed to fulfil its obligations under the Treaty. The first of these decisions led to the equal value regulations of 1983 (above).[1]

It will therefore be seen that Britain lacks a single comprehensive code of discrimination law. This has led to a number of difficult and, as yet, unresolved questions about, for example, the relationship between EEC law and domestic British legislation, and the relationship between the Equal Pay Act and the Sex Discrimination Act. These problems arise because historically the Equal Pay Act 1970 was enacted

117

before the United Kingdom acceded to the Treaty of Rome, and the Sex Discrimination Act 1975 came into force before the European Court of Justice had spelled out the implications of the Equal Pay Directive. Despite the amending regulations of 1983, there are still a number of respects in which the British legislation is narrower in scope than Art. 119 of the Treaty of Rome and the Equal Pay Directive. For example, Art. 119 is not confined to cases where a man and women are contemporaneously doing the same work and a woman may compare herself with a male predecessor in the same employment, while under the British Act they must be contemporaneously employed. Moreover, some provisions relating to death and retirement are covered by Art. 119, although not within the scope of the British legislation. There are certain groups of workers, such as those employed by British companies at establishments outside Great Britain, who are excluded by the British legislation but would fall under Art. 119. In the second infringement proceedings, by the Commission against the United Kingdom (Case 165/82) the ECJ decided that the United Kindom was not in compliance with Art. 4(b) of the Equal Treatment Directive 76/207/EEC because the legislation in force in the United Kingdom contained no provision regarding discriminatory provisions in non-binding collective agreements. It also appears that the Equal Value Regulations of 1983 do not fully satisfy the requirements of the Equal Pay Directive in respect of equal value (see below). These gaps between EEC law and British domestic legislation mean that a litigant in Britain may rely on Art. 119 and the Equal Pay Directive in civil proceedings. Questions of interpretation may then be referred to the European Court of Justice under Art. 177 of the Treaty.

The provisions in the legislation designed to prevent overlapping between the Equal Pay and Sex Discrimination Acts are complex and it is not infrequently difficult to determine whether a particular matter of complaint falls to be redressed under one Act of the other. In general terms, it may be said that where the discrimination relates to payment of money under a contract of employment, only the Equal Pay Act can apply and where the less favourable treatment relates to a matter which is not included in a contract, only the Sex Discrimination Act can apply. But there may be some situations in which neither Act applies, for example where there is indirect discrimination against part-time workers in respect of payment of money and all the part-time workers and full-time workers in the establishment are females (because the Equal Pay Act requires that there should be a man with whom the woman can compare herself, and the Sex Discrimination Act which covers the situation where there is no male comparator expressly does not apply to the payment of money under a contract of employment).

The British legislation has been criticised by Lord Denning (former head of the Court of Appeal) for its 'tortuosity and complexity', beyond the understanding of any 'ordinary lawyer'. The industrial tribunals, in which the legislation is enforced in employment cases, have had the greatest difficulty in understanding and applying the legislation and the Employment Appeal Tribunal and Court of Appeal (dealing with appeals on questions of law) have not infrequently been divided in opinion. The legislation provides many examples of the peculiarly British approach to the drafting of legislation. Instead of broad principles, the Acts of

118

Parliament and Regulations abound in detailed and obscure provisions. While the legislation goes well beyond mere symbolic adherence to the principle of equal opportunity, and provides specific remedies for individuals, it rests upon a compromise between conflicting political and social pressure groups. It represents an attempt at 'social engineering' in a situation in which there is no real social consensus.

This is reflected in particular in the legislation relating to racial discrimination. In the 1950s and 1960s, there was a remarkable campaign to improve the social position of Britain's immigrants from the New Commonwealth and of British-born black children. This campaign was not based on the trade unions but rather on organisations of ethnic minorities, sympathetic liberals, the Labour Party and other left-wing political organisations. The first Race Relations Act in 1965 contained criminal sanctions against incitement to racial hatred and prohibited the practice of discrimination in places of public resort and in the disposal of tenancies. A report by an independent research organisation, Political and Economic Planning (PEP), published in April 1967, documented the vast extent of racial discrimination in Britain and later in the same year a committee of lawyers led by Professor Harry Street suggested the forms of enforcement that a new anti-discrimination law might contain. This drew heavily on the experience of the American states and Canadian provinces. In the following year, the Race Relations Act 1968 made employment discrimination, with certain exceptions, unlawful and also covered discrimination in housing and the provision of goods, facilities and services. It gave power to an administrative agency, the Race Relations Board, to receive and investigate complaints of violation and to seek redress of the victims' grievances. Many weaknesses in the 1968 Act soon emerged, particularly in relation to the method of enforcement by the Board and the narrow definition of discrimination.

In 1973 PEP undertook another national survey and in a series of reports documented the persistence of massive discrimination against ethnic minorities in the field of employment. At the same time, perceptions of the scope of discrimination began to broaden, in particular as a result of the Equal Pay Act 1970. That Act was the result of a century of pressure by the TUC; as early as 1888 the TUC had unanimously passed a motion that 'in the opinion of this Congress it is desirable, in the interests of both men and women, that in trade where women do the same work as men they shall receive the same payment' and this was reiterated by Congress on more than forty occasions in the following seventy-five years. However, it was not until 1963 that Congesss called for legislative intervention to secure equal pay. The question of equal pay in the public sector had been examined by no less than three Royal Commissions and three Government Committees between 1912 and 1946 and following a collective agreement of January 1955 equality of pay in the Civil Service was achieved in 1961. The Labour Government elected in 1964 was committed to legislate on equal pay in the private sector but its Bill was enacted just before that Government lost office in 1970 and employers were given five years to prepare for the implementation of the legislation.

It was appreciated that the Equal Pay Act would be of little value

119

so long as the occupational segregation of women in low paid jobs, including those where trade unions are weak, continued. This is a particularly important problem in Britain where (by 1980) 40 per cent of the labour force consists of women, 56 per cent of those being full-time and 44 per cent being part-time, and two-thirds of them are in jobs done only by women. The Conservative Government, under Mr Edward Heath, was preparing legislation on the broader aspects of sex discrimination when it lost office in 1974. The Labour Government introduced its own Bill which was enacted as the Sex Discrimination Act 1975. This came into force at the same time as the Equal Pay Act. It allows aggrieved individuals a right of direct access to the industrial tribunals in employment cases, while at the same time entrusting strategic enforcement in the public interest to an Equal Opportunities Commission (EOC). The EOC deals with discriminatory practices by industries, firms and institutions and is expected to encourage positive action against discrimination. This Act was used as the model for a new Race Relations Act, enacted in 1976, which came into force in 1977. There is a similar system of enforcement through industrial tribunals and strategic enforcement by a Commission for Racial Equality (CRE) which has similar powers to the EOC. The two pieces of legislation are in many respects identical.

Has the legislation had any significant impact? A major study of the implementation and effect of the Equal Pay and Sex Discrimination Acts in twenty-six organisations (from 1974 to 1977) concluded that 'women have made tangible gains as a result of the Act, particularly with respect to pay. The vast majority of women in the organisations studied were entitled to and received some increase in their rates of pay as a result of the Equal Pay Act and most were getting equal pay as defined in the Act' (M.W. Snell, P. Glucklich and M. Povall, 'Equal Pay and Opportunities', Research Paper No. 20, DE, April 1981, p. 90). However, the study found that the Act did not have much success in achieving equal pay and opportunities in a wider sense. More recent evidence from 'The New Earnings Survey' (1970-82, Part A, Tables 10 and 11) shows that the initial effects of the equal pay legislation have now been exhausted. In 1970, women's average gross hourly earnings (excluding the effects of overtime, employees aged 18 and over) were 63.1 per cent of men's. They reached a peak of 75.5 per cent in 1977 and in the following years to 1982, settled in the range 73-75 per cent. When overtime earnings are taken into account the gap is even wider, because men work substantially more overtime than women. The earnings gap is widest among non-manual workers in the private sector where women's average earnings in 1981 and 1982 were just less than 53 per cent of men's (see Seventh Annual Report EOC 1982, Appendix 9, Part 4a). In view of the overwhelming social survey evidence of continuing occupational segregation of women, and of racial discrimination in employment, it is remarkable that very little use has been made of the legal remedies provided by Parliament. In 1976, the first year of operation of the Equal Pay Act, there were 1,742 applications to industrial tribunals; by 1982 this had declined to a handful of 39 cases. The number of applications to tribunals under the Sex Discrimination Act fell from 243 in 1976 to only 150 in 1982. Under the Race Relations Act, the number of applications to Tribunals reached a high point of 426 in the year 1979-1980, declining to 332 in 1980-1981. Those who use the law have relatively little chance of success. Only about one in every ten applicants who go through an industrial tribunal hearing on a complaint of racial discrimination win their cases. About two in every ten win their sex discrimination cases after a tribunal hearing. As will be seen later the scale of remedies which may be granted to successful complainants is derisory. It is against this background that the scope of the legislation and the present enforcement mechanisms must be judged.

DEFINITION OF DISCRIMINATION

The British legislation is based on the notion of equal opportunity rather than equality of outcomes or 'fair shares'. In other words, it is primarily concerned with the concept that likes must be treated alike, that it is wrong to treat two persons differently if there is no morally relevant difference between them. It aims to remove all formal and deliberate impediments to opportunity on the basis of ability or individual merit. This has been described as an essentially 'procedural' approach to equality. The legislation does not address directly the issue whether inequalities in the distribution of benefits based on wealth, inheritance, power, class, etc. should be removed. For this reason the critics of the legislation argue that 'equal opportunity' means only the equal right to become unequal.

The legislation covers both 'direct' discrimination and 'indirect' discrimination. The first concept is 'less favourable' treatment on one of the prohibited grounds. The case law has established that any deprivation of choice can amount to 'less favourable' treatment. There is no need to show that the act was inherently hostile or prejudiced against the interests of women or a particular racial group as the case may be. The only issue is whether that group was put at a factual disadvantage compared to the other group. For example, since the Act applies to both men and women, it would be no answer to a complaint by a man that women were being allowed to leave the plant five minutes earlier than men on grounds of 'chivalry' or that women were being given 'less dirty' work than men to protect their hair-dos. The Race Relation Act specifically declares that segregation is 'less favourable' treatment. The legislation has been interpreted to protect those who refuse to carry out discriminatory instructions by the employer, for example to refuse service to black persons. Moreover, the concept of 'direct' discrimination has proved wide enough to cover stereotyped assumptions based on race and sex. For example, it was held that an employer had acted unlawfully when he dismissed a woman with young children on the ground that in his experience such women were unreliable employees; and an employer was not allowed to refuse training to a woman on the ground of a generalised assumption that when she was qualified she would leave their employment to follow her husband to work in another town - employers may not assume that males are the only 'breadwinners'.

The second type of discrimination is 'indirect' or 'discrimination by effects'. This bears a close family resemblance and owes its origin to

121

the interpretation by the United States Supreme Court of the US Civil Rights Act 1964, in particular in Griggs v Duke Power Company 401 US 424 (1971). In that case the Supreme Court decided that it was unlawful discrimination under Title VII for an employer to use a practice or procedure that disproportionately affects blacks, unless this is a matter of 'business necessity' essential to the employer's operation. This ambiguous test was translated into the specific and complex language of the British definition of 'indirect discrimination'. The underlying theory is that in a society in which inequalities in the distribution of benefits are regarded as justifiable, the opportunity for attaining those benefits ought to be determined on a proportional basis of group entitlement. In order to establish indirect discrimination, the complainant must prove:

(i) the respondent applied a 'requirement or condition' to him which is applied generally to all work-seekers or employees. There is a significant difference between this and the test in the Griggs case because the English Court of Appeal has decided that the 'requirement or condition' must be an absolute bar, something which has to be complied with. It is not sufficient if it is simply one of a number of criteria taken into account by the employer. For example, in one case a native of Sri Lanka complained of indirect discrimination in that an interviewing board for the post of legal assistant in the Civil Service had taken account when assessing his personal qualities of a number of facts such as his experience in the United Kingdom, his command of the English language, and his age. It was held that since these were no more than a number of flexible criteria, they did not amount to an 'absolute bar' and therefore there could be no case of indirect discrimination.

(ii) The proportion of the complainant's racial group, or his or her sex, or of married persons, who can comply with that 'requirement of condition' is considerably smaller than the proportion of persons not of that racial group, or not of that sex, or single persons as the case may be, who can comply with it. This means that if an employer requires an applicant to pass an educational test for a job or promotion this would be discriminatory if it were shown that the test operated to disqualify black applicants at a considerably higher rate than white applicants. The test whether a person 'can' comply with a requirement is not whether it is physically possible for him or her to do so, but whether he or she can do so in practice. Applying this approach it was decided in one case that in determining the proportion of women who 'can' comply with an age limit of 28 years for entrance to the post of executive officer in the Civil Service, it is relevant to take into account the usual behaviour of women in this respect as observed in practice. Judicial notice was taken of the fact that a considerable number of women between their mid-twenties and mid-thirties are engaged in child-rearing and this was supported by statistical evidence, so leading to the conclusion that the age limit (17-28 years) for entry to the executive class in the Civil Service was one which it was, in practice, harder for women to comply with than for men. The courts have, as yet, given no real guidance on what constitutes a 'considerably smaller' proportion. Presumably, notions of 'statistical significance' should be examined but the courts have said that a common sense approach rather than elaborate statistical evidence should be used. In the British context, some of the most important examples of indirect discriminatory requirements or practices would include minimum height requirements; prohibition on wearing certain types of clothing (such as turbans by Sikhs); language proficiency in manual jobs; refusal to accept foreign qualifications; maximum age limitations; experience or training in Britain; recruitment by personal referrals within the existing workforce, sometimes called 'word of mouth hiring'; and recruitment through a network of contacts which excludes ethnic minorities, women, etc.

Once the complainant has proved that there is a requirement or condition which has a disproportionate impact, and that it is to his or her detriment, it is then for the respondent to prove that the requirement or condition is 'justifiable', irrespective of the sex of the person to whom it is applied or irrespective of marital status or irrespective of colour, race, nationality or ethnic or national origins. In the United States, in the Griggs case it was recognised that indirectly discriminatory policies and practices may sometimes serve valid ends: 'the touchstone is business necessity. If an employment practice which operates to exclude Negroes cannot be shown to be related to job performance, the practice is prohibited'. The British concept of 'justifiability' is, however, far broader than this American test. It appears from the Parliamentary debates on the Sex Discrimination Bill that one of the main reasons that the word 'justifiable' rather than 'necessary' was used in the British statute was to avoid the courts and tribunals finding that certain seniority rules were unlawful (such as the 'last in first out' criterion for redundancy selection which is likely to have a greater impact on women than men). This suggests, as the Employment Appeal Tribunal decided, that the tribunal must look at all the circumstances including necessity and the discriminatory effect of the requirement or condition. But the Court of Appeal has equated 'justifiable' with 'reasonable'. The employer, it is said, must 'advance good grounds', 'acceptable to right-thinking people'. A former President of the EAT was rightly apprehensive whether the tribunal had the capacity to make such evaluations. In his words: 'on emotive matters such as racial or sex discrimination there is no generally accepted view as to the comparative importance of eliminating discriminatory practices on the one hand, as against, for example, the profitability of the business on the other'. The point is that the Court of Appeal expects a process of fact evaluation in an area where no consensus exists amongst tribunal members, even less a social consensus. Although the House of Lords has recently thrown some doubt on the Court of Appeal's approach, the scope of the defence remains ambiguous. The concept of indirect discrimination is the legal expression of the concept of institutional or structural discrimination. If undue deference is given to existing practices, notwithstanding their discriminatory impact, it will be difficult to eliminate disadvantages which result from the effects of past discrimination, from entrenched ways of doing things, from networks which exclude women and ethnic minorities

123

and so on. If the defence of 'justifiability' is too wide, the objective of the legislation will be easily defeated.

GROUNDS OF DISCRIMINATION

The Sex Discrimination legislation covers discrimination on grounds of sex and applies equally to men and women. In all cases it is necessary to compare like with like and this has led a majority of the Employment Appeal Tribunals to decide that, since men cannot become pregnant, a woman with child has no masculine equivalent; with the result that dismissal on grounds of pregnancy is not covered by this legislation. However, the general employment legislation provides protection to women with more than 52 weeks' service against dismissal on grounds of pregnancy and also confers maternity rights on women with two or more years' continuous service with the same employer. The Sex Discrimination Act prohibits discrimination against married persons on grounds of marital status but this does not include discrimination against single persons. Discrimination against homosexuals or otherwise on grounds of sexual orientation or preferences is not unlawful in Great Britain, but several local authorities pursue non-discrimination policies in respect of these matters.

The Race Relations Act outlaws discrimination on grounds of colour, race, nationality or ethnic or national origins. The words 'ethnic origins' have been given a wide interpretation as meaning a group which is a segment of the population distinguished from others by a sufficient combination of shared customs, beliefs, traditions and characteristics derived from a common or presumed common past, even if not drawn from a common 'racial stock'. Accordingly, Sikhs are regarded as an ethnic group, although not distinguishable from other Punjabis, apart from the tenets of their religion. So too discrimination against Jews as a group with common ethnic origins would be regarded as unlawful. However, discrimination on grounds of religion as such is not covered in Great Britain (in Nothern Ireland, however, discrimination on grounds of religion and political opinion is prohibited by law).

Discrimination on other grounds, such as language, age, etc. are not **per se** unlawful but 'requirements and conditions' in relation to these matters might, in certain circumstances, constitute indirect discrimination (see above).

EXCEPTIONS

There are relatively few exceptions, although some of these are potentially important. The legislation excludes employment for the purposes of a private household. In the case of discrimination on grounds of sex or marital status, discrimination by those employing five or less persons is excluded, but in a recent decision (Case 165/82) the European Court of Justice has ruled that the total exclusion of persons employed in private households cannot be justified and goes further than is lawful under Art. 2(2) of the Equal Treatment Directive of the Council 76/206/EEC. EEC law has also led to a modification of the British legislation which excludes discrimination in relation to death or retirement. The ECJ decisions have enabled women to obtain equal treatment in respect of contributions to retirement pension schemes paid by the employer as an addition to gross salary, and in respect of special facilities after retirement which are granted as a term of employment. However, the legislation, like the EEC Treaty and Directives, does permit a different compulsory retirement age for men and women and consequently differential treatment directly linked to the State retiring age is not unlawful. There must be equal access to occupational pension schemes.

The Sex Discrimination Act has a list of circumstances in which being a man or woman is a 'genuine occupational qualification' and in these circumstances discrimination is lawful. These include models, actors, toilet attendants, hospital and prison staff, personal welfare counsellors and jobs to be fulfilled outside the United Kingdom in countries whose laws or customs require discrimination. The Act does not apply to employment as a midwife but the concept of male midwives is slowly being introduced in a manner which the ECJ (Case 165/82) has held to be in conformity with Art. 2(2) and 9(2) of the Equal Treatment Directive 76 6/207/EEC. There are special provisions regarding police and prison staff.

The Race Relations Act has a narrower list of genuine occuaptional qualifications, including actors, models, personal welfare counsellors and jobs including working in a place where food and drink is provided in a particular setting for which in that job a person of a particular race is required 'for reasons of authenticity' (e.g. Chinese restaurants). Both this Act and the Sex Discrimination Act and Equal Pay Act apply only to employment at establishments in Great Britain.

The Sex Discrimination Act and Equal Pay Act preserve the special protective legislation which applies to women; much of the nineteenth and twentieth century legislation relating to the hours of work, holidays and safety of women in factories, mines and certain other places of employment remains in force. The absolute prohibition of the employment of women underground was modified by the Sex Discrimination Act so that 'no female shall be employed in a job the duties of which ordinarily require the employee to spend a significant proportion of her time below ground at a mine which is being worked': this means that it is still impossible for a woman to become a face-worker in a coal mine but she could become an engineer or join any other occupation which does not involve spending a significant proportion of her time underground. These protective measures could be repealed or replaced by regulations laid before Parliament by the Secretary of State, and the Equal Opportunities Commission and Health and Safety Commission are required to keep the legislation under review. There have been reports on the issue whether the existing protective legislation should be retained by a working party of National Joint Advisory Council to the Ministry of Labour (1969) and the Equal Opportunities Commission. The present view of the TUC is that such legislation is still required to protect women in view of their position in the family, which may require lager social changes before the legislation can be repealed.

AFFIRMATIVE ACTION AND REVERSE DISCRIMINATION

Nothing in the legislation requires 'reverse' discrimination in favour of women, married persons or blacks. Indeed, the definition of discrimination means that, apart from a few exceptions, such discrimination is itself now unlawful. One exception is in respect of discriminatory training and education but a number of detailed conditions must be satisfied. Another exception is that trade unions and similar bodies may reserve seats on elective bodies for members of one sex.

On the other hand, affirmative or positive action to enable women and members of ethnic minorities to develop their potential and 'catch up' with men and the majority group is encouraged by both the Equal Opportunities Commission and the Commission for Racial Equality. This does not involve the imposition of quotas or permit discrimination in selection. The government policy statement which preceded the introduction of the legislation defined the need for positive action. It argued that a principle of non-discrimination, interpreted 'too literally and inflexibly' might 'actually impede the elimination of invidious discrimination and the encouragement of equality of opportunity' because it would exclude such measures as special training courses and special encouragement to disadvantaged groups to apply for employment which, for various reasons, they had not previously sought. The government therefore concluded that 'it would be wrong to adhere so blindly to the principle of formal legal equality as to ignore the handicaps preventing many black and brown workers (and women) from obtaining equal employment opportunities'. The CRE has issued a Code of Practice for the elimination of discrimination and the promotion of equality of opportunity in employment. This was approved by Parliament in June 1983 and came into operation in April 1984. Tribunals must take account of the provisions of the Code when dealing with cases brought before them. The Code recommends trade unions and employers to take positive measures to provide encouragement and training where there is under-representation of particular groups in particular work. A similar Code has been drafted by the Equal Opportunities Commission in respect of sex discrimination but is not yet in force. Among the matters recommended in the Code are advertising jobs in the ethnic minority press and using minority languages as well as English, emphasising that ethnic minority applicants are welcome, including areas of high ethnic minority population when running pre-entry training and other courses for adults designed to overcome a general deficiency of skilled workers in a particular trade, giving poor workers induction courses which include mutual awareness and appreciation of cultural differences and catering for the special needs of particular groups in relation to training for promotion and transfer.

ENFORCEMENT

The Race Relations Act 1968 was enforced by a Race Relations Board along the lines of a North American human rights commission and by voluntary industry disputes procedures in some forty industries covering about on third of the labour force. The industrial machinery failed to deal adequately with complaints of racial discriminsation. Only the Race Relations Board could bring cases before the courts, but it was required to investigate all individual complaints. This procedure was found to be 'costly and wasteful' and it created a degree of resentment and hostility among those whom it was designed to assist because they were denied direct access to the courts. On the other hand, it was argued that it was useful to have a public enforcement agency because private individuals do not have the resources to find and prove discrimination and it is through individual case work that patterns of discrimination are most likely to emerge.

The Sex Discrimination Act 1975 and the Race Relations Act 1976 tried to meet these points by allowing both individual enforcement, in some cases with the assistance of the Commissions, and also actions against discriminatory practices by the Commissions themselves.

An individual may complain to an industrial tribunal within three months of the alleged discriminatory act (the period may be extended) and the EOC and CRE may in their discretion assist individuals, for example by giving advice, procuring settlements, arranging for legal assistance and representation. Officers of the independent Advisory, Conciliation and Arbitration Service have to attempt conciliation, encouraging use where appropriate of voluntary industrial agreements and procedures. The most serious obstacle facing the complainant is that of proving unlawful discrimination, although a procedure does exist by which a complainant may obtain information from the respondent to help him or her decide whether or not to institute proceedings, and, if he or she does so to assist in presenting a case. Although the formal burden of proof is on the complainant, the tribunals have adopted a flexible attitude. The Employment Appeal Tribunal has directed them to take into account the fact that direct evidence of discrimination is seldom going to be available and that, accordingly, in these cases the affirmative evidence of discrimination will normally consist of inferences to be drawn from the primary facts. If the primary facts indicate that there has been discrimination of some kind, the employer is called upon to give an explanation and, failing clear and specific explanation being given by the employer to the satisfaction of the industrial tribunal, an inference of unlawful discrimination from the primary facts will mean the complaint succeeds. Normally it is regarded as sufficient for the complainant to show that he or she possessed the minimum objective requirements for the job and that after his or her rejection the employer continued to seek applicants or appointed one of the opposite sex or another racial group as the case may be. The employer must then give a 'clear and specific explanation' and the reasons he puts forward must be credible.

The EOC and CRE each operate within their own field but they are similarly composed and have similar functions. Each Commission has a Chairman and fourteen members (on a tripartite basis) and supporting staff. Their main functions are to conduct investigations and to take action to remove unlawful practices. Where investigation reveals discriminatory practices, a non-discrimination notice may be served on the respondent requiring him to cease, subject to an appeal to an industrial tribunal. If within five years of a non-discrimination notice becoming final, or of a finding by a court of tribunal of unlawful discrimination it appears that the respondent is likely again to act unlawfully, the Commissions may apply to an industrial tribunal to ascertain the facts and may then seek an injunction in the County Courts. The Commissions also have general functions, such as the promotion of research and education. They have made relatively little use of their powers of formal investigation, partly because of a number of restrictions which have been imposed on their use of these powers by the courts.

Equal pay cases are also enforced by individuals through the industrial tribunals. Either the employer or the employee may start the proceedings, as may the Secretary of State. The employee may claim arrears of remuneration or damages in respect of a time not earlier than two years before the date on which proceedings were instituted. Where the claim is for equal pay for work of equal value (in cases where there is not 'like work' or 'work rated as equivalent' under a job evaluation study) there is a much more complicated procedure. There has to be preliminary hearing by the tribunal to decide whether there are reasonable grounds for determining that the work is equal value. If the tribunal decides that the case can go ahead, then it must refer the issue to an independent expert, who may apply to the tribunal for orders against any person with relevant information or documents to furnish these for the purposes of the investigations. The expert's report may be challenged on a number of grounds and each party to the proceedings may call one expert of his or her own choosing. The independent expert, whose costs are paid by the State, may be cross-examined. Eventually the tribunal has to decide whether the work is of equal value, having regard to the report, and whether the employer has shown a defence that the difference in pay or terms of employment is due to a material factor other than a difference in sex.

The remedies which the tribunal may award in Sex Discrimination and Race Relations Acts are far less effective than those to be found in corresponding American legislation. The tribunal may
(i)   make an order declaring the rights of the party;
(ii) award compensation which is subject to a maximum at present of £7,500, including a sum is respect of injured feelings (usually in the vicinity of £150); and
(iii) recommend that the respondent take within a specified period action appearing to the tribunal to be praticable for the purposes of obviating or reducing the adverse effect of the unlawful discrimination on the complainant.

There is no power to order reinstatement or re-engagement or that the next job be offered to the complainant, although these measures may be recommended. If a recommendation is not complied with without reasonable justification, the amount of compensation may be increased but not so as to exceed the overall limit of £7,500.

CONCLUSIONS

The concept of equal rights in Britisch anti-discrimination legislation depends for its effectiveness upon the recognition of the collective deprivation of women and ethnic minorties as groups. In the case of direct discrimination, this requires proof as to the treatment of groups, and in the case of indirect discrimination of the consequences of rules and practices upon groups. This involves the determination and evaluation of social facts. The form of civil adjudication for the resolution of private disputes about individual transactions between the immediate parties to the litigation has proved to be ill-adapted to these tasks of 'social engineering'. In particular, the process of acquiring knowledge about the recurrent patterns of behaviour which go to make up social facts is different from the process familiar to lawyers for re-constructing occurrences between individual parties. The British 'solution' to this problem has taken two principal forms. One is simply to neglect the social facts; the other is to rely upon the intuitive common sense of the 'reasonable' man.

This prompts the question, what are the alternatives? One view is that the structure of anti-discrimination legislation is 'misconceived and self-defeating'. These critics maintain that equal opportunities laws should be simple and unambitious and used only as a basis for education and persuasion. On the other hand, there is still a powerful lobby which is committed to a more instrumental role for the law. From this viewpoint a number of reforms have been suggested. One is to allow the judge to refer issues to an independent agency for the investigation of social facts. Something along these lines has already been introduced in the case of claims for equal pay for work of equal value, although this has been wrapped up in a very complicated procedure which makes it difficult to utilise the expert's report. Another proposal being canvassed is to create a specialised court to deal with discrimination cases and other violations of human rights, or at least to confer jurisdiction on the High Court which has far greater powers than the industrial tribunals. This solution itself may be criticised on the ground that it involves the use of an adjudicative model which is incapable of taking account of the wide unforeseen repercussions for many persons other than the immediate parties. Instead of following an American pattern of 'structural' adjudication, it has been suggested that one should consider new forms of pubic arbitration which are perhaps better suited to considering interests of groups and employing a mixture of negotiation and compulsion.

Questions such as these are moving to the centre of the debate about equal rights, and they are not confined to the arenas of racial and sexual discrimination. Increasingly, there are demands for fair shares for groups such as disabled persons, low-paid workers, the unemployed, particularly young men and women. The consciousness of social deprivation among these groups has increased the intensity of demands for collective entitlements to remedial assistance and for the extension of indivual rights to equal opportunities. These pressures may push the concept of equal rights itself closer to one of substantive 'equality of results'.

NOTE

1. The legislation extends to the whole of Great Britain (England, Wales and Scotland). There is parallel legislation on sex discrimination in Northern Ireland where there is no Race Relations Act but the Fair Employment (Northern Ireland) Act 1976 provides a comprehensive remedy for political and religious discrimination in employment in Northern Ireland. This article is concerned exclusively with the situation in Great Britain.

9. Hungary

L. Nagy

I. INTRODUCTION

The equality of citizens means that citizens are, within the framework of society, in social, economic and legal relations in an identical situation with one another. A more restricted concept than this, the equality of civic rights, expresses that the citizens enjoy equal rights, their situation is identical, their behaviour is determined with equal measures.

The legal prescription of equality of civic rights only forms the basis of civic equality. The actual assertion of this cannot be separated from the political, social, economic, cultural, etc. circumstances in which the activity or conduct of life takes place. It follows from this that the equality of civic rights and duties does not mean a neglect of the actual differences between citizens. It does mean, however, that this distinction should be justified, consequently it should not be in contradiction with the principles of equal rights. This is expressed by the prohibition of disadvantageous discrimination, enumerating the conditions in respect of which no discrimination is admitted.

Within the framework of this paper we only investigate a single projection of the equality of citizens, or civic rights. That which is connected with work and labour conditions and the legal organisation of which falls within the scope of labour law.

II. HISTORICAL BACKGROUND

Until Word War II, Hungary was an agricultural country, with inadequately developed industry. This left its mark on the legal regulation of labour relations and had a bearing on several feudal traits of discrimination. This presented itself particularly strongly in the field of the disadvantageous discrimination of females. On the one hand, the employment of women was restricted **e.g.** generally women could not serve in public service posts and on the other hand, the labour conditions of women were less favourable, their wages were lower than those of males. The situation of young people was similar but aggravated by the fact that, for example, in the case of industrial apprentices, even the use of corporal punishments was permitted by law. In the case of farm labourers and domestics, it was permitted, by law, to hold them in their place of employment by non-physical coercion, that is if they left their workplace without the permission of the employer, they could be constrained in an administrative way to continue the labour relationship. This situation was not essentially changed by the international conventions of labour, ratified following World War I

131

(**e.g.** concerning the night-work of young people). The implementation of these ratified conventions either occurred extremely imperfectly or not at all. They were mostly suspended immediately before the War or later during it. The fact that the country had no written Constitution and no unified Civil Code played a part in the formation of legal regulations. In this way, the uniform regulations of the fundamental institutions, with regard to labour relations and of the fundamental rights and duties originating in these relations, was missing. This situation was even made worse in the period between the two World Wars in the course of which several discriminative dispositions of racial and political character were issued.

Following World War II, in the field of labour-law regulations, one of the most urgent tasks was to quash those rules of a discriminative character offending the equality of civic rights. The declaration of the right to work appeared in our country in Act I of 1946, at first, manifesting among 'human rights' the 'right to work and to a worthy human liveli-hood', as well. Already created by this period were rules of law promoting the predominance of the right to work and eliminating the inequality of citizens in the field of labour relations, as well. We are emphasizing here only the most important of these rules of law. Thus Act XXII of 1946, giving equal rights to women in the field of vocational education, necessary for the equality of employment of females. Act XLIII of 1948 provided for the elimination of the disadvantageous position of women existing within the public services and in other professions. From among the rules of law eliminating the inequality of employees, some of the first were those cancelling the provisions of fascist laws containing political and racial discriminations. These rules of law ensured, however, only that every citizen should have the possibility, without any distinction, to make contracts of work and labour. The rules of law, introducing the free Labour Exchange or restricting the dismissal of industrial or commercial employees, took steps in the direction of ensuring the possibility of undertaking a job. Further important advances followed in the course of concluding collective agreements, particularly in the field of the equal rights of females and young people.

The Constitution enacted in 1949, the first written constitution of the country, unambiguously declares the equality of civic rights and the right to work. The rules of the Labour Code, enacted in 1951 (the freedom to create labour relations, prohibition of discrimination, etc.), serve the realisation of the latter. In the course of the following decades essential steps were carried out for creating the conditions for the right to work. This was indicated from one side, by the complete termination of unemployment; from the other side, by the rules on the measures for creating the equal rights of females, or the Act on youth. Regarding legal regulation, Labour Code II, enacted in 1968, partly summarises and develops further the legal regulation brought about since World War II. About this, we will speak in detail.

III. EQUALITY OF RIGHTS

The fundamental manifestation of the equality of civic rights in the field of labour relations is the declaration of the right to work, **i.e.** the right of every citizen to undertake work and, through this, partly to be able to ensure his living, partly to express his spiritual and physical capacities, to realise himself. Art. 55, sec. 1 of the Hungarian Constitution clearly declares that the Hungarian People's Republic guarantees to its citizens the right to work.

The constitutional declaration of the right to work does not entitle any citizen to a concrete place of work. This means the State has a double duty. Partly, to create those conditions from which a place of work is available to each citizen. This demands for example wide political, economic and educational organising activity. Act. 55, sec. 2 of the Constitution, mentioned above, refers to this. This establishes, namely, that the right to work is realised by the Hungarian People's Republic 'by means of developing the productive forces of the People's Republic according to a plan and implementing it with labour-force economy, founded on a plan'. The aim of the other requirement is that the State should create such a situation in which the citizen can use the possibility ensured to him and is really able to undertake a work placement. This already requires legal regulations and the creation of legal guarantees. This legal regulation should particularly be directed to the following:

- it should ensure the unimpeded utilisation of institutions during which process a place of work can be found,
- possibility should be given to the free choice of a place of work and to a free, unforced conclusion of an agreement concerning the establishment of a labour relation,
- it should provide for regulating the security of the place of work,
- it should ensure identical labour conditions and pay.

To promote workseeking, labour law regulates the functioning of two institutions. One of these is occupational counselling; the other, the labour exchange. Both are entirely gratuitous. Everybody may have recourse to them without any restriction.

In connection with undertaking the work, Art. 18, sec. 1 of the Labour Code guarantees the right of citizens to enter into labour relations on the basis of their own free will. In the interest of this, the Labour Code regulates the legal capacity and capacity of action of citizens. Art. 16, sec. 2, in accordance with the International Convention of Labour on the subject, declares every citizen over the age of 15 legally capable if he has completed his general-school studies successfully or he has been exempted from attending school. The rule of law ensures a capacity for concluding labour contracts to a legally capable person. Such a person can, therefore, conclude this contract himself. There is only one exception to this; in the case of an under 16 years old it requires the permission of his legal representative to undertake the first labour relation.

In the interests of the security of the place of work, there are necessarily two kinds of measures. On the one hand, during the labour relations the conditions established in the labour contract should remain unchanged. On the other hand, it should be guaranteed that the labour relations of employees should not be terminated groundlessly.

Art. 24 of the Labour Code declares as a general rule that those conditions contained in the labour contract should only be changed with the common agreement of the parties. Exceptions are only permitted in a very narrow field, for the employer, primarily in the case of disciplinary calling to account.

Labour relations are generally of lasting character. During a long period, in the case of either party, some changes may easily occur which could make the further maintenance of the labour relationship become inconvenient, and even unnecessary. In the case of the agreement of the parties, the labour relationship may be terminated jointly, at any time. But if there is no such agreement, both of the parties should have the right to terminate the labour relationship with a unilaterial declaration. When, therefore, we speak of the security of the place of work, we should take into consideration the possibility of terminating the labour relationships which have already lost their purpose or cannot be maintained from any other point of view. The security of the place of labour should not mean for the employer the absolute exclusion of the possibility of terminating the labour relationship. The legal regulation should be directed towards excluding the unjustified cases. According to § 26 /2/ of the Labour Code, the enterprise is obliged to offer an explanation of notice. The law does not enumerate the reasons justifying notice. According to the standpoint of the Supreme Court only such a circumstance can justify notice which makes the termination of a worker's employment relationship necessary to the enterprise. Such circumstances may arise either within the enterprise; reoganisation, changing to a new product, a need for workers with other qualifications; or on the part of the worker, improper working activity, unjustified absence. If the enterprise terminates the employment relationschip not for the reasons mentioned above but because of personal conflict, then the law has been misused and the notice of dismissal is invalid. In the case of an unlawful termination of employment the enterprise must fulfil the following duties:
- the worker must be employed in his original job,
- wages and other benefits must be paid,
- possible damages must be refunded, including the costs of the claim of unlawful dismissal.

IV. POSITIVE DISCRIMINATION

Above we have outlined a positive description of the equality of rights. The equality of rights, as referred to, cannot, and should not, leave out of consideration the differences existing in life which are justified and are to be maintained. The legal regulation chooses in this connection a double solution. On the one hand, it determines which differences should be allowed and taken into consideration. This is formulated by the general norm concerning the prohibition of discrimination. On the other hand, it determines the exceptions i.e. the cases in which the discrimination is allowed.

The Constitution has also certain provisions in respect of the prohibition of discrimination. This is formalised by the Labour Code in respect of labour relations. According to Art. 18, sec. 3, 'in the course of establishing the labour relation and determining the rights and duties originating in the labour relation, we should not make any discrimination between employees according to their sex, age, nationality, race and descent '.

This general rule is completed by Art. 19, sec. 2 of the Act with a provision of positive formulation. According to this, 'the employment of a pregnant woman or a mother should not be refused, with regard to this circumstance '.

As to young people, Act. IV of 1971 on Youth, prescribes, in harmony with the former provisions, that 'the material-moral appreciation of working young people should be ensured on the basis of the principle of distribution according to the work, in the same way as with other employees'.

As already mentioned, there are necessarily certain exceptions to this prohibition of discrimination. The grounds of the exceptions are, in Hungarian Labour Law, the following:
- qualifications and the work performed,
- the security of the State,
- the public interest,
- labour safety and the protection of special categories of employees. Among the exceptions we should speak about two factors, meaning certain distinction, which present themselves in connection with creating the labour relation. These are: the establishment of the qualification required to perform the work and of the remuneration due on the basis of the work. (These are, in our opinion, apparent exceptions. The notions of discrimination have always had an illegal character. These are real distinctions which are necessary just in the interest of the development, the advancement of the single employee and of the society.)

The aim of production and commerce, is, in our opinion, to satisfy the needs of society as completely as possible, to raise the living standards of citizen. One of the essential preconditions of this is that it should take place on the highest possible level and organisation of activities. This is, however, only possible if the person performing the work always has the necessary up-to-date qualification which would, therefore, be in the interest both of the whole of society and of the individual citizens.

In connection with the qualification, we should notice that this may only be one without the existence of which the scope of activity cannot duly be managed. A qualification, therefore, which is otherwise not obligatory on the basis of the character of the scope of activity, should not be prescribed in order to make possible the exclusion of certain employees from the employment. Thus, for example, it is prescribed by the rule of law that in ceratin types of telephone exchanges blind switchboard operators should be employed. Certain employers try to elude this ruling by extending the responsibilities of the switchboard operators to include certain tasks e.g. taking over supervising deliveries, which cannot be performed by a blind person. And, referring to this extended responsibility they refuse to employ blind switchboard operators in that office. In such a case, the Court of Labour, where the employee initiated a labour dispute, always obliged the employer to employ this employee. Otherwise, as referred to above free education and the development of the school system serve only the prevention of indirect discrimination, induced possibly by requiring the qualification.

The situation is similar in connection with the remuneration of labour. According to our Constitution, the quantity of the work performed and its quality are to prevail in establishing the remuneration. Correspondingly, Art. 44 of the Labour Code establishes: 'Remuneration is due for the work implemented. The system of remuneration should be established taking into consideration the quantity, quality of the work implemented and social utility.' It follows from this rule that he who gives a higher, better performance, obtains a higher remuneration than he whose performance is of lower level or quality. This, at any rate, is a justified, righteous distinction.

In this way, neither the prescription of a special education or training nor a remuneration according to the quantity or quality of the work implemented may be brought into the scope of discrimination, they are not discriminative measures. Of course, the rules serving as basis of the prescription of special education and of determining remuneration, should be valid uniformly and without any exception for the employees performing an identical range of activity. (Therefore, it is not right to prescribe a different book-keeping training in this type of activity for women from that of men, or it would be wrong if the scope of activity is the same, to determine the wages of adult and young persons on the basis of different scales of wages.)

Concerning the safety of the State Hungarian rules emphasise Hungarian citizenship and a clean record. In the area of public administration and of the administration of justice, only a Hungarian citizen may be employed and only if he has a clean record. Outside this scope, i.e., in an enterprice, a non-Hungarian citizen may be employed. But, of course, he should have a labour permit issued by the competent Hungarian authority.

The clean record requirement is valid more widely, for example in enterprises, where employees have positions of responsibility, in which they manage financial affairs or materials (e.g. a cashier, an official charged with the handling of stored good).

Not only the safety of the State in a strict sense but public interest, as well, may justify differentiation to a certain degree, in employment. The rules already mentioned which require proof of a clean record in the area of work connected with managing mooney and store-keeping belong here.

Discrimination in the public interest is meant by the provisions which forbid the employment of those suffering from certain diseases, mainly infectious, in activities where they could spread the disease widely. Thus, for example, in the food industry and public catering. Similarly, it is required, in the public interest, that special education or certain qualifications should be compulsory in the case of fields of work or activity where an inadequate performance may cause an increased danger of accidents or any other danger (boiler- or fireman, driver, etc.). Public interest also plays a part in the rules which require a pre-determined age for performing certain work. The prevailing idea is that activities which demand increased responsibility require circumspection which can only be supposed after reaching a certain age. Thus, for example, for the range of work performed in public administration only a person over 18 years may be employed.

Some exceptions in other directions may also be needed from the point of view of labour safety and labour health. Three cases belong to this sphere: (a) physical and psychological state; (b) the protection of women; and (c) the protection of young people.

(a) The Hungarian law attributes great importance to the adequate physical and psychological state of the workers. The aim of regulation in this matter is to render it impossible for anyone to be employed in a job where his or her health could be impaired or where he/she might suffer accidents. The law in certain cases establishes general prohibitions. In certain jobs the law makes employment contingent upon a medical examination. The law prescribes the investigation into psychological fitness in addition to that into physical fitness. In such cases **e.g.** in the case of a driver, the worker should be subjected to the so-called vacational selection.

(b) The rule of law forbids or restricts the performance of certain types of work or activity in the case of women. In such situations, therefore, women are not permitted to enter into labour relations. The cause of this differentation may be twofold. One is of a general character: the physical constitution of females means their ability to manage physical tasks is different from that of males. The other is specific: the protection of motherhood.

According to prevailing medical opinion, work which requires major effort **e.g.** lifting of large loads, or the work of miners working below the ground may cause physical damage and induce diseases in women. Here the regulation of labour law applies three kinds of solutions. Partly, the rule of law itself excludes women from carrying out certain types of activity **e.g.** from lifting up loads larger than 20 kilogrammes. Partly, the rule of law entrusts the exclusion of some further types of activity to the enterprise rules on labour-safety which, with regard to the possibility of their deteriorating health, cannot be filled by women. Finally, according to the provision of the rule of law, before being employed in physical work, every woman should be submitted to a medical examination, in order to establish whether she is suitable for performing the given range of activity, which is otherwise not forbidden to females. Insofar as, according to the medical investigation, the woman may be employed in the given activity then she should not be in a more disadvantageous situation than men in respect of the recompense for her work.

The protection of maternity already demands a more complicated regulation. The regulation should exert an effect in two directions. It should prevent the pregnant woman or the mother with a small child from performing a range of activity which could be detrimental to her own health or to that of the child to be born. This only means a temporary distinction. After the termination of this state, the woman can be employed in any activity which does not fall within the above-mentioned general restrictions. However, it may be that pregnancy occurs during the existing labour relations and the pregnant woman is working in an activity which is detrimental to her health, according to medical opinion. In such a case, the employer is obliged to transfer her temporarily, from the time of establishing pregnancy till the child is six months old into a type of activity more suitable to her state of health, or satisfactorily modify the conditions of work in her existing activity. The employee must consent to being transferred to a different activity. The earnings of the employee temporarily transferred should not be lower than her earlier average pay.

We should mention here, also, the rule whereby women in employment should not be obliged to work in a different setting or to do night-work from the beginning of the fourth month of pregnancy until her child is one year old. Extra work, overtime, being on call should not be ordered at all until the child is 6 months old. And following this, until the child becomes one year old, these should only be ordered with the consent of the mother.

(c) In the case of young people, under 18 years of age differentiation in labour relations is also justified on health grounds. The rule of law uses solutions similar to those in the case of females. Partly, in the case of determined types of work, it forbids the making of labour relations. Partly, it trusts to the labour safety regulations of the enterprise to determine some further labour conditions and situations where young people should not be employed. In the case of the physical demands of the work, a preliminary medical examination is necessary for young people, as well. Beyond this, the rule of law prescribes a certain degree of differentiation within the labour relationship. Thus, young people should not be assigned to night-work, and under 16 years old to extra work, overtime, being on call and waiting time, either.

V. INDIRECT DISCRIMINATION

The legal regulation, made known so far, only gives protection against the direct forms of discrimination. Discrimination may also take place insofar as the citizen cannot exert his right to work because he is not in possession of the requirements for the work. For example, he does not possess the necessary qualifcation or physical state. The start of work may possibly be hindered by the lack of accommodation or of other conditions. This may occur over a wider field, too, like the cases of discrimination, enumerated in the rules of law. Thus, the decreased capactty for work may also result in a disadvantageous situation. A wrong approach frequently occurs, as well, for example in connection with the employment of women. It is shown, also, by the examples enumerated that indirect discrimination is, in part, the consequence of some factors which cannot be excluded by labour law. Thus, the termination of the wrong approach may primarily be influenced by social means. While the difficulty of employment, resulting from the lack of qualification may be diminished by developing free education. In the framework of this paper, we only deal with solutions falling within the scope of labour law.

The rules of labour law first of all pay attention to those who can find a place of work but encounter difficulty owing to their social situation or their physical health condition. In this area, too, we find different solutions.

Thus, according to Art. 19, sec. 2 of the Labour Code, the pregnant woman and the mother with an infant or small child should be given preference in the case of identical employment conditions. Also, sec. 3 allows giving preference by a rule of law to other persons, on the basis of their social situation, health or other conditions.

The exclusion of indirect discrimination is similarly achieved by the provisions prescribing the temporary or definite change of the scope of work, in order that the citizen is able to exercise his right to work or is not obliged to move his home. These rules primarily affect females, young people and employees of limited work capacity.

We should mention here the rules which prescribe advantages for pregnant women and mothers. Thus the following are to be mentioned:
- The working woman with a child is entitled to additional leave.
- The pregnant woman is due to twenty weeks maternity leave, maintaining her average earnings.
- The employer should allow unpaid leave to the employed woman, at her request, after the maternity leave period for nursing and care of the child up to his third birthday, but in case of a seriously handicapped child, till the end of his sixth year and in case of the ill child till the end of his tenth year. During unpaid leave, the mother receives provision under social security rules.
- The working woman is due to a reduction in her worktime to enable her to feed her child.

For employees with a decreased work capacity the rule of law determines legally binding prescriptions in great detail. The description of these would exceed the reference of the present paper.

The above immediately affect the creation or maintenance of labour relations. It should be mentioned that a number of the social benefits and services, which should be provided by the employer on the basis of labour relations, serve similarly to prevent the elimination of indirect discrimination. The following are particularly to be mentioned:
- Children's institutions (nurseries, crêches, etc.), maintained by the employer, making return to work easier for women with children.
- The employer is obliged to contribute to the travelling costs of those living in another locality.
- The employer may maintain a workers' hostel for employees working a distance from their homes.

The rules referring to the above should be determined in the collective agreement.

The obstacle to the possibility of women undertaking work, is often that they do not have the required education. Cabinet Decision No. 1013/1970/V.10./Korm., dealing with the tasks necessary to improve the economic and social situation of females, prescribes that enterprises and other organisations of employers should emphasise, when developing the plans for continuing education, the importance of participation of women. At the same time, the competent national organs should pay particular attention to the position of women when developing further the education system using forms of instruction favourable to them. And they should promote the increased participation of women in education and training, even by granting them benefits.

In the case of young people, the ensurance of progression, development, is particularly important. The duty of the employer, originating in labour relations, is, in the case of every employee, to give benefit directed to the continuation of their learning and performance of work of a higher value. In the case of young people, however, Cabinet Decision No. 1043/1971/X.2./Korm., on the execution of the Act on Youth, prescribes, among other things that particular attention should

be paid to young people, ensuring work, at first, for five years. To this end it should investigate, together with the youth organisation whether:
- the placing of young people corresponds with their education and abilities,
- whether their remuneration is in proportion to the work implemented,
- whether in their place of work healthy and safe work conditions are guaranteed,
- whether there is opportunity for their special development and the continuation of their learning.

VI. LEGAL SANCTIONS

In the following, I turn to the legal fact of the means of law at our disposal in the case of an offence against the right to work in respect of the prohibition of discrimination. The questions belonging here may be classified within two groups:
- In the first group belong those which ensure remedy to the employee having suffered grievance.
- In the second group belong those which contains the sanction against those committing a violation of the law.

If an infringement of legal rule took place, the citizen suffering grievance may appeal against it. But the situation is different, depending upon whether the infringement of legal rule was committed by a public administrative body or by the employer.

There falls within the scope of the first **e.g.** the case of the Labour Exchange, functioning within the framework of the local council which refuses to give information about work vacancies or is not inclined to recommend the citizen to the work place he wishes. Or if the result of a medical examination, preliminary to employment, is false or contains wrong data. In such a case, in accord with the regulations on public administration the citizen may appeal to the superior public administrative organ, asking for a remedy. This process, however, falls outside the framework of Labour Law and it will not be dealt with here. But we note that if because of the illegal decisions, the citizen suffers, for example, if he was not employed because of an inaccurate medical examination and in his home area he could only find low paid employment which did not match his ability then he may apply, according to the rules of Art. 348 of the Civil Code, for compensation if the administrative procedure was wrong.

If the grievance took place in the course of creating the labour relation or later during its existence, on the basis of the rules of labour law, remedy may by found in the framework of the labour dispute.

If the employer does not employ the person presenting himself for work because the worker does not meet his requirements or because he selected somebody else, the by-passed aspirant cannot appeal against the employer as the declared right to work does not mean any subjective right to a specific place of work. However, it may be that behind the outward cause discrimination is concealed **e.g.** the person was not employed because she was a woman or a gipsy. This behaviour is injurious and such a person may commence an action against the employer within the rules governing labour disputes. People are often employed in seasonal work or to substitute for somebody for a determined period. It may heppen that the work lasts for a longer time than was predicted. In such cases, after agreement with the employees, the duration of labour contracts will be prolonged. However, it does happen that a female employee, becoming pregnant, will not have her labour contract prolonged because the employer wants to avoid his obligations to pregnant women. It is the standing practice of the Courts of Law that in these cases, if the employee commences an action against the employer, he will be obliged to continue the employment.

Two cases of discrimination may occur in the course of determining wages, other allowances or labour conditions. One of these is when the employee does not get the full value of the wages or allowances determined in a rule of law or in the collective agreement. This does not raise any considerable theoretical or practical problems as in the course of the labour dispute the wages or allowances of a stipulated amount are adjuged to the employee. However, freqently the rule of law or the collective agreement determines the wage or other allowance not as a fixed amount but as lower and upper limits and, within the framework of this, the employer is entitled to determine the amount due. In such a case, the employee has only a (subjective) right to a measure corresponding to the lower limit of wages or allowances. Therefore, he cannot begin a labour dispute to get a higher rate. However, insofar as the employer exercises his right in such a way that he is discriminating **e.g.** in the case of identical education and achievement, a female employee does not get so much as a man or a juvenile employee so much as an adult, then the employee is entitled to begin a labour dispute. In this case, the behaviour of the employer comes into collision with the rule of law forbidding discrimination.

Where, in the cases discussed above, some damage is suffered by the employee, **e.g.** owing to the non-prolongation of his labour contract for a time fixed, he is deprived of certain social insurance services, then beyond remedying the wrong, he may also claim compensation, according to Art. 62 of the Labour Code.

We have discussed the means to be applied for remedying the grievance. However, it should be mentioned that the trade union may also take measures in the interest of the employee. It has two possibilities open to it. One of these is: on the basis of Art. 14, sec. 3, it lodges an objection to the injurious action taken by the employer. (This may also be applied, in addition to the violation of a legal rule, in the case of the employer's behaviour which contravenes the manner of treatment, appropriate to a socialist philosophy.) The objection has delaying force. If the employer does not agree with the objection, he should submit it to the Labour Court. The other is: the trade union begins a labour dispute in the interest of the employee. It is entitled to do this on the basis of the law and the involvement of the employee is not needed.

Beyond the possibility of remedying the offence, the rule of law ensures sanctions in the case of discrimination. These are partly of labour-law, partly of criminal-law character.

As a means of sanction within the framework of labour law, disciplinary responsibility and material liability come into consideration.

The manager who discriminates violates his labour relations duty. Because of this, on the basis of Art. 55-56 of the Labour Code, he may be called to account and disciplined. In the course of this, if his conduct is serious, he may even be dismissed. And insofar as the injurious measure of the manager caused damages, in addition (e.g., in case of the former example, the employer had to pay damages to the employee in recompense for the missing social insurance allowance), on the basis of Art. 57 of the Labour Code, he may be obliged to recompense the damaged person in total or in part.

The rules of criminal law contain sanctions on two levels. One of these is the Act on petty offences, the second, the Criminal Code.

The Criminal Code orders the punishment of those committing discrimination. According to Art. 156, 'he who causes to a member of a national, racial or religious group, because of membership of that group, a serious physical or mental affront, commits a crime and should be punished with imprisonment between 2 and 8 years'.

Art. 75 of the Act on petty offences expressly provides sanctions on the behaviour which results in some discrimination. According to this, the employer commits a petty offence if he 'illegally refuses to employ a person because of his sex, age, nationality, race or descent'. Indirectly other legal facts pertaining to petty offences also contain some sanctions in connection with this. Thus, according to Art. 75, point b, a petty offence is committed by the employer, 'who violates the rules on the conditions or prohibitions of employment'. Art. 76 similarly defines more than one petty offence rule in this connection. Thus, a petty offence is committed by the employer who 'terminates the labour relationship of the employee giving a false reason in the notice, or otherwise abuses his right to terminate the labour relation.' Similarly there are qualifications if he violates the 'provisions concerning worktime, the protection of labour conditions for women, young people and persons with a reduced capacity for work', as well as the employer who does not guarantee 'the wage, leave or other conditions due to the employee on the basis of labour relations'.

VII. CONCLUSION

We have endeavoured to present the prevalence of equality of civic rights and of the prohibition of discrimination in Labour Law. In conclusion, it should be emphasised that in creating equality of civic rights, the social, economic, cultural etc. conditions played an essential part. Law, and in the present case, Labour Law, is therefore just one of the factors, though no negligible factor, in the field of creating equality. Thus, for instance, the considerable development of industrial democracy of recent years promoted to a high level the formation of a social atmosphere within the enterprise which, even alone, reduces the occurrence of discrimination. Or, for example, the development of eduction, and particularly the increase of the ratio of females in secondary and higher vocational education and training, considerably promotes the cessation of inequality in the employment and wages of women. One of the essential causes of this phenomenon, at present, is still the lack of necessary qualification.

10. Italy

T. Treu

I. HISTORICAL INTRODUCTION AND SOURCES

In Italy as in other countries the principle of equal treatment has been historically proclaimed as a fundamental tenet of private and public law. But for a long time it was applicable only to state action and not directly to private acts, including employment contracts and regulations.

A turning point is marked by Art. 37 of the Italian Constitution (1947), which gives women workers 'the same rights as men, including the right to equal pay for equal work', and minor workers only the right to 'equal pay for equal work'. Italian courts began to interpret this norm, especially the latter part concerning equal pay, as applicable also to the employment relationship. Therefore, the principle of non-discrimination became effective in labour law to the extent whereby wage discrimination against women, and later against minors, was prohibited; and so it remained until the nineteen seventies.

Subsequently, the problem of non-discrimination because of union activity (and also religious and political positions) was faced by the legislature. Act 604/1966 declared null and void all dismissals which are discriminatory because of union activity, religion or political opinion. The rule is extended by Act 300/1970, the so-called Statute of Workers' Rights. Art. 15 declares null and void all acts and agreements related to the employment relationship - hiring, dismissals, transfers, disciplinary sanctions and any others which are a detriment to the employee because of his or her union activity, affiliation or non-affiliation, religion or political opinion. Moreover, the unions are given the right of a special judicial action (Art. 28) in case of unfair labour practices by the employer, including discriminatory acts on the grounds mentioned above: the judge may issue a cease and desist order - penally sanctioned - following an emergency procedure.

A third landmark is represented by Act 903/1977 on the equality of male and female workers; it is currently the main text regulating this subject matter.

Therefore, the legislature has played a major role in this area of the law. Judicial interpretation was rather important in the '50s and '60s, particularly in implementing the general constitutional directive on equal wages for women and subsequently for minors. Collective agreements do not explicitly regulate the matter, but union presence and grievance procedures at plant level are a major factor in implementing the principle of non-discrimination, specifically in defense of union freedom of action and less so in the case of sex discrimination.

So far, governmental and administrative action has not been particularly important in this area, due mostly to the lack of specific enforcement agencies such as the EEOC found in other countries. Monitoring and inspection regarding the application of the law prohibiting discrimination are left to the ordinary offices of the Ministry of Labour (labour offices and labour inspectors), both at central and local level. But they are traditionally rather inefficient in general, and even more so in the relatively new field of discrimination law.

II. SCOPE AND GROUNDS OF ANTI-DISCRIMIATION LAW

The broadest rule of non-discrimination in Italian law is presently stated by Art. 13 of Act 903/1977, which has partly reproduced and partly extended Art. 15 of Act 300/1970. Art. 13 declares null and void all acts and agreements on hiring, dismissals, transfers, etc. related to the employment relationship (of any kind) which are detrimental to women because of their sex. The same sanction is applied to discriminatory acts against any employee because of race, colour, ethnic and national origin, in addition to religious or political opinion and union memberschip or non-memberschip.

Other grounds of discrimination are treated by more limited norms. Age is considered (Art. 37 of the Constitution) only with respect to minors - meaning employees under 18 or 21 - and only as far as wages are concerned in much the same way as for women (we will return to this aspect in reference to equal pay for women). The principle of equality apparently does not apply to other aspects of the employment relationship in the case of minors, who are subject to extensive protective legislation (limits to work capacity, hours of work, prohibition of night work, etc.). Moreover, statutory law contains provisions directed to promote employment of young workers between 15 and 29 years of age as per Act 285/1977 and the more recent decree 94/1984 (see below).

Art. 1 of Act 903/1977 forbids discrimination against women even though it is pursued in reference to the marital, family or pregnancy status. Act 7/1963 had already nullified any clause in agreements or factory rules providing that the employment relationship be terminated because of marriage; and for any dismissal of a female employee occurring between the banns and one year after the marriage (except for serious misconduct by the woman).

Private life is protected against discrimination by Art. 8 of Act 300/1970, which forbids the employer to investigate in any way - even prior to hiring - political, religious, union and ideological opinions and any aspect of the employee's life which is not relevant to the professional qualifications required for the job. The norm is explicitly intended to prevent discrimination on the same grounds and is penally sanctioned. A few major cases have been decided by the courts against the prehiring and selection techniques of large firms (FIAT, Alfa Romeo), openly or indirectly aimed at ascertaining the 'employee personality'. The practical effectiveness of the prohibition on current employer practices is however questionable, particularly in the case of sophisticated questionnaires and interviews practices. The employer is in no way obliged to disclose these techniques except in the case of court action brought by the individual employee and with reference to the facts of the individual case.

Discrimination because of linguistic and ethnical origin has been of some practical importance in certain regions of the country which have large minority groups. No race discrimination problem is reported in Italy.

Regional legislation not only confirmed the prohibition of direct discrimination on these grounds but it provided for a series of seemingly effective affirmative actions and reverse discrimination. Linguistic and ethnic minorities are recognized, particularly the right to be hired in public posts in proportion to their number (in each area); some geographical job stability and limits to possible transfers; the right to be represented proportionally or even on equal terms in some key public positions, **e.g.** local courts of justice, and administrative bodies; and - functional to all this - the right to be taught at school in the mother tongue; to use the same language in all public offices; plus basic protection of cultural identity and activities. (The widest ranging provisions are indicated in the basic law of the Trentino-Alto Adige region).

As in many countries, foreign workers are required to have a special work permit (apart from EEC members for whom the rule of free movement applies). This requirement, together with the desire to reduce labour costs and avoid taxation, accounts for the fact that many foreigners work under illegal conditions.

Finally, a widely shared scholarly opinion holds that discrimination is forbidden, **i.e.** discriminatory acts should be considered null and void, also on grounds not covered by Act 903: **e.g.** social origin, personal status or any frivolous or illegal motive. This opinion is derived from the general principle of equality stated in Art. 3, para. 10 of the Italian Constitution. Indeed, the traditional view that the constitutional rule of equality does not apply to private acts is slowly being eroded.

Along these lines some courts have decided that the terms of collective plant or enterprise agreements (governing wages in particular) should be applied to all employees of the unit including non-union members, contrary to common rules and according to the principle of equality. This does not yet imply that the principle of equality is 'absolute'. It imposes equal application of terms that have been agreed upon collectively, but is would not forbid the employer to bargain individually over these terms or pay extra bonuses only to some individual employees and not to others, according to their 'merit' or for any other reason judged suitable by the employer (as long as no specific illegal ground for discrimination is proved).

In practice, the areas of discrimination law which have been most extensively debated and applied in Italy relate to discrimination because of sex and union activity. We will concentrate on the first area now, though most of the issues and solutions might well be applied to discrimination on grounds other than sex.

III. DEFINITIONS OF DISCRIMINATION AND MAIN PROVISIONS ON SEX DISCRIMINATION

Discrimination is not explicitly defined by the law. Proposals to define the term, including indirect discrimination, in Act 903 were rejected by Parliament. However, the wording of the act is broad enough to include all forms of discrimination related to all aspects of the employment relationship, irrespective of the ways and means by which it is practiced. The prohibition of indirect discrimination can also be derived from the law, **e.g.** Art. 1 prohibits the practice of setting requirements linked to the employee's marital status.

The scholarly definition is similar to those accepted in other countries: **e.g.** any practice, including apparently neutral criteria which have a disproportionate impact on employment opportunities for women and are not justified by a recognized business necessity.

In practice the effectiveness of the non-discrimination principle varies according to many factors.

A. Equal pay and job classification

The principle of equal pay for equal work has received a great deal of attention from Italian courts and in collective agreements. An early interpretation of Art. 37 of the Italian Constitution held that equal work was to be considered as work having not only the same duration and position according to job specification schemes but also the same intrinsic value and economic result. The existing practice of underpaying women and minors was therefore justified on the grounds that their work was on average less productive than the corresponding work of men. (In the mid-sixties average wage differentials between men and women were estimated as over 35 per cent and between minors and adults between 20 and 30 per cent, varying according to age group: 15-16; 16-18; 18-21).

This opinion was abandoned during the sixties first for women, later for minors, and since then the expression 'equal work' or 'work of equal value' has been interpreted in a strict sense as work having the same professional content as normally evaluated by collective agreements or company practice irrespective of group or individual productivity. No differentials were permitted because of higher costs for women as a group (costs for social security, higher absenteeism, etc.). In the case of piecework or incentive schemes the principle was held to imply that same criteria to evaluate production must be applied to men and women. As a consequence of this judicial attitude a number of collective agreement clauses which applied reduced wage rates or specific grades for women were declared null. Collective bargaining and company practices were adopted correcting at least the most blatant cases of wage discrimination, first for women then for minors (in the mid-seventies). Collective agreements have also reduced the traditional wage differentials for young apprentices: they may receive from 70 to 82% of ordinary employees' pay, according to age and education. In this respect Art. 2 of Act 903 of 1977 confirmed a well-entrenched judicial rule. There were two specifications, both following the EEC directive - (1) in order to apply the principle of equality, men's and women's work must be equal or of equal value; (2) job classification systems must adopt common criteria for men and women. The former provision makes explicit the point which was already clear through interpretation. Indeed it may be interpreted to extend to work of similar or equivalent professional value (a concept already applied by courts in other respects on the basis of common contractual or company criteria of job evaluation). The latter norm, again anticipated through interpretation, implies for instance that it is not permissible to give a man more points for a particular factor, in a job classification system whatever its form, than to a woman regardless of economic justification. It also implies, according to legal scholars, that it is illegal to adopt separate classification schemes for men and women (separation is **per se** discriminatory) or to distinguish between male and female jobs, even though somehow disguised, for instance presented as a distinction between 'heavy' and 'light' jobs. This opinion has not however been tested in the courts, also because discriminatory practices of this type seem hardly to persist. The Ministry of Labour with circular letter No. 92 of 1978 explicitly directed its regional offices to abolish the distinction between male and female jobs used in the formation unemployment lists preferred by the public placement service and to unify the lists for men and women. Italian law has been interpreted very widely by Italian courts and collective agreements, so as to include any economic benefit in cash or in kind granted by the employer to the employee in respect of the employment relationship. This includes fringe benefits, seniority allowances, sick pay benefit, preferential loans, etc. From this point of view, too, therefore the protection of the law seems quite complete and in line with Art. 1 of the EEC directive.

In spite of this, discrimination because of sex still exists, according to common knowledge confirmed by basic data on average wages and job classification. Complete and recent statistical data are not available, but in 1977 national average wage differentials per hour between men and women were over 23 per cent in the industrial sector, well down from the sixties but still considerable. The average income differentials are considerably greater, with women earning about 60 per cent of men's wages, due to the reduced number of hours worked (34 hours per week on average as against 39 for men), less overtime and fewer extra allowances for night shifts, etc. (see table). Moreover, general rates of pay in the female-dominated industries, for instance the textile retail trade, tend to be lower than in the male-dominated industries, for instance the steel or automotive industries. Inter-sector differentials have been slowly decreasing in the last decade due to the egalitarian wage policy of Italian trade unions (not related to sex parity), but they are still considerable and they seem to be increasing again under pressure of economic crisis. The reasons for these differentials and the ways in which they are built in depend on historical tradition and are multi-dimensinal. Some aspects appear particularly indicative of sex discrimination. Clearly this is the case with wage differentials linked to different productive sectors. The problem is not to enforce equal pay **per se** but to overcome historical sex segregation by opening up traditionally male professions to women through education, training, etc. A second aspect, related to indirect wage discrimination has to do with possible bias built into existing job classification schemes. Such a bias can be claimed for instance when classification criteria are adopted, whether unilaterally or contractually that evaluate factors such as physical strength, common to men, more than manual dexterity and accuracy (skills which are considered typically female); the result in fact is the under-valuing of certain kinds of jobs which are female-dominated. Similar bias may be found in practices which place less value on certain kinds of jobs in traditionally female-dominated sectors than jobs common in male-dominated industries. For instance in the textile industry a skilled female job, such as master weaver, is rated less than a skilled male job such as a printer in the printing industry. These systems of classification have never been challenged in court and indeed are barely discussed by trade unions or in collective bargaining. This is due also to the fact that a bias of this kind cuts across the job structure in different productive sectors and overlaps therefore with discrimination due to job segregation. The discriminatory effect indeed appears more clearly when comparing typical female jobs in the textile or pharmaceutical sectors with typical male jobs in the metallurgical and mechanical sectors. These latter are better rated because they are considered to be heavier or perhaps simply because male workers have more bargaining capacity and stronger representation in the unions than the former, despite being less skilled. The available data, although partial, clearly show the existing discrimination in job classifications (see table).

On the other hand the concentration of women in the lowest paid jobs within a single sector or across sectors may be justified not by bias in the classification system but by historical gaps and discrimination in education and the social organisation of work. These factors can be again redressed only by positive action rather than by the legal prohibition of formal discrimination. This is underlined by both employers and union representatives.

Italian courts are however very reluctant to recognise wage and other discrimination unless they appear to be direct. The court of cassation (decision 329 of 1979) stated that the concept of equal work or work of equal value is in itself generic and needs further specification. When this specification is made by collective agreements following the proper procedures and technical evaluations by the parties it cannot be annulled, according to the court, unless the criteria adopted are openly discriminatory, that is they apply similar treatment to obviously different jobs. Indeed one may wonder whether the decision would have been different if the job classification system had been adopted unilaterally by the employer, as is the case in a minority of companies not adequately unionised or for specific groups of employees not represented by unions such as managerial employees and technical employees.

The Supreme Court in the same decision also established that the principle of equal wage and treatment works fully only in favour of women and does not provide absolute protection to men, for instance if they receive comparatively lower wages. In this respect the court decision seems hardly in line with Art. 2 of Act 903 where the principle of equal treatment in wages is stated as being bilateral or bi-directional (this however does not preclude positive discrimination if directed to redress substantial inequalities of opportunity in favour of women).

This exsisting wage differentials between men and women may be due to other causes. One is, for instance, personal merit bonuses paid above contractual rates. These bonuses fall in principle under the provision of the law, but are hardly controllable in practice either for men or women when they by-pass the unions. This now occurs more often than a few years ago as a reaction of employers to excesses in the unions' egalitarian wage policy. The granting of these policies on an individual basis (but possibly to a considerable number of employees) is justified as a reward for employees' qualities such as actual presence on the job, willingness to undertake specific work performance (over-time, rotating shifts, etc.) which are in fact more easily found among men than among women for social and family reasons. A special kind of bonus recently bargained for, the so-called attendance bonus, is linked to the number of days actually worked in the year and aimed at combatting absenteeism. This might be considered discriminatory if not carefully worded so as to exclude legitimate reasons for absence (maternity, child care for both parents, etc.). No court decisions however are known.

Two major wage elements in the Italian system are linked to company-wide seniority. The so-called seniority allowance paid at the end of employment in proportion to the years of continuous service, and the periodic seniority wage increases, that is wage increases granted every two years of service in proportion to the basic wage or in a lump sum. They certainly contribute to increased wage differentials in favour of men, who typically have a more continuous working career than women (the available data confirm this common judgment). But they have never been challenged in court nor in bargaining practice and indeed are commonly held to be justified on legitimate grounds such as length of service. In recent years however their relative weight on the total wage of all workers has been decreasing because the merit of rewarding continuous seniority as such has been questioned. In the public service a minimum seniority is still required for entitlement to the seniority allowance which may well disadvantage women.

Other reasons for legitimate wage differentials which favour men are allowances for overtime and shiftwork, both most widespread among men for obvious reasons.

B. Equal treatment

The other norms of Act 903 which prohibit discrimination in all aspects of the employment relationship have received less attention than the principle of equal pay, and their application has been uneven.

Such is the case of Art. 1, which forbids sex discrimination in access to a job, irrespective of hiting techniques and sectors of activity, in educational and professional training initiatives regarding both content and admission requirements.

In spite of this wide-ranging provision, control of discriminatory hiring is not effective. Here, more than anywhere else, major difficulties arise in proving discrimination and finding remedies (see below).

A relatively greater control is possible in public and semi-public employment where general, publicized screening systems are adopted. For instance, banks have considerably increased their hiring of women after adopting an impartial screening system. The same holds true for many public institutions, although here too the requisites may in fact lend themselves to a reduction in the number of women hired.

Discrimination is in itself excluded for employees hired through the public placement service; the employer is obliged to request employees not by name but by number and qualification from a special list that includes both men and women. This rigid hiring system is however often avoided and in actual fact it applies only to a small minority of unskilled unemployed workers looking for a first job. Over the past few years (less frequently now due to the economic crisis), the system enabled a goodly number of women to be hired because they had more lengthy periods of unemployment and hence were at the top of the unemployment list. Indeed the number of women registered with the labour offices has been on the rise in the past few years. This indicates a greater willingness of women to apply for jobs officially, possibly also a result of Act 903. The female labour supply increased rapidly during the seventies (over 15 per cent over the decade). This increase was not matched however by a parallel increase in available posts. The ratio of unemployed women is still much higher than that of men; in 1983 over 48 per cent of the unemployed were women.

Vocational training and education lie at the base of subsequent discrimination in employment. In spite of Act 903, vocational training is still often organized separately for men and women, or in such a way as to discourage women.

Another particularly difficult problem is discrimination in job assignments and career opportunities (prohibited by Art. 3 of Act 903). Promotions and career development are handled mostly by management in the private sector except for the lowest job levels. In this area, there have been few attempts to control sex discrimination which prevents women from reaching highly rated jobs proportionately to men. The obstacles are the same as above. But the statistical evidence for promotions should be even more conclusive than for hiring, because it applies to a definite number of men and women to be promoted who by definition start out with the same professional qualifications, and because men and women should be offered equal treatment in training according to the law. In practice, the lowest job levels at which women are often hired are the ones where training opportunities within the enterprise are fewer. In the public service, seniority is more widely used as one, but not an exclusive, requisite for promotion. This might work against women, although their continuity of service is higher in the public service than in the private sector due to the fact that the facilities provided in the former are better. Distribution by sex in higher career echelons is also uneven in the public service.

Obviously, dismissals raise the most delicate problems, particularly in a period of economic recession which traditionally tends to affect women most seriously. Taking this into account, Act 675 of 1977 provides for special protection against discriminatory collective dismissals of women in cases of industrial restructuring (individual and other collective dismissals fall under the general rule of Act 903).

Act 675 states that a prerequisite for public assistance to an emplc.
interested in restructuring and in the consequent labour mobility i.
that the ratio of women in the labour force remains stable throughout
the process. Therefore, the legislature provides an automatic guarantee
in favour of women.

The application of Act 675 however has been rather limited in this
respect, also because the protection is interpreted as applicable not
in all cases of economic crisis of the firm, but only when the company
resorts to a special position of mobility which is rather cumbersome
and often avoided.

The principle of maintaining the ratio of women employed in case
of economic difficulties or to favour them in cases of new hiring and
turnover (sometimes mentioning employment in traditionally male jobs)
is explicit in some company-wide agreements. This is one of the areas
where collective bargaining has worked positively to improve and
expand the law. But the actual impact of these provisions, particularly
in the case of serious crisis, is uncertain.

In general, the priority criteria for collective dismissals in the
confederal agreement of 1966 are as follows: business needs, seniority,
economic and family conditions. In fact, all three may be used in a
way that is indirectly discriminatory against women. Seniority may be
discriminatory for the reasons indicated above; business needs, because
they may be used to justify forced dismissals of less-qualified employees
(women); family conditions if they are interpreted as favouring the
male head of the family with respect to women (but this interpretation
should no longer be legal following Act 903, which equalised the sexes
with respect to family responsibilities).

Until recently, however, the average rate of official terminations
of employment does not indicate a clear detriment to women. Some
observers however claim that the situation may have worsened in the
last two years.

Another provision which can be found in most national collective
agreements and may be useful for promoting equality commits the
employer to give periodic and detailed information to trade union
representatives with respect to female employment (hiring, mobility,
turnover, future employment prospects) and sometimes to the state
of application of the legislation on equality.

Equal treatment has been implemented by Act No. 903 in the
area of social security, as well as in the form of possible equalisation
of the retirement age for men and women (with the option given to
women either to retire at 55 or work until 60 like men) and equal
rights to receive family allowances, pensions granted in case of
survivors, etc.

IV. EXCEPTIONS

(a) The concept of **bona fide** occupational qualifications is not explicitly
adopted by Italian legislation; it may be inferred to some extent
through interpretation.

Art. 1 of Act 903 does not consider it discriminatory to subordinate
to a gender requirement hiring in artistic and fashion activities and

of public performances when such is essential to the nature
Beyond these exceptions no reason for excluding women
/ment in principle is admitted by law, irrespective of
as business needs essential to the nature of the work.
s type may be considered in judging the appropriateness of
irements for hiring, but may not justify an **a priori** exclusion
of women.

For instance, the norm makes it illegal to exclude or limit the
hiring of women on the basis of stereotypes concerning their quality
as a group: **e.g.** insufficient aggressiveness as salespeople and unsuit-
ability for the business environment.

Despite the lack of explicit mention and definition of indirect
discrimination in the law, a widely-shared opinion considers it illegal
to condition hiring on certain physical requisites such as minimum
height or weight lifting requirements which are detrimental to women
and irrelevant to the work. A minimum height has traditionally been
required for railroad personnel and some other public servants (now it
is being abandoned). The administrative tribunals annulled the exclusion
of a woman from competing for a post in the urban police force due
to the fact that she was under 1.65 metres tall. But another tribunal
did not hold the same requisite illegal for police officials. Similarly,
mobility within the country might be considered an illegal requirement
particularly when not strictly connected with the nature of the job.
Strict age limits, for instance below 35, which is common in the
public service and in semi-public companies (sometimes with an
increase of two years per child), are also considered illegal. But
these issues have rarely been tested in the courts nor in no way have
they been adequately raised by unions or public representatives.

However one court did decide that unnecessary skills or basic
qualification requirements which are unfavourable to women are to be
considered illegal. Requisites such as single status or having no children
under a certain age are banned explicitly by the wording of Art. 1 of
Act 903. Indeed, the very fact of asking this type of information is
considered **contra legem**; but such questions are still frequent in hiring
practices and the refusal of jobs to pregnant women, mothers with
young children or sometimes even to married women appears to be
persistent, according to union representatives, and may be difficult
to prove (see below).

(b) The major (possible) exception to the principle derives from special
protective measures in favour of women workers which have traditionally
been rather widespread in Italy.

In Italy probably more than in other countries, protective legislation
was the main reason for the special status of women workers (see
Act 653 of 1934). The criticism claiming that this legislation was at
least partly responsible for women's disadvantaged position in the
labour market and therefore indirectly conducive to discrimination, has
been almost totally accepted by the law. Art. 19 of Act 903 in principle
abrogates all previous protective legislation incompatible with its
provisions. Although this provision is somehow controversial (for
instance, the problem of rest periods mentioned above) it encompasses

152

more than required by the EEC directive. Protective legislation for the unions has escaped this criticism and is still in force.

The traditional prohibition of heavy work for women was lifted by Act 903, but at the same time the law empowered collective agreements to restore the prohibition of 'particularly heavy jobs'. A different approach was followed with respect to night work: Act 903 maintains the prohibition for women but empowers collective agreements to restore it.

The unions have hesitated to use their power to reintroduce limits on the hiring of women by agreement even for protective reasons (no more than 20 local agreements are reported in 1979). Recently, there has been a wider use of the power to allow night work (over 200 agreements reported).

These rules on heavy and night work have given rise to controversy. The courts have ruled that the heavy nature of the job and even the possible health risk do not justify **per se** the refusal to hire women. The same conclusion holds for the prohibition of night work; even though the Court of Cassation held unconstitutional the absolute prohibition of night work in the previous legislation, the prohibition remains in principle. The refusal of an employer to hire women for this reason was held illegal by the courts, since the employer himself organized the night shift. This might imply that in order to avoid discrimination only men should be burdened with night shifts.

The legal prohibitions on heavy and night work have been criticised. It is argued that the net result of work provisions, not being compensated by any positive measures to control or improve working conditions, could entail a worsening of the status of equal rights for women to the detriment of their health. It would have been better to adopt a more cautious attitude, as has been done elsewhere including the EEC directive; that is, not to repeal the protective legislation altogether but provide for progressive revision, if necessary subject to controls by administrative agencies, and to positive measures for guaranteeing better safety and health conditions for both sexes.

A traditionally protective measure (Art. 18 Act 653/1934) imposed for women a one-hour break after six hours of work. This provision has been held unconstitutional by courts and is considered to have been repealed by Act 903.

The major piece of protective legislation still in force for women concerns pregnancy and maternity (Act 1204 of 1971). The fact that it is linked to specific female characteristics and aimed at protecting basic interests such as the health of the mother and child has saved it from the kind of criticism directed at other protective legislation. The same interests of health protection justify the protective legislation in favour of minors.

Some rights reserved to the mother by Act 1204 have been granted by Act 903 (Art. 7) to the father in lieu of the mother or when the children are in the father's custody: namely, the right to abstain from work for six months after the compulsory period of leave without loss of seniority and with 30 per cent pay; the right to unpaid time off work in the case of a child's illness until the age of three.

According to some court decisions, the father should also be entitled to all rights stated by Act 1204 which are not linked to the physical aspects of maternity; but it is controversial whether this should also apply to the right to two hours' time off work a day, which the law recognises for women and is not explicitly extended to men. These opportunities have rarely been used by working fathers, due to traditional social resistance, but also because a father's wages are higher than a mother's and hence the reduction is not economically worthwhile for the family.

There is discussion as to whether these rights can also be granted to a working father when married to a woman who is an independent worker, **i.e.** self-employed.

Art. 6 of Act 903 extends the same rights, plus the compulsory paid leave, to adoptive mothers or to women who are given official custody of a child under a certain age. This provision is under consideration in the European Court of Justice because it limits these rights to women.

No other general exception to the principle of non-discrimination exists in Italian law. A specific exception concerns enterprises with a special (political, religious or ideological) vocation, where a certain loyalty is demanded of the employees; hence they can be refused a job or dismissed if they do not meet these requirements.

V. AFFIRMATIVE ACTION AND REVERSE DISCRIMINATION

This area of the law is hardly developed in Italy. In fact, a major weakness of Italian legislation on equality, denounced by many commentators, is the lack of positive measures - legislative, administrative, judicial and contractual - directed at promoting equal opportunities for women, minors and other desadvantaged groups.

A few legislative provisions have already been mentioned in favour of ethnic and linguistic minorities (see above). Some attempts have been made to promote youth employment by Act 285 of 1977 (see above), but the results are sparse. Recently, similar but more effective provisions were enacted in 1983 and 1984 to favour the hiring of young employees under the so-called education contracts (half-time work, half-time education). The employer receives financial incentives (social security contributions and fiscal reductions) for each young person hired. Secondly, s/he is free to hire young employees on fixed terms (whereas fixed-term contracts are admitted only in limited cases for adult workers), and outside the rigid prescriptions of public placement law: **i.e.**, the employer is entitled individually to choose the employee instead of following the general rule which obliges selection from a list provided by the public placement services. Apparently these new provisions have shown better results than those of 1977.

A few measures to promote female employment can be found in the law and collective agreements. Art. 3 of Act 903 provides for specific preferential treatment in favour of female workers designed partially to reduce the negative effects of motherhood on their professional status. In fact, it stipulates that the legally recognised periods of abstention from work for maternity count towards seniority in cases where collective agreements do not establish special requirements. The meaning of this exception is controversial. It may be left to collective decision and hence reffered to any clause which links promotion not to simple seniority but to seniority qualified by actual work done as a means of testing experience acquired. This is often the case with promotions from the lowest job levels where they are based on seniority. In fact, this reduces the impact of this legal positive discrimination in favour of women particularly when the requirement of actual work done is not actually aimed at increasing the employee's professional skills.

A few agreements condition promotion on requirements such as participation in training courses and rotation to different job positions, possibly including three-shift systems.

Art. 8 of Act 903 puts the burden of wages in cases of abstention from work during maternity periods on the State budget (with the aim of reducing the costs of protection).

A similar reduction of some employer-paid social security contributions (for illness) has also been provided with the same aim. These kinds of financial provisions are advocated mostly be employers, but they are costly and probably too sweeping. More specific and diversified measures might be comparatively less costly and more effective.

A few other measures in favour of women workers have been tested through collective bargaining with limited success. For example, additional time off to working mothers, and sometimes to fathers, for family duties; use of a number of previously bargained hours (maximum 250) for general education purposes in favour of all workers in order specifically to promote women's education and professional training or retraining.

In a few cases professional training for women, particularly in typically male jobs, has been organized mostly by regional governments usually following agreements with the social parties and in accordance with EEC programmes.

Recently a similar local government initiative (in Liguria) was held illegal by a criminal court as being against the principle of 'formal equality', i.e. discriminatory against men. The decision was bitterly criticized and appealed, but the present effect has been to block this kind of initiative specifically promoting the professional training of women.

At present the question of affirmative action is under discussion and some proposals have been submitted by the National Committee for Equality (instituted by a ministerial decree in 1983) to Parliament: e.g. to provide better administrative control over hiring by giving the regional labour office the power to ask employers with a record of disproportionate male/female hiring for information and the reasons for their hiring practices; to subordinate the approval of the education contract project by regional employment commissions (required by law) to the condition that (young) women be hired proportionately to the number of unemployed women in the area (usually higher than for young men); to apply a similar hiring ratio in the public service under the exceptional programme now being discussed by Parliament; special leave for women (and possibly men) during the peak period of family responsibilities (possibly partly State-financed), along with special retraining programmes directed to favour the re-entry of women into the labour market after this period.

VI. ENFORCEMENT

Enforcement is a major problem and a serious weakness of the current Italian legislation. In fact, the application of Act 903 has been minimally tested in the courts (and indeed it has not been pushed to any great extent in the trade unions).

The annual reports of the Ministry of Labour acknowledge that those parts of the Act which have been more fully applied are the ones requiring a minimal, if any, judicial test or party initiative, **e.g.**, repeals of limits on women's work or extension of social security benefits. This limited implementation of the law is due in part to the weakness of the enforcement system.

A first key point concerns proof of discrimination. Italian courts seem to exclude the need to prove subjective elements such as the employer's intention to discriminate, only requiring objective evidence of the negative effects of the employer's decision on employment for women. Some scholars have suggested that the interested woman should present only **prima facie** evidence of discrimination, **i.e.** she was denied hiring or promotion while meeting all requirements, and the employer should prove objective, not sex-linked, criteria to support his or her choice. Recourse to statistical data has also been proposed as indicative - and not conclusive - evidence. The fact that women are statistically underrepresented in hiring and/or in highly rated jobs is not definite evidence of discrimination in hiring and promotion practices because it may be due to the fact that women are historically disadvantaged with respect to professional qualifications. And these historical factors can be remedied not simply by applying the legal rule of equal treatment but by positive measures designed to promote equal opportunities.

Italian courts - like the Italian tradition in general - appear reluctant to admit statistical evidence of discrimination. An amendment to the law proposing the application of quota systems to the hiring of women has been rejected.

A further difficulty in proving discrimination concerns the lack of information. In the absence of objective and publicized systems of recruitment or promotion, as is the case in most private firms, an interested woman would in any case not have basic information about applicants and selected employees sufficient to prove her case. Interestingly enough, most of these difficulties of evidence have been overcome by Italian courts in the cases of anti-union discrimination, even though the burden of proof is similarly distributed by law. In fact, the courts have made wide use of presumptions to infer discrimination based on circumstances against union activists (particularly in cases of transfers, dismissals, discipline).

Other major weaknesses of Italian legislation on discrimination concern the nature of judicial action and the available sanctions. First, suits aimed at declaring the nullity of discriminatory acts can be brought to court in principle only by an individual woman, which is a serious limitation in itself. The only partial exception, provided for by Art. 15, concerns discrimination in hiring where the action is still individual, not collective; but the woman may be represented by a union of her choice. No public agency such as the EEOC exists to promote and assist the parties in the enforcement of the law.

Second, the basic sanction is nullity. Criminal sanctions are provided only in cases of violation of Act No. 903, Art. 1, 2, 3, 4 (fines of up to one million lire), Art. 5 (night work, with fines of up to 100,000 lire per day per woman employed) and Art. 6-7. The sanction of nullity is not sufficient to guarantee a positive result for the discriminated woman in cases of so-called 'acts of omission', **e.g.** refusal of promotion. Art. 15 empowers the judge to order the hiring of the discriminated woman only in the case of a discriminatory refusal to hire. Moreover, the consequences of these sanctions raise doubts: must the judge also nullify the hiring or promotion of a man chosen in place of the discriminated woman? This consequence seems to follow from the general rules of civil law, but it is hardly satisfactory. The other alternative of simply ordering the hiring of the individual woman would imply imposing upon the employer a higher number of employees than originally planned.

Indeed, the problem could be successfully resolved only by giving the judge wider powers to order positive action on the part of the employer, directed at restoring the balance between women and men in a given period of time. These powers are presently lacking, and so the possibility for the judiciary to promote women's employment is greatly reduced.

Public agencies aimed at promoting and assisting the parties in the enforcement of the law (not only in the field of discrimination) are alien to the Italian tradition. Only in 1983, and following EEC directives, the Ministry of Labour set up a National Committee for Equality where social and political party experts and women's associations are represented. On paper the Committee is provided with relatively wide powers: research and information on employment problems and prospects for women, investigation and inspection of enforcement of the law (through the labour inspectors), assistance to women subject to discrimination, intervention in disputes (conciliation proposals), submission of regulative proposals and advice to public institutions on anti-discrimination measures. In fact, the initiatives of the Committee are limited by the composition of the body itself and, first and foremost, by the lack of financial resources and technical staff.

11. Japan

T. Hanami

I. HISTORICAL INTRODUCTION

1. The Meiji Restoration of 1868 abolished discrimination based on the social status of the feudal society such as that of the samurai (feudal warriors), the shōnin (merchants) and the nōmin (farmers). The Constitution of the Empire of Great Japan of 1889 admitted equal rights of all Japanese subjects to be qualified to enter public service and to participate in politics. However, in the prewar period equality under the law was limited in several respects. [1] The Emperor was the ruler based on his birth and the subjects were destined to be ruled by their birth. [2] A peerage system existed and a peer was entitled to be a member of the House of Peers. [3] Women were not entitled to suffrage. They were not able to vote or to be elected to the House of Representatives. The different status of men and women was self-evident in various laws, particularly in family law. Women were discriminated against not only in customs and practices but also in their legal status. [4] Japanese nationals and foreign subjects were given a different legal status in many respects.

2. After the Second World War the Allied Occupation authorities were determined to introduce the principle of equality before the law and **inter alia** they ordered the abolition of the peerage system. The Draft Constitution suggested by the Supreme Commander for the Allied Powers (SCAP) included an article guaranteeing equality before the law for all human beings and prohibiting discrimination in political, economic and social relations based on race, creed, sex, social status, caste or national origin. The 1964 Constitution of Japan declared the equality of all people before the law and Art. 14 prohibited discrimination in political, economic and social relations because of race, creed, sex, social status or family origin.

Art. 24 stipulated essential equality of both sexes in family life. Art. 26 provided the right of all to equal education and Art. 44 prohibited discrimination because of race, creed, sex, social status, family origin, education, property or income in connection with the qualifications of members for both Houses and their electors.

3. The Constitution also abolished several types of privilege granted to certain kinds of persons. Art. 14, Section 2, prohibits aristocratic titles. Section 3 of the same article provides that no privilege shall accompany any award of honour, decoration or any distinction and it also prohibits the inheritance of such honours. Lese-majesty was abolished from the Criminal Code. Based on the principle of equality between both sexes, the Family Law of the prewar period was

159

completely amended. The prewar family system based on patriarchy was abolished. The system of a recognised head of the family, primogeniture, the incompetancy of wives, inequality of chastity between husband and wife etc. were abolished. Equality of parental rights and in inheritance was recognized. The husband's control of the property of his wife was also abolished.

The Civil Service Law provides equal treatment of all people regardless of race, creed, sex, social status, family origin or political opinion or affiliation.

4. In spite of the heritage of unequal social status from the prewar period, the equality issue in the postwar period has not been very controversial. The generally accepted reason is that the Japanese nation is a homogeneous nation and discrimination because of race or national origin is not serious. Thus the most frequent issues raised in the law courts in the field of equality have been those concerning the legality of discrimination because of political creed, union activities and gender. Also as a result there are neither significant public measures nor machinery implemented to protect those suffering from discrimination and the only remedy available is the court of law. The Committee for the Protection of Human Rights located in cities and villages and the Bureau of Protection of Human Rights at the Ministry of Justice have the function only of providing information and advice in order to promote human rights. The only significant exception is the Special Measures for Assimilation Act of 1969 which protects a minority group called the burakumin (see below, III, 1).

5. In the field of labour law Art. 3 of the Labour Standards Law of 1947 prohibits discrimination in wages, working hours and other working conditions because of nationality, creed or social status. Art. 4 stipulates the principle of equal wages for equal work between both sexes. The omission of sex from the prohibited reasons for different treatment in Art. 3 is generally explained by the protection admitted specially for women in the Labour Standards Law such as restrictions on overtime or dangerous jobs, the prohibition of underground or night labour, maternity leave etc. However, this omission has caused serious problems in recent years in connection with the promotion of equal opportunity for women in employment (see below, III, 2).

Art. 5 of the Trade Union Law of 1949 provides that nobody shall be disqualified from membership because of race, religion, sex, social origin or status.

This provision does not prohibit different treatment because of political opinion or affiliation. This omission has also caused some problems in connection with political unionism (see below III, 3). However, except for discrimination because of political opinion or affiliation, there is no serious discrimination between members by trade unions, especially since minority problems are not so serious in employment because of the strict policy against foreign immigration after the Second World War (see below, III, 1). Since the most frequent and prevailing discrimination in employment is because of sex, the most significant discrimination, sometimes supported even by unions, is sex discrimination. The typical example is different retirement age by gender, **i.e.** a younger retirement age, retirement by marriage or at child-birth for women workers, some of which are stipulated in collective agreements.

6. Government action has not been very significant except in the field of discrimination based on union affiliation and union activities where special remedy is provided through the Labour Relations Commissions against unfair labour practices. In recent years there has emerged a strong impetus for the introduction of equal employment opportunity legislation for women workers. A government bill is now under preparation (see below, III, 2).

II. DEFINITION OF DISCRIMINATION

7. The constitutional guarantee of equality is interpreted as protecting Japanese nationals only. However, it is an established theory that equality under the law is also guaranteed to foreigners except in connection with state affaires such as the suffrage. Thus a legal judgement which upheld a provision of the constitution of a company excluding foreigners from membership of the board of directors and auditors should be seriously criticized. In the field of employment too discrimination against foreigners should be prohibited as long as they have work permits (see below, III, 1).

8. The words of Art. 14, Section 1, 'equal before the law' mean that legally all people should be treated equal although in fact every person is different in terms of circumstances, relationships, attributes etc. This leads to the conclusion that different treatment is justified so long as it is reasonable. For instance, different treatment because of different ability may be justified. In other words the contention is that substantial equality rather than formalistic equality, relative equality rather than absolute equality, and proportional equality rather than mechanical equality should be guaranteed.

9. Section 1 of Art. 14 of the Constitution also prohibits discrimination because of race, creed, sex, social status or family origin. This prohibiution is interpreted as the natural result of the principle of equality before the law. Thus the grounds stipulated in this article are not exclusive but only illustrative of important grounds prohibited by the Constitution. There is no doubt, for instance, that discrimination because of colour or national origin is also prohibited.

10. The difference between direct discrimination and indirect discrimination has not been very much discussed in Japan. There is no doubt that any indirect discrimination which brings discrimination as a result is regarded as prohibited discrimination. The typical case is that of the burakumin who live in certain areas, so discrimination because of one's birth place should be regarded as discrimination on grounds of social origin or ethnicity (see below, III, 1).

III. GROUNDS

1. Race, colour, ethnics and national or social origin

11. It is generally accepted that there is no serious problem of discrimination because of race, colour or ethnicity since the Japanese nation is fairly monolithic and homogeneous. The largest ethnic minority is the Koreans and Japanese of Korean origin who are estimated as about 600,000 in number. Chinese and Japanese of Chinese origin are smaller in number (less than 50 thousand). The total number of foreigners living in Japan is about 750 thousand, of whom only 25 per cent are economically active. They constitute less than 0.4 per cent of the total labour force. This rather extraordinarily small number of foreign workers in Japan is a result of the very restrictive immigration policy of the Government.

Work permits are granted only to those whose jobs are indispensable and not easily done by the available Japanese labour force. A typical example is that of Chinese cooks for Chinese restaurants or teachers of foreign languages.

12. Since Art. 3 of the Labour Standards Law prohibits discrimination in working conditions because of nationality and social status, direct discrimination against minorities in working conditions is rarely known. The most vital problem is discrimination in employment itself. A legal judgement has granted reparation of damage by an employer who refused employment to a Korean who had been promised a job without disclosing his nationality; the promise was later rescinded on discovery of his nationality. The absence of legal cases involving discrimination in employment because of race, colour or nationality does not mean that there is no such discrimination; it is rather explained by the small number of employees of foreign nationality or race. The expected growing number of foreign workers as part of the increasing internationalization of the Japanese economy will cause the problem to become more conspicuous in the future.

13. There are small numbers of minority groups in Japan whose national origins are not necessarily foreign. One is the minority called the Ainus who once occupied Hokkaido and the northern part of Honshuu (the main island) and have been oppressed by their Japanese conquerors. Today the pure-blood Ainus are estimated as a little over 10,000 and many of them have lost their identity by intermarriage with Japanese. Another minority group who are Japanese have also traditionally suffered from discrimination; they are not of a different race but are treated as a lower class because of their jobs, such as slaughtering animals and grave digging. They used to be called by various names meaning 'filthy', 'non-persons' etc. and are now often referred to as mikaihō buraku min (inhabitants of an unliberated village). The government has been trying to eliminate discriminatory attitudes to these people. The above mentioned Special Measures for Assimilation Act is one of such government efforts.

14. In connection with the employment of such minorities and Koreans

the use of the family register is a vital problem. An employer usually asks a would-be employee to submit a copy of his or her family register. A person from mikaihō buraku can be identified as originating from a certain village. Koreans, who often change their name into Japanese versions, could also be identified by their real names from their family registers.

In recent years, in order to avoid such misuse of the family register, offices of cities, towns and villages refuse a request to see the register by other persons than the registered one unless ther is a legitimate purpose.

15. As already indicated, the Labour Standards Law prohibits discrimination in working conditions only after exmployment, but not in hiring, recruitment or advertisement for employment. The Employment Security Law prohibits discrimination because of race, nationality, creed, sex, social status or origin or union membership by the Public Employment Offices. Thus there is no direct legal provision prohibiting discrimination in hiring by employers. The Supreme Court has laid down that Art. 3 of the Labour Standards Law only prohibits discrimination after employment and Art. 14 of the Constitution only regulates the relationship between government and individuals but not that between private persons. Thus, according to the Supreme Court decision, employers have the freedom to choose employees and refusal of employment because of thoughts or creed is not to be deemed illegal. According to this precedent, employers are granted complete freedom to refuse employment on grounds of race, colour, ethnity, national or social origin, sex, marital status and the like. This Supreme Court decision should be criticized because of its narrow interpretation of the effects of constitutional provisions on relationship between private persons. Some legal doctrines hold that refusal to employ certain workers because of reasons prohibited as discrimination constitutes a tort and that at the least reparation of damages should be granted to the victims, since it might prove impossible to order the employment of certain persons in the absence of such legal provision.

2. Sex

16. Discrimination on grounds of sex is perhaps the most significant field of discrimination in contemporary Japan because of the number of female employees, nearly 35 per cent of the total number of employees, with a tendency to increase in recent years. The number of female employees almost doubled between 1970 and 1982. The average age of female workers also went up rapidly from 26.3 years old in 1970 to 35 years in 1982. The percentage of female workers older than 35 years among the total of female workers increased from 39.2 per cent in 1970 to 54.8 per cent in 1982. The percentage of married female workers also increased from 44.7 per cent in 1962 to 68.5 per cent in 1982. The average length of service of female workers also rose from four years in 1970 to 6.3 years in 1982. Such a change means that women who used to work for a few years and then leave to get married have started to remain in employment or to return to work after

marriage or after they have raised children. As a result they have begun to be interested in equality in employment, working conditions, and particularly in promotion.

17. Art. 4 of the Labour Standards Law lays down the principle of equal pay for equal work for both sexes. But Art. 3 does not include sex among the grounds of prohibited discrimination. This omission is explained by the protection provided by the Labour Standards Law for women workers. The protection for women in this law is rather extensive. There are provisions restricting overtime and working on holidays and prohibiting night labour, underground labour and other dangerous jobs to women. They also provide maternity leave, nursing time and menstruation leave. Because of such extensive protection for women, it is asserted, the Law might be contradictory if it declared equality for both sexes.

18. In 1978 the Labour Ministry's Study Committee on the Labour Standards Law raised the suggestion that these protective provisions, except maternity protection, should be abolished since they contradict equality; it also proposed the introduction of new legislation for equal opportunity for women in employment. The Advisory Committee on Problems of Women and Minors of the Labour Ministry and its Committee of Specialists on Equality of Men and Women also proposed the introduction of such legislation in 1979 and 1982. In early 1984 the Advisory Committee finally issued its report which suggested the abolition of some of the protective provisions of the Labour Standards Law and the introduction of legislation to guarantee equal opportunity for women in employment. However, at the time of writing public opinion is still seriously split about the scope of the protection to be abolished and whether the enforcement of the equality provisions to be introduced should be with or without punishment; whether the legal effects of measures violated by the employers should be null and void or only accompanied by sanctions such as warning and guidance by administrative agencies; whether remedies should be provided through law courts or through special administative agencies; and whether such administrative agencies should possess power or only recourse to conciliation.

19. In the Contemporary practice of industrial relations in Japan women are discriminated against in various respects. Many companies employ women only for temporary, part-time or lower jobs (the percentage of part-time workers among the total of employed women is about 20 per cent while that of part-timers of both sexes among the total employed persons was 10 per cent in non-agricultural industries in 1982). They do not employ women university graduates. Only 27 per cent of companies which recruited universitary graduates offered employment to female graduates (Labour Ministry's Survey on Personnel Management of Women Workers, 1981). The· Labour Ministry began to issue administrative guidance for the abolition of the lower retirement age for women in 1980 when there were 18,000 companies with such a discriminatory retirement age. At the end of the fiscal year 1982, 70 per cent of these companies abolished such treatment. In 1980

2,900 companies had compulsory retirement on marriage, pregnancy or child-birth, of which 90 per cent had abolished such retirement system by the end of the fiscal year 1982. Also in promotion women tend to be discriminated against the practice of most companies. The above mentioned Survey in 1981 by the Labour Ministry on Personnel Management of Women Workers shows that there are women in jobs above that of supervisor in fewer than 40 per cent of the companies surveyed. In 20 per cent of the companies surveyed no training is provided for women workers. 40 per cent of companies provide a different kind of training for women and men. In view of the importance of in-house training in Japanese enterprises because of the life-time employment system, such discriminatory training practices have a serious impact on the promotion of women. Thus, in spite of the legal principle of equal pay for equal work, the average wage difference is still substantial (women's average wage was 52.8 per cent of that of men in 1982).

20. The courts have been active in promoting equality by holding to be discriminatory dismissal of women contradictory to the equality guaranteed by Art. 14 of the Constitution. According to the established legal decisions dismissal because of marriage, pregnancy or child-birth, regardless of whether or not it is based on retirement clauses of the work rules or collective agreement is regarded as null and void. Also, the ending of a contract or dismissal based on the earlier retirement system for women is held to be null and void. At the time of writing in 22 cases the courts have declared such discriminatory systems and dismissals based on them null and void, while only in two injunction cases have the courts rejected the claims of the women. The courts have held null and void discriminatory dismissals without such systems in eight cases. The plaintiffs lost nine cases in which they challenged the legality of discriminatory dismissals. In certain of these cases dismissals, based on the standards of collective dismissals, of women with working husbands, were regarded as reasonable because they entailed dismissal of workers suffering less than others, since these women worked for a second income in the family. In some cases the courts found that there are some reasonable grounds to dismiss women in cases of redundancy because they may suffer less from dismissal for similar reasons or because of the difficulty of providing alternative jobs for women in cases or redundancy. There has only been one case in which discrimination in promotion was held to be illegal. There has also been one case in which discrimination in wages was held to be illegal.

21. The above mentioned trend in legal cases shows that the courts are rather active in nullifying the legal effects of dismissals based on discriminatory systems or reasons. In cases of discrimination in promotion or wages there are only a few cases, partly because the plaintiffs find less prospect of winning cases and also because the courts see a difficulty in finding discrimination since the employers might provide excuses based on different jobs, ability or experiences between men and women although often these are caused by discriminatory treatment of companies in training or job assignments. There is no case where refusal of employment has been challenged, probably

because of the above-mentioned attitudes of the courts, which refuse to find illegal the discriminatory refusal to employ (see above, 15). This trend in case law and the pattern of cases involving sex discrimination suggest a number of interesting points for discussion. First, the lack of provision prohibiting sex discrimination in the Labour Standards Law (except in connection with wages) is not necessarily derogatory as far as discrimination in dismissals is concerned, since the courts nullify discriminatory dismissals by utilizing the constitutional provisions guaranteeing sexual equality and the freedom of marriage (in cases of retirement at marriage). Secondly, the courts' approach definitely has certain limitations. For one thing the courts tend to refuse to admit remedies for refusal of employment and, needless to say, for discriminatory recruitment policy. Thirdly, the victims of discrimination in promotion and job assignments are not keen to seek legal remedies. They know that in such cases, as well as in cases of refusal of employment, providing evidence of discrimination is difficult, while employers may have numerous possibilities to provide various reasons and excuses for the different treatment of men and women. Fourthly, in these cases the courts' remedies might be insufficient even if the courts admitted discrimination. The most the victims could expect from the courts for such types of discrimination might only be the recovery of damages but not affirmative orders, since under the Japanese legal system such orders could not be issued without specific legal provisions. All these points lead to the necessity of establishing special administrative agencies such as the EEOC in the United States or EOC in the United Kingdom.

22. In spite of the situations described above the expected government proposal for new legislation for equal employment opportunity may not be sufficient to meet the needs. The government is expected, at the time of writing, to propose the establishment of administrative agencies whose function would mainly be to provide advice for both parties, employer and labour, and to carry out mediation to settle the cases. This rather hesitant stance of the government is caused by strong pressure against effective legislation from the employers' side. In particular the employers are strongly opposed to the introduction of any provision prohibiting discrimination in recruitment and hiring with legal effect. Thus at the moment theres is a strong possibility that government proposals may prohibit discrimination in working conditions and dismissal with legal effects and may include some provisions to encourage equal treatment in recruitment and hiring as a moral obligation. Thus, the bill might be a result of a compromise of seriously divided opinions in Japanese society. The labour side is strongly opposed to any attempt to abolish the protective provisions of the Labour Standards Law while the employers insist on abolishing protection other than maternity protection as a **quid pro quo** for accepting equality. Certain groups of women workers, particularly women managers and white collar or professional workers are in favour of abolishing certain protection such as the limitation of overtime, the prohibition of night labour and menstruation leave which they view as obstacles to promotion and wider opportunities for their career. The government

is at present seeking to find a point of compromise among these divided opinions.

3. Religion and political opinion

23. Discrimination because of religion has never been a serious problem in Japan, perhaps because the Japanese people are rather indifferent and tolerant of the difference of religious creeds. Our society has been ready to accept new religions from abroad starting with Buddhism from China in ancient times. Only during the mediaeval age and the Second World War was Christianity oppressed but since World War II complete freedom of religion has been sustained in practise as well as in law. There is no legal case of discriminatiuon because of an employee's religion. Discrimination because of political opinion is more serious but most cases are ones in which employers have dismissed workers because of their Communist Party membership or because they are fellow travellers.

Around 1950 a number of companies dismissed employees by taking advantage of the so-called 'red-purge' by the Occupational Forces; this expelled Communist Party leaders from major public offices. A number of cases were brought to the courts arguing that such dismissals are unlawful, violating the Constitutional provision guaranteeing equality because of creed and freedom of thought. A majority of legal judgements have held that dismissal is unlawful and therefore null and void when occurring because of an employee's political views or party membership but not necessarily so when occurring because of subversive activities in the enterprise as a meber of such a party or supporter of such political views.

24. Political opinions also cause some problems in internal union affairs. More than one-third of organized labour is organized by unions affiliated to the Sohyo (General Council of Trade Unions in Japan), a national centre closely connected to the Socialist Party. Some 17 per cent of them is organized by the unions affiliated to the Domei (Japanese Confederation of Labour), which is another national centre connected with the Social Democratic Party. Some unions are still influenced by the Communist Party. These unions with certain political orientation often support certain candidates or certain parties in political elections at national level as well as local level. There are a number of legal cases in which members of minority groups were expelled from the union or disciplined when they refused to support the endorsed candi-dates or parties or to pay political contributions by the unions for the endorsed party or to work for political campaigns for such parties. A majority of these legal decisions have held that such expulsions or disciplinary measures are illegal. In particular there have been cases in which these minority members were dismissed on the basis of the union-shop clause. In such cases the courts also held dismissals illegal when they founds expulsion illegal.

4. Marital status

25. As already mentioned (2, 19), some enterprises have a system or practice of retirement on marriage. The courts have held that such systems or practices and dismissals based on them are unlawful because they contradict the constitutional guarantee of freedom of marriage and sexual equality (see above, 2, 20). The expected government proposals on equal opportunity in employment are expected to declare illegal such systems, practices and dismissals.

5. Age

26. Age discrimination in employment is not a very serious problem in Japanese industrial relations. The reason is not altogether clear. One reason may be the established practice of retirement age at the end of so-called life-time-employment. Regular employees employed fresh from school and remaining in their particular company accept retirement at a certain prescribed age. The companies normally pay fairly large retirement allowances, the amount of which is calculated on the basis of the amount of the last monthly wages and the number of years of the employee's service. Furthermore, employees of larger companies are often provided with new employment opportunities after retirement in subcontracting and other related companies. These are reasons why Japanese employees have thus far accepted retirement at ages of between 55 and 60. However, because of increasing life expectancy in recent years, such retirement ages today mean that retired employees are going to live for more than ten years. Thus in recent years many companies have been levelling up the retirement age from 55 to 60 years old. In contrast with the trend in Europe and the United States, unemployment is more frequent in older age groups than among the younger generation. However, because of technological innovation, including the introduction of high technology, the unemployment of older people will be more serious in the future. Thus in these few years the unions and opposition parties have been making proposals to introduce age anti-discrimination legislation.

6. Private life

27. Discrimination because of private life is also not very serious, perhaps because homosexuality and lesbianism are not very common or at least not so conspicuous in Japan as in Europe and the States. Divorce also does not cause much discrimination because there is no strong religious inhibition against divorce. This might be another difference between Western countries and Japan.

IV. EXCEPTIONS

1. Bona fide occupational qualifications

28. **Bona fide** occupational qualifications are accepted as a legal concept to excuse the different treatment of different groups. A typical case is that of different treatment because of sex. Traditionally certain jobs have been regarded as women's jobs, such as nursing, telephone operator, typist or secretary. Job segregation by sex is still common. The jobs in which the percentage of women among the total labour force is high are service and clerical jobs. Among professional jobs women are concentrated in teaching, music or acting, and nursing. The percentage of women is low in technical jobs, science and research, journalism, accountancy and legal businesses. The percentage of women in managerial jobs is also very low. The courts take the position that only a few exceptional jobs such as that of a maiden in the shrine service could be one with a **bona fide** occupational qualification of being female. However, there is almost no case in which the policy of companies to refuse women for employment in certain jobs has ever been challenged. The reason for the reluctance of women to challange job segregation is the above mentioned courts' attitude of respect for the employers' freedom to hire. The expected new legislation will change the present situation by providing the Labour Ministry with the authority to issue administrative guidance to correct such job segregation by sex. There are certain jobs in which beauty and youth may be important qualifications, especially in the service industries. In a few cases women have challenged dismissals or transfers done on the grounds that they had become old or had lost their beauty after serving as air-hostesses or TV announcers. In such cases the courts have denied the employers' arguments in the final analysis but have not said directly whether or not youth or beauty is a **bona fide** occupational qualification.

29. In the public sector until a few years ago women were disqualified by law from certain jobs such as defense officers, the emperor's palace guard, some special categories of jobs in the prisons, police, tax offices, immigration offices, and even the post office. After 1979 the government began to allow women to take exams or to participate in training for such jobs. Women are now qualified to take exams to qualify as navigation control officers and to enter the Aviation Safety School and the Navigation Safety School, but they are not yet permitted to take exams to enter the Defense University and therefore to take higher positions in the Defense Force. The justification for this exception is not very convincing; it is based on traditional notion that warfare is a man's job.

2. State security

30. The National Civil Service Law and the Local Civil Service Law provide equal treatment regardless of race, religion, sex, social status, family origin and political opinions. However, they disqualify from

169

employment those who have established or have engaged in the activities of subversive organizations which intend to destroy by violence the Constitution and the government based on the Constitution. Both laws prohibit government employees in general categories[1] to engage in political activities such as fund-raising for political parties, standing as candidates for elected public office, and being officers of political parties. This principle of the political neutrality of government employees has been challenged as a violation of freedom of political thoughts and political opinions. The courts have held that such prohibition of political activities by government employees of general categories is reasonable since they are the servants of all the people and are obliged to carry out the efficient administration of the government with integrity, continuity and stability.

Although civil service laws guarantee equality regardless of race, those of foreign nationality are not eligible to be government employees. The constitutional guarantee of equality is interpreted as applying only to Japanese nationals. This is justified by the argument that the Constitution applies only to the Japanese nation. And this is reasonable insofar as legal rights such as voting in elections or candidacy for public posts such as membership of the Diet, Upper House or Cabinet members are concerned. However, such broad disqualification of foreign nationals from all kinds of government jobs is hardly justified. The state security argument is not sufficient to justify disqualification of foreigners except for certain types of government jobs which allow access to state secrets or confidential information. Recently the government changed the regulation which admitted foreigners only for part-time teaching jobs in public schools and now foreigners are admitted as professors of national and other public universities, an amazingly delayed step at a time of internationalization.

3. Special protective measures

31. The Labour Standards Law provides protection for women, restricting overtime, holiday work, prohibiting night labour, underground and other dangerous work and providing maternity leave, menstruation leave and nursing periods. There are special measures to promote the employment of aged (45-65 years old) and handicapped persons, including providing subsidies from government funds to the employers who employ such persons or give training to them.

The government has also specified quarters, a prescribed percentage of handicapped or workers older than 55 years among the total number of employees of a particular undertaking, to promote employment of such persons.

V. AFFIRMATIVE ACTION AND REVERSE DISCRIMINATION

32. Since there is no special administrative agency to enforce equality in employment, the only enforcing procedure is through the courts. Under orthodox doctrine the courts have no power to order specific performance without special legislative provision to that effect.

However, Japanese courts have usually taken a position which declares the existence of the employment contract when they have found dismissals unlawful and therefore null and void. The result is the same as an affirmative order to reinstate and, in a sense, more effective since the dismissed employees are always provided with retroactive payment of wages. The same is also true in cases of discriminatory transfer, since the majority of court decisions regard an order to transfer as a legal action and declare the order null and void if it is discriminatory. The employee unlawfully transferred is admitted to the legal right to work at the former work place, the result being the same effect as an affirmative order. The same may be also true in cases of promotion but there is only one case so far other than in the field of discrimination because of union membership and union activities.

33. However, in those cases of discrimination in actual treatment which are not regarded as legal actions such as a refusal to hire, recruitment policies, training policies, there is no way in which the courts could provide effective remedies, perhaps except at most by providing reparation of damage depending on the individual cases. The latter is greatly dependent on whether the plaintiffs can give evidence that their legal rights to expect employment or training have been damaged by such discrimination in employment policy or training. In any case the courts have no power to order employers to change their policies.

34. There are no legal cases of reverse discriminatuion. The argument on reverse discrimination is thus far only a matter of theory. This reflects the underdeveloped stage of equality in Japanese industrial relations.

It is quite obvious that there is no reverse discrimination because according to the present law employers are given fairly extensive freedom regarding hiring and promotions.

VI. ENFORCEMENT

1. Proof

35. The courts basically put the burden of proof of discrimination on the plaintiffs who challenge the legality of discriminatory action. However, the courts often switch the burden of proof to the defendants when the plaintiffs have reasonably convinced the courts of the probability of discrimination. In other words, the defendants will lose the case if they cannot submit enough evidence that differential treatment occurred for lawful reasons, not discriminatory reasons. However, even with this shift of the burden of proof it is very hard to prove discrimination, especially in cases of discriminatory hiring, recruitment or promotion, since the courts acknowledge extensive freedom to employers in such cases. This is why new legislation is necessary to establish an administrative agency to support victims of discrimination

in obtaining evidence and to carry out legal procedures as a sort of public procecutor.

2. Enforcement agencies

36. As repeatedly mentioned, the law courts are the sole enforcement agency in the field of discrimination except for the Labour Relations Commission for cases of unfair labour partice. The expected new legislation against sex discrimination will probably introduce local agencies, however, with the role of mediation. Thus there is no prospect in the near future for the establishment of an effective enforcement agency in Japan.

3. Remedies

37. As already mentioned (V, 32, 33), affirmative action is not admitted under the present system. In cases of discrimination by legal action such as dismissal or transfer the courts in effect provide remedies similar to reinstatement by declaring such discriminary legal action null and void. In most cases payment of wages for the period between dismissal and the court decision is also ordered. In other cases of actions without legal effects, such as refusal to hire or promote, the only remedies are reparation of damages even if such actions are regarded as unlawful and therefore a sort of tort.

VII. CONCLUSION

38. The major area of discrimination in present-day Japan is that of gender. Discrimination because of nationality or race might become more serious in the future because of the expected increased internationalization of the Japanese economy. In view of the lack of serious problems except for sexual discrimination, the present attempt at new legislation for sexual equality in employment is a good opportunity to promote the development of anti-discriminatory law. However, because of strong opposition from the employers and the division of opinion among women, there is little prospect that any effective legislation will be introduced this time. However, no matter how inadequate the bill it will nonetheless promote a change of employers' attitudes towards sexual equality in employment. The result of the government's efforts remains to be seen.

NOTE

1. General categories of government employees include most government employees in administrative jobs. Diet members, Upper House members, and Cabinet members belong to the special category of the civil service.

12. The Netherlands

I. Asscher-Vonk

I. HISTORICAL INTRODUCTION

In the Netherlands the history of battling against discrimination in employment is rather limited. Of the international treaties concerned with the prohibition of discrimination the International Convention on the Elimination of all forms of Racial Discrimination (1965) is particularly significant. On the subject of sex discrimination the EEC-Treaty (Art. 119) and the Directives of 10 February 1975 (75/117 EEC) and of 9 February 1976 (76/207 EEC) are of the greatest practical importance for the Netherlands.

The Netherlands Constitution, which has long contained guarantees of the freedom of religious belief, has since 1963 contained a provision (Art. 1) in which discrimination on the grounds of religion, political creed, race, sex or any other grounds is forbidden. As far as discrimination between employer and employee is concerned, the inauguration of the legal battle against discrimination can be observed in a national law of 1927. Art. 1, para. 3 of the Act on Collective Agreements (1927) declares null and void any provision requiring the employer to hire solely or not to hire employees of a certain religion or political creed or members of a certain association. This rule does not forbid in itself discrimination, but it prohibits the assumption of the obligation to discriminate by means of a collective agreement.

The 1937 law on the extention of collective agreements was the next step. Art. 2, para. 5, of this act prescribes that provisions in collective agreements that force employers or workers to unite in a certain union or provisions that bring about unequal treatment between organised and unorganised workers cannot be declared generally binding. This is, from the point of view of fighting discrimination a rather minimal rule: firstly it is not forbidden to discriminate, but it is forbidden to lay the duty to discriminate on those who are not yet bound by collective agreement. Secondly it is only the coercion to join a certain organisation, which may mean discrimination on grounds of religion or political creed and discrimination between union members and non-union members that is the subject of this provision. An attempt at prohibiting discriminatory dismissal on grounds of age may be seen in the extra extension of the term of notice for workers of 45 years of age and older (Art. 1629j, para.1, Civil Code) and in the minimum period of notice of 3 weeks established for workers of 50 years of age or above, both introduced in the Civil Code in 1968. The ban on dismissal because of a person's marriage or during pregnancy introduced in the Civil Code (Art. 1639h) in 1976 may be seen as protection against discriminatory dismissal on grounds of marital status or pregnancy. Regulations forbidding discrimination in employment were also introduced in the Penal Code in 1971: Art. 137 of the Penal Code prohibits provisions that discriminate on grounds of race in the carrying on of a business or occupation. This amendment of the Penal Code was a consequence of the United Nations Convention on the elimination of all forms of racial discrimination. As a result of this legislation, the article of the 'Wet CAO' quoted above had to be adapted so that any agreement to discriminate on grounds of race is also null and void.

The next step making possible the legal struggle against discrimination was the Equal Pay Act of 1975. This Act prescribes equal pay for men and women and gave effect to the EEC Directive of 1975 and Art. 119 of the EEC Treaty. Then came the Equal Treatment Act of 1980 which forbids discrimination between men and women in access to work, occupational training, and labour conditions. In 1981 there came into force an amendment of the provisions of criminal law concerning the prohibition of racial discrimination. The modification, among others, added the possibility of reverse discrimination (preferential treatment) as an exception to the ban on discrimination. The explicit prohibition of discrimination in employment, in constitution or law, therefore, is of rather recent date. Older decrees, in the Constitution, are very general and refer to a number of fields, including employment. Governmental action to assess the extent to which unequal treatment occurs resulted in a programme of the Ministry of Culture, Recreation and Social Work in which rules governing differential treatment on grounds of sex or marital status were drawn up as well as an inventory[1] which did the same for discrimination on the grounds of race, national origin etc.

Government action to advance equality in employment has resulted in a number of specialized labour market regulations for the young, for older people and for part-timers. The trend is now to discontinue these regulations, mainly because there are serious doubts about their effectiveness. The employment exchange and labour offices are instructed to enforce the provisions on dismissal of the Equal Treatment Law. Jurisprudence concerning equality in employment is in part somewhat hidden. On the one hand there is legal doctrine concerning rightful dismissal etc., in which elements relating to discrimination may be found. For example, in one case the judge ruled on the dismissal of a teacher who belonged to a certain religious sect and wanted to wear the clothes belonging to his religious creed (see under IV, 1). However, there is very little doctrine relating to the specific acts prohibiting discrimination. The minimal use that persons make of the rights they have under the law is one of the problems of enforcing anti-discrimination legislation.

The Foundation of Labour, a superbody with representatives of the central organisations of unions and employers, issued a report in 1980 calling for the elimination of discrimination in the labour market market and in trade and industry. Trade and industry were called upon to put forward a policy aimed at equal opportunities for employees of equal value, regardless of age, sex, sexual disposition, marital status, religion, colour, race or ethnicity, nationality or political opinion, so that no conflict would arise with objective occupational qualifications. This recommendation has been followed, mostly in the

174

form of declarations of intent in about 20 collective agreements.[2] There has been some publicity concerning the fact that one school also incorporates a non-discrimination clause in its Statute.[3]

There is a general trend in the Netherlands to restrain the role of the legislation in many fields. Therefore it is not to be expected that in the short term more legislation concerning equality will be drafted, with one exception. There is in preparation the draft of a bill against discrimination on grounds of sex, homosexuality and marital status in public life. In the field of employment, however, this bill will not alter much compared with the Equal Pay and Equal Treatment Acts in existence. Insofar as the government is aware of a duty in the banning discrimination, stress is laid on the stimulation of developments in trade and industry. For instance the responsibility for the drawing up of Positive Action Programmes, looked upon by the government as a means of attaining equal treatment, is completely left to trade and industry.[4]

II. DEFINITION OF DISCRIMINATION

Certain problems arise with the definition of discrimination. In the first place, there seems as yet no consensus about what should be considered as discrimination. Secondly, there is the question of whether there should be one definition of discrimination, regardless of the grounds, or different definitions depending on whether discrimination is based on race, sex, religion or whatever. Thirdly, there is the question of whether the same definition can be used for example both in regards to labour law and social security.

Perhaps we have the beginnings of answers to some of the questions formulated above. Where specific legislation has been promulgated concerning discrimination, a definition can be found in the law and/or in the preparatory parliamentary works. Art. 90 of the Penal Code gives a general definition of discrimination as used in this Code. The article reads: 'Discrimination is every form of distinction, every exclusion, restriction or preference, aimed at or having the effect that the acknowledgement, enjoyment or exercise on an equal footing of fundamental rights and fundamental freedoms are set aside or impaired'. What is intended to be prohibited in Art. 429 of the Penal Code as amended in 1981 is not quite clear, considering the legal history. The text of the article forbids 'distinction between persons because of their race'. It is not quite clear whether every distinction of this kind is forbidden or only less favourable distinctions. The explicit exception is para. 2 of this article for reverse discrimination seems to indicate that the term 'distinction' in para. 1 is meant to be neutral. In Penal law, as in Civil law, it is irrelevant whether discrimination is intentional or not.[5]

At the time of the discussion of the Bill in Parliament, the Secretary of State stated that discriminatory effect would determine the applicability of the article.

Lastly, there is the question of whether Art. 429 only forbids unjustified distinction. This question has not been under discussion a propos Art. 429.

The way in which discrimination is prohibited in the Equal Pay Act does not seem to leave room for any exception. Art. 2 states: 'An employee is entitled to the same pay as an employee of the other sex for work of equal value generally receives'. The Equal Treatment Act, on the other hand, forbids 'the making of distinctions, directly or indirectly, between men and women'. This last distinction, between direct and indirect discrimination, is in conformity with the EC Directive of 10 February 1976 (76/207/EC), Art. 2, para. 1. The explicit exception in the Equal Treatment law of reverse discrimination seems also to indicate that distinction is meant to be a neutral term. The legal history gives a particularly broad definition of indirect discrimination: reference to a quality that has nothing to do with a person's sex, but happens to refer to persons of one gender in particular, has to be considered indirect discrimination. This definition appeared to be too broad in practice, as it also included, strictly speaking, **bona fide** occupational qualifications. In applying the Equal Treatment Act the need was felt by the Equal Treatment Commission to outline more clearly and precisely the concept of indirect discrimination. The Commission considers a statistical disproportional effect as presumed discrimination.[6] Counterproof can be furnished and must be that there is objective justification for the policy, act etc. that causes the disproportional effect. It should be pointed out that the Commission only accepts counterproof in cases of indirect discrimination. Every direct distinction between men and women, that is distinction that points to a person's gender or qualities inseparably linked with a person's gender, are forbidden by the Equal Pay Act and Equal Opportunity Acts, unless one of the legal grounds for exception (see under IV) exists.

III. GROUNDS

1. Race, colour, ethnics and national or social origin

Procedures attacking discrimination on these grounds (as on other grounds) are fairly scarce. C. Groenendijk[7] has counted five procedures in recent years. There are a number of possibilities for fighting discrimination in employment on these grounds. There are general rules forbidding discrimination (among others) on these grounds. These are found in the Constitution (Art. 1) and in international treaties. Leaving aside the complicated question of whether the international rules are self-executing or not, these general rules are important in giving meaning to the vague national norms pertaining to labour law, for example the duty to perform as a good employer. With a decision on short procedures concerning the dismissal of a number of workers, all foreigners, by a shipping company, the possibility was opened that such dismissal is unlawful on the grounds that the Constitution explicitly forbids discrimination.[8]

There are specific rules against discrimination on grounds of race in employment, notably Art. 429 of the Penal Code. A person suffering from discrimination as prohibited in this article may initiate action for tort. Clauses in collective agreements and individual labour contracts forbidding discrimination on these grounds make it possible for this obligation to be enforced as one arising from a labour contract. A number of reasons can be adduced for this minimal use of legal means; these are also partly valid for discrimination on other grounds. Specifically with discrimination on grounds of race and the like there may be a difficulty in that it is mainly through penal law that the norm is elaborated. This means that the possibilities of litigation against discrimination in a civil lawsuit are indirect. Furthermore there is no specialized enforcement agency. The suggestion made at the time of discussion of the Bill amending Art. 429 that there should be an Independent Committee has not up to now been followed. Lastly there are a number of problems connected with bringing about an individual claim. As causes of the minimal use by civil parties of the rules of law forbidding discrimination on these grounds one can note both unfamiliarity with the rules and fear of victimisation. The opportunities for class actions are fairly limited.

2. Sex

It is clearly under the pressures of EC obligations that legislation forbidding sex discrimination in employment has come into being. At present the most elaborate legislation on discrimination concerns sex discrimination in employment. There are three acts on sex discrimination in employment. The Equal Pay Act of 1975 gives a person a claim against his of her employer for equal pay with a person of the opposite sex for work of equal value. This law only forbids direct discrimination. In 1980 the Equal Treatment Act came into force. This law forbids both direct and indirect discrimination in access to work, conditions of employment, occupational training, and dismissal. Under this Act there can also be filed a claim of indirect discrimination in the field of wages. In 1980 there also came into force the Equal Treatment Law for civil servants. This act forbids discrimination in employment, by unequal pay or otherwise, against those working as civil servants. Together the three acts forbid discrimination, direct or indirect, because of sex. Of the different ways in which indirect sex discrimination can take place, the act explicitly mentions marital status and family situation. It should be noted that not all discrimination on these last grounds is forbidden, but only when that which in practice entails sex discrimination. [9] Making distinctions in hiring and firing between married and unmarried persons has also been explicitly prohibited.

There are several reasons why the many questions about these acts remain unanswered. One reason is that there is very little litigation over the rights guaranteed under these acts. This in itself is part of the problem; though reports show that these acts are still systematically breached, persons do not seek legal remedies. A number of reasons may be adduced for this phenomenon. Firstly, there seems to be considerable fear, and this fear is not groundless, of jeopardizing one's position in an organisation by seeking equal rights. The proportionally higher number of complaints about not having been hired (where there is not this danger) seems to corrobate this. Secondly, it is not always clear what claim has to be filed. Thirdly, women seem to have difficulties in getting legal advice and help. In the fourth place, the fact that nearly all claims have to be filed by an individual, and that only in the case of discriminatory advertisements is a class action possible, seems to keep down the number of complaints under the law.

3. Religion and political opinion

We have noted a number of rules that prohibit discrimination on many grounds, among which are religion and political opinion. There are not many provisions dealing specifically with discrimination on these grounds. In the Act on Labour Contract, which is part of the Civil Code, provisions exist which may be considered as guarantees of the enjoyment of freedom of religion or political opinion, no protection, however, is given in these provisions against discrimination on these grounds, nor is there protection from victimisation. The provisions are:
Art. 1638c of the Civil Code: The employer must give time off to exercise the right to vote;
Art. 1638v: The employer should make it possible for a resident employee to fulfil his or her religious duties;
Art. 1638w: An employer is not allowed to let his of her employee work on Sunday or similar days.

4. Marital status

The Equal Treatment Act explicitly prohibits distinctions between married and unmarried persons in hiring and in dismissal. In these cases, therefore, discrimination between persons of the same sex is forbidden. Discrimination on the grounds of marital status as a way of discriminating indirectly between men and women has also been forbidden where labour conditions etc. are concerned (see above). Since 1976 the Civil Code has had a provision prohibiting dismissal on the grounds that an employee is or intends to get married. A dismissal on this ground is null and void.

5. Age

Prohibition of discrimination in employment on grounds of age has taken a special form in the Netherlands. There is no ban on using age as a reason for termination of employment. In the Civil Code, however, the term of notice for an employee of 45 years of age has been extended, and a minimum term of three weeks has to be observed on behalf of employees of 50 years of age and older. This protection of older workers against dismissal can also be noted in regulations about compulsory retirement; these almost all use age and seniority as a criterion for (non-)dismissal and let age and seniority influence the level of severance play. It should be noted, however, that these regulations seem to have a reverse effect on the hiring of persons above a certain age. The difficulties and costs of firing older employees make many employers reluctant to hire them.

6. Private life

In the Provisions of the Labour Contract Act, in the Civil Code, some attention is given to the protection of a worker's private life: in a number of cases, such as the confinement of the employee's spouse or the death and burial of members of the family, the employee is entitled to some time off without loss of pay. Though these provisions constitute some kind of protection of a worker's private life, they cannot be considered more than a very small step towards the prohibition of discrimination on the grounds of private life.

Recently, there has been some discussion of whether a person's homosexuality can be a valid reason for dismissal or failure to hire, and whether a person is under obligation to mention his or her homosexuality when applying for a job. Firstly, there arose a broad discussion when the pre-draft of a law on equal treatment, issued in September 1980 [10] forbade discrimination in employment and in other fields of public life on the grounds of sex, marital status and homosexuality. In particular the question of whether schools may be an exception to the rule that an employer may not discriminate betwee homo- and heterosexuals received considerable attention. Because of the reactions and the ensuing debate, the pre-draft is being studied by the government and a definite draft has been promised before the end of 1984. [11] Secondly, the case of a social worker, who was not hired when his homosexuality became known to his employer (who, incidently, happened to be the Royal Household) gave rise to questions in Parliament. In response the Government stated that although it may generally speaking be considered irrelevant whether an applicant for a job is a homosexual or not, there may be instances when it is better for the person, the employer, and the persons the employee has to work with, if the homosexuality is known at an early stage. Suppressing this fact may be a breach of trust in some circumstances. Homosexuality can also in some circumstances cause a security risk, namely when the homosexuality has been kept a secret and the person for that very reason has become vulnerable. [12]

IV. EXCEPTIONS

1. Bona fide occupational qualifications

The use of **bona fide** occupational qualifications as an exception to the prohibition of discrimination has been under discussion in the case of sex discrimination and religion as well as of discrimination on grounds of religion or political opinion. The potential for making an exception on the grounds that a person's sex is a **bona fide** occupational qualification is given in the EC Directive of 10 February 1976 (76/207/EC), Art. 2, para. 2. The Netherlands Equal Treatment Act has adopted this possibility in Art. 1637ij BW. Though in practice there has been no appeal against this rule, it has been under discussion because of the possibility that because of its open character it may be in conflict with the EC rules in the Directive. Pressure from Brussels has resulted in a statement to Parliament (18 269, 2 Parliament Papers) promising to draw up a list, so that the number of instances in which an appeal could be made on the basis of this exception under the Equal Treatment Act will be limited.

When freedom of religion and political opinion is concerned, there is some jurisprudence that seems to allow limitation of this freedom because of **bona fide** occupational qualifications, though no explicit appeal has been made on the basis of this exception. There was one case in which a Bhagwan teacher insisted on wearing the clothes belonging to his religion while on duty as a teacher in a Roman Catholic school. The judge ruled that this teacher no longer complied with the reasonable qualifications that a Roman Catholic school could demand. The judge ruled that the treaty does not prevent a person from giving up to a certain extent the rights it aspires to protect (NJ/AB 1983/277).

In another case, membership of the Communist Party and the fact that the person concerned held public offices at municipal level for the Party was considered incompatible with the orders the Catholic school where he worked could reasonably give him (NJ/AB 1979, 347 idem AB 1975, 115). As private life, incompatible with the necessary occupational qualifications, was considered the fact that a teacher (of a Catholic school) left his wife and children to live with a married woman. The same was the case with a teacher who entered a sexual realtionship with his assistant.[13] In a number of cases judges have ruled that open living as a homosexual, and especially the fact that the homosexuality thus became known to colleagues and others constituted a valid reason for termination of employment.

2. Security of state

The fact that for a number of public offices it is a necessary requirement that the person has Netherlands nationality may be explained by reasons of state security. Security reasons were explicitly mentioned by the government in the case of the homosexual who applied for a job as social worker in the Royal Household and was rejected on the grounds that he had kept his homosexuality secret in the course of the selection procedure and that a homosexual who keeps his nature a secret is vulnerable and thus can be considered a security risk.

3. Special protective measures

Special protective measures that may conflict with equality of employment are traditionally established for women and young persons. These special protective measures are for the most part of statutory origin. The Labour Act includes regulations about the period for which a woman is not allowed to work before and after her confinement and maxima for overtime hours for men and women etc. The ban on women working as stevedores still exists. A bill, modifying the ban on night work for women in industry is at present under discussion in Parliament (17 038). The special regulations for young persons in the Labour Act have recently been under revision.

V. AFFIRMATIVE ACTION AND REVERSE DISCRIMINATION

At the first stage of an affirmative action programme we may consider the drawing up of an inventory detailing where persons of a certain group are differently treated. Inventories such as these for discrimination on grounds of sex and marital status are provided in legislation (1978) and several studies of different treatment and (indirect) discrimination in collective agreements have been made by the Service for Collective Labour Conditions. For discrimination on grounds of race, etc. an inventory of different treatment in legislation was publicised in 1983 by the Ministry of Justice and details of discrimination on these grounds in collective agreements were issued by the Service for Collective Labour Conditions, also in 1983. Labour market measures especially aimed at certain groups have for some time existed for women, for young persons and for older persons. There is a tendency now to omit special measures such as these.

In a recent Statement (1984) to Parliament, the government stresses the importance of positive action programmes, especially for women, at the level of the enterprise. The importance of the employers' council in this sphere is stressed. For the Civil Service, a kind of positive action programme mainly related to training, is developed in the so-called CIER Reports (Ministry of Internal Affairs, 1983).

Affirmative action by way of preferential treatment is explicitly envisaged on behalf of racial minorities in Art. 429 of the Penal Code. The Equal Treatment Law also envisages affirmative action. This law deems affirmative action possible for members of both sexes. There is some possible debate whether the opportunity for the preferential treatment of men is in accordance with Art. 2, para. 4, EC-Directive of 9 February 1976.

VI. ENFORCEMENT

1. Proof

The well-known difficulty in proving the fact of discrimination has somewhat been diminished by the decision of the High Court of 10 December 1982. In a case concerning the housing of a family of minority ethnic origin the High Court ruled that the fact that since there was clearly a disproportional effect of housing policy against the minority, the burden of proof shifted to the Housing Office. When the Housing Office could not give a reasonable explanation for the disproportional effect, it was presumed that discrimination had occurred. There are two elements important for litigation in discrimination cases in this decision: firstly the importance of statistical material for the shifting of the burden of proof, and secondly the fact that it was not necessary that the intent to discriminate was proven: it was sufficient that there had been no reasonable explanation that made clear that there had been no discrimination. Since there is very little litigation, the impact of this decision on jurisprudence is not yet clear.

2. Enforcement agencies

Setting aside the general possibility of filing a complaint with the Ombudsman, a possibility not limited to cases of discrimination but including other complaints against the government, there are specialised enforcement agencies only in cases of sex discrimination. There are two Committees for Equal Treatment, which also deal with questions concerning equal pay: one for those working for a private enterprise or employer and one for civil servants. It is expected that these two committees will be merged as from 1 January 1985 (18 269). The powers of the committee are and will remain very limited. The committee is competent to give a judgement on a complaint about violation of the Equal Pay Act or Equal Treatment Act (or for the Committee for Civil Servants: the Equal Treatment Act for Civil Servants). In cases under the Equal Pay Act, it is even obligatory to have the judgement of the committee in order to be able to file a complaint under that act. The judge, however, is completely free to use or to ignore the committee's judgement. Court decisions show that the judges as often as not follow the committee's view. Another impediment to the functioning of the committee is that while its members are representatives of unions and employers' associations along with indepent members, it has only a small secretariat and does not have its own budget. The committee is helped in its task of investigating a complaint by the Service on Technical Problems concerning Wages, a government office.

There is no specialised agency for complaints concerning rare discrimination. Suggestions to institute an agency such as this have as yet been rejected.

3. Remedies

The remedies for discrimination on grounds of race, nationality etc. are in the first place of a penal nature. In civil law such an offense may create an unlawful act and be cause for compensation. The remedies for sex discrimination are given in the Equal Pay and Equal Treatment Acts. The acts are part of Civil Law. No penal sanctions exist for violations of the law. The civil sanctions, especially in the Equal Treatment Act, are not very clearly delineated. It is still not clear what claim can be made, for instance, when an employer has refused to hire a person for discriminatory reasons. The sanction for discriminatory dismissal seems to be a claim for damages, but what damages remains unclear. The Equal Treatment Act (not the Equal Pay Act nor the Equal Treatment Act for Civil Servants) offers protection against victimisation by dismissal. Such dismissal is null and void.

Recent cases have made clear that the prohibition of discrimination of any kind, as is now stated in the Constitution, can help to have declared unlawful an act or null and void an agreement in which discrimination has been an issue. The apparent minimal effectiveness of the legislation concerning the prohibition of discrimination has given rise to criticism in the relevant literature. Possible causes of the fact that very little use is made of the legal remedies possible in non-discrimination law include the fact that there is almost no opportunity for class action; the fact that, especially in sex discrimination cases, it is not very clear what claim has to be put; and the fact that there is very little protection from victimisation: only the Equal Treatment Act prohibits dismissal on the grounds that the employee has filed a complaint under the law. As it is known that a person's position in his or her work more often than not becomes very difficult when s/he has appealed for his/her rights under the lasw, as seems the case with sex discrimination, it may be presumed that this is one cause of the minimal use that is made of the law (cf. Annual Report 1982 of the Commissie Gelijke Behandeling).

NOTES

1. Ministry of Justice, 1983.
2. The text of the formula most used reads as follows: 'Considering objective occupational qualifications, it is not allowed to keep employees of equal value from equal opportunities for work and equal opportunities in the labour organisation on grounds of factors as age, sex, sexual disposition, marital status, religion, colour, race or ethnicity, nationality or political opinion.'
3. Academie de Horst in Driebergen.
4. See Parliamentary Papers, 18 269.
5. C. Groenendijk: 'Recht tegen rassendiscriminatie op de arbeids-markt', Sociaal Maandblad Arbeid, 1983, p. 660.
6. Cf. High Court 10 December 1982 Nederlands Juristenblad, 1983, nr. 687.
7. Sociaal Maandblad Arbeid, 1983, p. 1.
8. Injunction, 1983, 341.
9. J.J. van der Weele, De Wet Gelijke Behandeling van mannen en vrouwen, Kluwer 1983, p. 61.
10. Voorontwerp van Wet Gelijke Behandeling, Ministerie van Cultuur, Recreatie en Maatschappelijk Werk.
11. Parliamentary Papers, 18 269, 2.
12. Zitting 1982-1983, Tweede Kamer der Staten-Generaal, Aanhangsel p. 707 en 708.
13. See B.J. van der Net, Kringenrechtspraak voor leerkrachten bij het bijzonder onderwijs, proefschrift 1977.

13. Sweden

B. Flodgren

I. INTRODUCTION

§1. Ethnic origin

1. Sweden was for a long time a very homogeneous country with regard to ethnic origin, race and religion and consequently did not experience very much social conflict due to such factors. Until the middle of the 20th century the only large minority groups were the Laps, the Finnish-speaking population in Northern Sweden and, to some extent, the Jews. However, increasing immigration after the Second World War changed the picture drastically. In the immediate postwar period it was the demand for labour that caused this immigration, mainly from Finland and from countries in Southern Europe such as Greece, Yugoslavia and Turkey. At the beginning of the 1970's immigration policy once again changed its character and labour immigration is now permitted only in exceptional cases.

2. Swedish immigration policy at present rests on the following principles: 1) the free movement of labour within the Nordic countries, 2) restrictiveness with regard to non-Nordic immigration labour, 3) a fairly generous attitude towards immigration on political or humanitarian grounds. The main element of present immigration consists of refugees and their next of kin who receive permission to stay in the country mainly for political and humanitarian reasons. The number of immigrants, or rather the number of movements to Sweden (some have moved several times) during the period 1968-1982 was, according to official records, 555,000, of whom 311,000 were citizens of Nordic countries (236,000 Finns). The number of emigrants from Sweden was during the same period about 314,000 of whom 214,000 were citizens of Nordic countries (150,000 Finns). These figures do not include Swedish citizens. The different categories of non-Nordic immigrants during this period were as follows:

Non-Nordic immigration to Sweden 1968-1982 [1]

Immigration of labour	27,100
Refugees or persons with refugee-like reasons	66,000
Next of kin etc.	150,900
Total amount	244,000

3. Among Sweden's 8 million inhabitants roughly 650,000 were born in a foreign country and of this population about 300,000 are still foreign citizens. 10-15 per cent of the persons entering the labour market in

185

the 70's were immigrants and although this figure is expected to decline somewhat in the future, there will remain a large number of non-Swedes in the Swedish labour force.

§2. Sex

4. Some background figures should also be presented with regard to the issue of sex on the labour market. In Sweden, as in other countries, women have entered the labour market in large numbers during the last decade. Figures from 1983 show that 67 per cent of the women aged between 16 and 74 were gainfully employed, as compared to 77 per cent of men; about half the Swedish work force now consists of women. However, on an overall basis women have a weaker position on the labour market inasmuch as they are more frequently unemployed, more often work part-time, receive less pay and are found in more menial jobs than men.

§3. International Conventions regarding discriminatiuon

5. In 1962 Sweden ratified the ILO Convention and Recommendation (No. 111) concerning Discrimination in Respect of Employment and Occupation (1958). According to this Convention Sweden is bound to declare and pursue - by methods appropriate to national conditions and practice - a national policy designed to promote equality of opportunity and treatment in respect of employment and occupation.

6. Furthermore, in 1962 Sweden ratified the ILO Convention (No. 100) and Recommendation (No. 90) concerning Equal Remuneration for Men and Women Workers for Work of Equal Value (1951). According to this Convention Sweden has a duty 'by means appropriate to the methods in operation for determining rates of remuneration, to promote and, insofar as is consistent with such methods, ensure the application to all workers of the principle of equal remuneration for men and women workers for work of equal value'. This Convention gives the State the option to implement the principle of equal remuneration by means of either 1) national laws or regulations, or 2) legally established or recognized machinery for wage determination, or 3) collective agreements between employers and workers, or 4) a combination of these methods. Sweden has chosen collective bargaining as the prime method of implementation and since 1980 there also exists the Equal Opportunities Act which protects the goal of equal remuneration set up by the ILO Convention.

7. In 1970 Sweden ratified the UN Convention on Elimination of All Forms of Racial Discrimination (1966) under which Sweden 'condemns racial discrimination and undertakes to pursue by all appropriate means and without delay a policy of eliminating racial discrimination in all its forms and promoting understanding among all races'. Under the same convention Sweden has also undertaken to 'engage in no act or practice of racial discrimination against persons, groups of persons or institutions and to ensure that all public authorities and public institutions, national and local, shall act in conformity with this obligation' as well as 'not to sponsor, defend or support racial discrimination by any persons or organizations'.

8. The European Council adopted a Convention on the Legal Status of Migrant Workers (1977) which has been ratified by Sweden. The Convention deals with such issues as recruitment, work permits, residence permits, conditions of work, housing etc. for migrant workers and their families.

9. Sweden has long been bound by agreements which constitute an open inter-Nordic labour market. The agreement now in force (from 1982, ratified in 1983) prescribes equal access to jobs in the Nordic countries for citizens from these countries, **i.e.** Denmark, Finland, Iceland, Norway and Sweden.

10. Finally, as a point of clarification, it should be emphasized that Sweden is not a member of the EEC and subsequently not bound by Art. 7 of the EEC Treaty which prohibits discrimination on grounds of nationality.

§4. Constitution

11. The Swedish Constitution (Regeringsformen) stipulates in general terms that men and women shall be guaranteed the same rights. Furthermore, it stipulates that the opportunities for ethnic, linguistic and religious minorities to keep and develop their own cultural and social life shall be promoted (Chapter 1, paragraph 2). In more specific terms the Constitution outlaws discriminatory regulation (not discrimination as such). The types of discriminatory regulation that is refers to concern racial/ethnic discrimination on the one hand and sex discrimination on the other hand, and it deals with each type separately. Chapter 2 paragraph 15 states: 'No statute or other regulation may imply the discrimination of any citizen who - due to race, colour of skin or ethnic origin - belongs to a minority.' Chapter 2 paragraph 16 reads as follows: 'No statute or other regulation may imply the discrimination of any citizen due to his/her sex, unless the regulation aims at establishing equality between men and women or regards military service or any similar duty to serve.' This paragraph does not outlaw sex discriminatory regulation that is already in force, nor does it prevent such regulation to be renewed in its discriminatory form. Chapter 2 of the Swedish Constitution contains provisions that establish fundamental rights and freedoms for Swedish citizens. Most but not all of those rights and freedoms are also guaranteed for 'foreigners in this country' (Chapter 2 paragraph 20).

§5. Criminal Code

12. The Swedish Criminal Code contains provisions which deal with discrimination. Here only racial/ethnic discrimination has been the subject for regulation, not any other form of discrimination. Chapter 16, paragraph 8, as amended in 1982, makes it criminal to publicly express or disseminate an opinion which involves threat or disrespect vis-à-vis any ethnic group or other such group of people with reference to race, colour of skin, national or ethnic origin or religious creed. Paragraph 9 of the same chapter makes it a criminal offence of unlawful discrimination for an entrepreneur in the operation of his firm to discriminate against a customer/client because of race, colour of skin, national or ethnic origin or religious creed. The same goes for employees or others who act on behalf of the entrepreneur as well as for civil servants.

13. Unlawful discrimination also exists if someone arranges a public meeting to which certain persons are not admitted on the same conditions as others due to race, colour of skin, national or ethnic origin or religious creed. The provisions of the Criminal Code do not apply particularly to the labour market but aims at curbing racial/ethnical etc. discrimination in society as a whole.

§6. General Labour Law Regulation with Anti-discriminatory implications

14. The Swedish Employment Protection Act of 1974, as amended in 1982, stipulates that an employment relationship may be terminated by the employer only with just cause. Factors such as race, colour of skin, national or ethnic origin, sex or religious creed are not considered just cause for dismissal/discharge, nor may they constitute grounds for any other discriminatory action with regard to an employee within the employment relationship.

14. According to the same act, dismissal due to redundancy shall adhere to the principle 'first in - last out' unless the union and the employer agree otherwise. Seniority lists made up by the employer and the union in redundancy situations are accepted by the law so long as they are not discriminatory with regard to the above-mentioned factors. The Labour Court has also made it clear that a lack of knowledge of the Swedish language is not accepted as a factor for selection of whom should be dismissed in a redundancy situation, unless such knowledge is actually needed for the performance of the jobs that are left.

15. The Working Environment Act of 1977 puts on the employer a general duty to organize and carry out work in the safest possible way. This includes, for instance, with regard to employees who do not speak Swedish or who are not familiar with Swedish conditions, a particular duty for the employer to inform and to give necessary instructions to such employees.

16. The Co-determination Act of 1976 provides the unions with the right to bargain and to enter into collective agreements with the employer. Through this right to negotiate unions are equipped with a tool which could be used to curb discrimination, for instance, with regard to hiring new employees. However, unions have not been active

188

in trying to establish collective agreements for the protection of minorities. So far only collective agreements regarding sex discrimination have been established, but no major collective agreement exists with regard to ethnic/racial discrimination.

§7. Particular anti-discriminatory regulation with regard to the employment relationship

17. It is only recently that the Swedish legislature has become occupied with the need for anti-discriminatory regulation, particularly for the labour market. The two factors of sex and ethnic origin are so far the only ones that have been subjects for the legislature's attention. As far as ethnic origin is concerned, no legislation has yet been passed, but at present (June 1984) the issue is subject to legislative efforts that will most likely lead soon to legislation - in one form or another.

18. The first and so far only anti-discriminatory legislation that has been introduced for the labour market is the Act on Equal Opportunities for Women and Men at Work of 1980 (see below, paragraphs 36 - 43).

19. Apart from sex and ethnic origin there are several other factors that might cause discriminatory treatment on the labour market. Since the labour market is a competitive market, people who deviate from the ideal labour force, for instance, due to old age or due to extremist political opinion, will - in times when jobs are scarce - be subject to discriminatory treatment. The negative effects of the labour market's way of functioning for such categories have been dealt with through special protective measures as well as through more general protective measures, not always, however, successfully. As a special protective measure one could mention the Act of 1983 regarding Youth Teams in Public Employment which makes it compulsory for the government and the municipalities to offer employment in so-called youth teams for young people until they reach the age of twenty (see below, paragraph 74). As a general protective measure one could mention the protection against dismissal without just cause in the Employment Protection Act which outlaws dismissal due to such factors as, for instance, political opinion, old age, the private life of the employee etc.

20. As a general statement one could say that Swedish Labour Law and labour market regulation only to a limited extent contain legislation, collective agreements etc. with an explicit anti-discriminatory purpose, but to a large extent contain provisions - in statutes, collective agreements etc. - which in a more general sense aim at providing equal treatment, equal pay and equality in general between different categories of employees. There is a certain difficulty involved in determining whether a certain regulation or a certain provision which might have anti-discriminatory repercussions in a wider sense should be included in a article such as this which deals with the more explicit concept of discriminatiuon.

§8. Future developments

21. The growing immigration during the post-war period has changed the homogeneous picture of the Swedish labour market. Today a large number of the people included in the Swedish work force are immigrants or children of immigrants. Racial/ethnic discrimination in Swedish society has become a matter of public concern and in the near future one can expect legislation not only with regard to the labour market but also legislation that outlaws racist organizations and discrimination in housing.

22. Also with regard to sex the picture has changed. Today almost half the work force are women. Discrimination with regard to sex has been dealt with in the recently introduced Equal Opportunities Act with particular reference to the labour market. No further legislation regarding sex discrimination is to be expected in the near future. The act admits that certain of its provisions may be replaced by collective agreements, and such agreements are in fact in force for essentially the whole labour market. They usually do not go beyond the provisions of the act. If any alteration takes place in the regulations regarding sex discrimination in the near future, it will probably be through collective agreements. The agreements that have so far taken shape often for intance require complementary local agreements.

23. Discriminatory treatment due to age will be dealt with in different ways dependent on whether it refers to young people or to elderly employees. Growing unemployment among the young will probably also in the future be regarded as a social evil and therefore become the target of different attempts by government to try to solve this problem. Unemployment among elderly people, on the other hand, will probably become more and more accepted as the number of available jobs continues to decline. Different forms of early retirement are already encouraged by labour policy and no political effort is nowadays put into the issue of providing the elderly with appropriate occupations, a goal which in 1979 caused the appointment of a Government Committee with the explicit instructions to find ways to strengthen the position of elderly people on the labour market. [2]

II. THE CONCEPT OF DISCRIMINATION

§1. The general meaning of the term discrimination

24. Discrimination is a concept that implies making distinctions in a negative sense between human beings on grounds that have to do with their personal traits or personal situations. The concept of discrimination stems from the idea of equality, **i.e.** that human beings should be treated equally and have equal access to societal goods such as jobs, education, health care etc.

25. Furthermore, the concept of discrimination implies a minority-majority relationship. In its relationship with the minority the majority

190

may take advantage of the fundamental difference in power between majority and minority, and this difference in power is often a prerequisite for the possibility of discrimination.

§2. Discrimination as a legal concept

26. In the ILO Convention (No. 111) concerning Discrimination in Respect of Employment and Occupation of 1958 the phenomenon of discrimination is described as 'any distinction, exclusion or preference made on the basis of race, colour, sex, religion, political opinion, national extraction or social origin, which has the effect of nullifying or impairing equality of opportunity or treatment in employment or occupation'.

27. When discrimination is used in legal contexts it is usually given a particular meaning with reference to the type of discrimination the legal act tries to prevent. Such is, for instance, the case in the Swedish Equal Opportunities Act and also in the Bill now pending in Sweden regarding ethnic discrimination. Discrimination in the legal meaning of the word is thus a more technical concept than is the case with the concept of discrimination used in everyday language.

§3. Actual existence of discrimination in employment

28. It is commonplace to state that discrimination in the sense of negative special treatment exists on the Swedish labour market with regard to different categories of human beings. According to a recent government report more than 60 per cent of immigrants interviewed had experienced - according to their own opinion - discrimination in one form or another on the labour market.[3] They particularly emphasized the problems they encountered when trying to get a job. It is not only employers who are accused of discrimination but such criticism is often heard with regard to the public employment agencies and other public authorities. According to the above-mentioned government report immigrants experience more discriminatory treatment in their contact with the authorities than they do in their private lives or with regard to their legal status in Sweden.

§4. Direct and indirect discrimination

29. Looking at the legal system in regard to the labour market one finds regulation that implies direct as well as indirect discrimination. Direct discrimination is prescribed, for instance, in the Aliens Act of 1980 which restricts foreigners' access to the Swedish labour market by setting up conditions regarding work permits. Such discrimination is open, direct and intended. Other regulation might have discriminatory repercussions for certain groups which might neither be intended nor easily recognized. The women's movement have drawn attention to the fact that although a certain provision might look neutral on the surface with regard to sex, it may still have a discriminatory effect on women as a mere result of the way it affects women in practice. Such is the case, for instance, with some of the benefits of the social welfare system which may only be enjoyed by employees who work more than 17 hours a week. Many people, particularly women, work less than this and thus are excluded from parts of the welfare system.

30. Furthermore, one can talk about indirect discrimination when regulation aimed at protecting and helping certain categories of employees has instead the effect that these categories become less attractive on the labour market. Such is considered to be an effect of the Education in Swedish Act of 1972 which gives foreign employees the right to study Swedish for 240 lecture hours at their employer's expense. As a result, employers often try to avoid employing foreigners in order not to have to pay for their Swedish lessons. When these indirect discriminatory effects became apparent, the government put forward a proposal to change the regulation. If this proposal passes, the foreign employees' right to study Swedish will be financed through a fee which will be paid by all employers, not only those who employ foreign employees.

III. GROUNDS FOR DISCRIMINATION

§1. Race, colour, ethnicity and national or social origin

31. Access to the Swedish labour market is restricted for foreigners by the Aliens Act and the Aliens Ordinance, both of 1980. The restriction refers to nationality only, and grounds such as race, colour of skin, ethnicity and social origin are not formally relevant, either for access to the labour market or for conditions of employment.

32. According to the Aliens Act, a foreign citizen must have been granted a work permit and must at all times have a valid work permit in order to have the right to take and hold employment in Sweden. The lack of a valid work permit constitutes grounds for discharge. A foreign citizen who takes employment without the necessary permit may be fined. The employer may not only be fined or sentenced to prison (maximum of one year), but will also have to pay a special fee to the government for each illegally employed foreign citizen. In principle, the work permit should be applied for from abroad; once in Sweden the foreigner has only a minimal chance of obtaining such a permit. But even if a foreign citizen applies from abroad, the chances of obtaining a permit are very small. As has already been mentioned, Swedish labour immigration policy is very restrictive. The restrictions do not apply to citizens from the other Nordic countries, however.

33. Once the foreign citizen has received a work permit and entered the Swedish labour market s/he should, in principle, be given the same treatment, pay and opportunities as a Swedish employee. However, it is generally known that discrimination takes place and that, for instance, unemployment is twice as high among foreign citizens as among Swedes. At this time (June 1984) a bill has been put forward for the purpose of curbing ethnic discrimination on the labour market. The proposed legislation has been designed on the pattern of the Equal Opportunities Act which will be described in more detail below (see paragraphs 36 - 43). The proposed legislation has been met by criticism, mainly from the employers, but it will probably be enacted in some form or another in the near future.

34. The Employment Protection Act requires of the employer a duty not to dismiss an employee without just cause. Race, colour of skin, ethnicity, national or social origin are not just causes for dismissal. However, the ability to speak Swedish is required for certain jobs and does in fact exclude foreign workers from large segments of the labour market. Inability to speak Swedish may constitute a just cause for dismissal only if such knowledge is actually necessary for the job in question. In a recent case (Labour Court 1983: 107), the Labour Court rejected a seniority list made up by the employer (in this case a shipping company) and the union. According to the seniority list all non-Swedish speaking employees would have to leave the company first. The employer argued that the ability to speak Swedish was a prerequisite for safety reasons (the employees in question spoke only Finnish). The Labour Court did not find evidence for this argument and declared the seniority list discriminatory and void with regard to these employees.

35. Swedish immigration policy and labour market policy have as one of their goals the creation of equality between Swedes and foreign citizens living in the country. During the last decade strong efforts have been made to reduce differences in rights between these two groups. Only a few differences remain. According to a recent government report regarding the legal status of aliens some differences are intended to remain also in the future.[4] However, differences - if they continue to exist - will be rationally based and concern any of the following matters: (1) the independence of the State, (2) the security of the State, (3) the relationship to foreign states or international organizations, (4) an important public or private economic interest, (5) decisions concerning individual rights, or (6) the exercise of public authority. In such matters the rights of foreign citizens, say to achieve employment, may be limited as compared to the rights of Swedish citizens. Regulation that limits the rights of foreign citizens in these respects is not considered discriminatory. For instance, the Constitution limits the rights of non-Swedes to hold certain public positions, among others the position of judge. According to the Public Employment Act of 1976 positions in the military service, in the police force and as public prosecutor may be held only by Swedish citizens. The same act gives the government the right to prescribe or decide that positions in the government administration, in the Department of Foreign Affairs, and positions that might involve insight into security issues may be available to Swedish citizens only. A fairly large number of positions in the public sector have been declared by the government to be available only to Swedes. Limitations on the rights of foreign citizens with reference to security of state will be discussed further below (see paragraphs 66 - 67).

§2. Sex

36. Sex discrimination on the labour market is outlawed by the Act on Equal Opportunities for Women and Men at Work. This statute came into force on 1 July 1980. In the public sector there is also in force a particular Equal Opportunities Ordinance for State Employees. Furthermore, in the public as well as in the private sector there also exist Equal Opportunities collective agreements. This article will deal mainly with the Equal Opportunities Act.

37. As its title suggests, the Act on Equal Opportunities for Men and Women at Work only deals with discrimination on the labour market, not in society as a whole. The act contains two types of provision to curb discrimination, one which outlaws acts, and conditions that constitute sex discrimination under the act in individual cases, and another type of provision which encourages affirmative action programmes and intends to further equality between the sexes as a collective goal.

38. The first kind of provision outlaws sex discrimination by employers in individual cases (§§ 2-4). Discrimination occurs when an employer hires, promotes or in connection with education for promotion selects one person instead of another of the opposite sex although the latter is better qualified for the job or education in question, unless the employer can demonstrate that his/her decision has not been influenced by the employee's sex or makes evident that his/her selection of employees is part of an affirmative action programme or that s/he has some other **bona fide** reason for his or her behaviour. Discrimination also exists if an employer (1) for no objective reason does not apply similar conditions to men and women who perform similar work, (2) for no objective reason organizes and distributes work in such a manner that one sex is obviously less favourably treated than the other, or (3) dismisses, transfers, lays off or discharges an employee due to the employee's sex. The act finally outlaws any agreement which prescribes differences in working conditions between men and women or permits such differences in treatment which are outlawed as sex discrimination under the act.

39. The question of whether unlawful sex discrimination has taken place in a particular situation is adjudged by the local courts (if the employee does not receive the support of the Equality Ombudsman or his or her union) or directly by the Labour Court. If the case has started in a local court it may be appealed to the Labour Court. If sex discrimination is found to have occurred, the employer has to pay damages to the employee. In addition, the discriminatory act shall be declared void unless it consists of the appointment of a person to a job. In such case that person may keep his or her job and the discriminated person only receives damages.

40. The Equal Opportunities Act differs from other Labour Law regulations hitherto introduced in Sweden inasmuch as its protection is not limited to the already employed. The provision regarding unlawful sex discrimination also covers job applicants.

41. In its very extensive paragraph 6 the Equal Opportunities Act prescribes that the employer shall carry out a purposeful affirmative action programma in order to efficiently promote equality in working life. For this purpose the employer is obliged to take such measures - within the resources and general framework of his/her operation - that will make working conditions equally suitable for men and women. This might, for instance, imply the installation of technical equipment in order to reduce the need for physical strength in certain jobs. The act also prescribes that s/he should encourage both sexes to apply for jobs and should - through education and other appropriate means - promote equality between men and women in different types of work and among different categories of employees. Equality in the meaning of the act exists when each sex represents at least 40 per cent of the work force in each type of work and among each category of employees. Unless there are special reasons mitigating against it, an employer must strive particularly for equality at the work place when hiring new employees. This does not mean that s/he is obliged to hire an applicant from the underrepresented sex in a case where two applicants (of different sexes) are equally qualified. The affirmative action provision in § 6 only encourages him or her to do so, but, formally, s/he is free to make his/her own choice. If the employer is bound by additional equal opportunities provisions, for instance, a collective agreement or, if s/he represents the state, the special Equal Opportunities Ordinance for State Employees, s/he might be obliged according to such regulation to hire the applicant from the under-represented sex - usually the woman - if a male and a female applicant are equally qualified. What of the employer's right to hire a less qualified applicant rather than a better qualified of the opposite sex? In principle, in the private sector the employer is free to make such a choice but it might be questioned from the point of view of the sex discrimination provision (see paragraph 38). In the public sector, where the selection of applicants for a job is more formalized, the employer may make such a choice only if s/he can prove that the decision is part of a conscientiously drawn up affirmative action programme.

42. The affirmative action provision described above may be set aside by collective agreements (§ 7). Such collective agreements have to a large extent been achieved by the top organizations. In the public sector agreements between the higher organs (both state and munici-palities) become valid immediately even on individual work sites. In the private sector the top level agreement must be approved by the national union and employers' association of each particular branch of industry. Several branches, for instance construction and transportation, have not signed the equal opportunities agreement and, as a conse-quence, instead of the agreement, the affirmative action provision of the act is still in force in those areas of the labour market. The equal opportunities agreements entered into so far are usually very general in character and do not go beyond the affirmative action provision of the statute.

43. A particular question with reference to the issue of sex discrimination is that whether pregnancy has any significance in regard to employment. First it should be pointed out that in no way may pregnancy be regarded as a just cause for dismissal. According to the Working Environment Act a pregnant employee may, however, be transferred from one job to another for medical reasons. The employer may not transfer a pregnant employee from a job for reasons that have to do only with attitudes, for instance, because the employer finds her less representative in her state of pregnancy.

§3. Religion and political opinion

44. Freedom of religion and freedom of political opinion are two of the fundamental freedoms that are guaranteed in chapter 2 of the Swedish Constitution. Freedom of religion according to the Constitution is formulated as follows:
'Every citizen shall vis-à-vis the State be guaranteed freedom of religion: freedom to exercise his religion alone or together with others.'
The political freedom and the freedom of religion is further guaranteed in the following words:
'Every citizen is vis-à-vis the State protected against coercion aimed at making him reveal his opinion in political, religious, cultural or similar matters. He is also vis-à-vis the State protected against coercion aimed at making him participate in any gathering for the purpose of influencing public opinion or in a demonstration or any other expressing of opinion or for the purpose of making him join a political organization, congregation or other gathering for political, religious, cultural or similar opinions.'
The Constitution also outlaws any registration of citizens due to political opinion in public registers without the consent of the citizen. This protection does not include foreigners.

45. Some of the political and religious freedoms/rights protected by the Constitution may be limited by statute or other regulation for the purpose of 'furthering a goal which is accepted in a democratic society'. Such encroachment is not permitted for political, religious, cultural or similar reasons only.

46. Religion is not a controversial issue in Sweden where the Lutheran church has for long been the State religion/church. Compared to many other countries Sweden appears not only religiously homogeneous but also very secularized. On the labour market religion and differences between religious creeds have so far played no role. The only position – apart from acting theologians such as ministers, reverends, bishops etc. - that requires membership in the State church is the position as chief administrator in the diocese. For all other categories religious belief or membership or lack of membership in any particular church

196

are unimportant for their employment rights. If a religious creed carries with it a demand for particular clothing, for instance a turban, this might, however, collide with the employer's demand for certain clothing, for instance the demand to wear a uniform. No such case has - to my knowledge - been tested in the Labour Court, but if the employer's demand in such a situation were justified, the employee's refusal to wear the uniform might in exceptional cases constitute a just cause for dismissal.

47. Women are nowadays allowed to hold positions as clergymen within the Swedish Church. The most controversial issue with regard to religion and employment in recent times has been the question of whether male clergymen may refuse to hold sermons and communion together with female colleagues. Until recently, they had the right to refuse to do so under a particular clerical privilege called the Conscience Clause, a clause that was introduced when women were admitted to clerical positions.

48. The refuse by some - not many - male clergymen to serve together with female colleagues still creates a problem for the church as an employer. An important question with regard to this problem, concerning employment conditions - or rather promotion principles - within the Swedish clergy, will soon be determined by the government. This involves a case of a male applicant for a position as reverend who has been declared unqualified for such a position by the diocese in spite of the fact that he fulfilled all the necessary formal qualifications. The reason why the diocese declared him unqualified was that he had explicitly made clear that he absolutely refuses to work together with any female clergy. His complaints regarding the diocese's decision will be heard by the government soon.

49. Political opinion as such is not a just cause for dismissal. This is true even for extremist political opinions. In a case dating from 1981 which drew much attention (Local Court of Stockholm DT 276/81) a union-owned construction company had dismissed an employee, Z, who was working as a computer operator and had been in this employment for about a year. The reason for dismissal was that Z was active in a racist organization called 'Keep Sweden Swedish' (which had come to the company's attention through a television programme the evening before the dismissal). In court the company argued that it did not want to keep Z employed because in his capacity as computer operator he could easily get hold of confidential information about immigrants from the company's computer system. There was no evidence that Z had actually tried to get access to such information; on the contrary, evidence showed that he had performed his job quite satisfactorily during the time he had been employed. The court made the statement that 'the political views of a person can be just cause for dismissal only in the rare cases where the employer manages to show that these views make the employee unfit for the job'. In this case the dismissal was declared void because 'working as a computer operator did not have anything to do with any particular political or religious opinion'.

The importance of political opinion as a **bona fide** occupational qualification is discussed further below (paragraph 65).

§4. Marital status

50. The question of whether or not a person is married is not considered relevant for determining his/her employment conditions or employment protection in Sweden.

§5. Age

51. In times of growing unemployment the question of age becomes increasingly important in the discussion regarding who should get and maintain the jobs that are available. The right to employ is free and this means that it is not against the law to refuse to give a job to a person due to age. This in turn has had the effect that the unemployment figures are high among young people as well as among the elderly part of the population.

52. To start with the elderly, it is necessary first to make a distinction between employees who have reached pension age (normally 65), on the one hand, and other elderly employees, on the other hand. The old age pension system usually - but not always - requires that the employee leave employment in order to benefit from the old age pension.

53. A person who has reached pension age and remains in or regains employment does not enjoy the regular legal protection provided for other employees. For instance, the otherwise very restricted right for the employer to employ for a limited period of time is available with regard to people who have reached the pension age according to the Employment Protection Act (§ 5). The following discussion regarding employment rights for elderly people refers only to persons who have not yet reached pension age.

54. One of the main goals of the Employment Protection Act is to provide employment security for elderly employees. The act declares it principally important to make it possible for elderly people to stay employed and it puts on the employer a duty to try all possible means to keep an ageing employee in employment. The employer must, for instance, try to transfer the employee to less strenuous work when the employee's capacity to work diminishes as a result of old age. If it comes to the point where an employee due to age cannot perform any work of importance, the employer may as a last resort dismiss the employee but before doing this s/he must try to find a solution in co-operation with the labour market authorities.

55. It is particularly in redundancy situations that the employment security of elderly employees is threatened. To make up for this, the Employment Protection Act makes age a factor that strengthens employment security inasmuch as the act lets the time of employment determine some of the most important rights under the act, above all the seniority right and the right to re-employment. The seniority principle according to the act is 'first in - last out' which means that the employee who has been employed for the longest period of time shall be the last one to leave. If two employees have the same period of employment, the younger must leave first. The same principle is applied if the employer starts to hire anew within one year after the employee's employment ended. If the employee is over 45 years of age the act prescribes that s/he has the right to count one extra month for every actual month of employment after the age of 45. An employee may add at the most 60 such exxtra months to the actual time of employment when it comes to determining his or her seniority rights or the right to re-employment.

56. The seniority principle 'first in - last out' prescribed by the act in situations of redundancy has proved difficult to apply in practice. The principle is negotiable, i.e. the union and the employer may agree otherwise. The seniority lists negotiated by unions and employers often stipulate that elderly employees should leave whereas young - often better educated - employees are permitted to stay. Employers often threaten to close the whole plant if they are not allowed to keep the most efficient - which usually do not include elderly - employees. In such a situation the union often accepts that other seniority principles are applied than the one prescribed by the Employment Protection Act.

57. It is not only the elderly population but also the young who are exposed to discriminatory treatment on the labour market. The Employment Protection Act only covers those already employed and, thus, does not provide any help for the unemployed. It is generally considered that strong employment protection for those already employed contributes to making it harder for the unemployed to ever enter or re-enter the labour market. In order to make it possible to employ a person for a trial period the Employment Protection Act was amended in 1982 and now permits employment for such a purpose for a limited period of time, six months at the most. At the enactment of this rule the chances of young people to enter the labour market were particularly taken into consideration. Recently, the government has also taken measures for the purpose of easing young people's entrance into the labour market by creating so-called youth teams (see further below paragraph 74).

§6. Private life

58. An employer often tries - through tests and interviews - to get information about a person's private life before offering employment. If an applicant gives false information about him or herself in such a test/interview s/he may later be dismissed if the information can be considered relevant for his or her fitness for the job and for the employer's decision to employ him or her. The extensive employment protection now in force and the growing tendency among employees to remain for longer periods of time with the same employer make it important for an employer to find out as much as possible about an applicant before determining whether or not to employ him or her.

59. Formally, there are no limits as to the questions an employer may ask a person who applies for a job with the employer. The women's movement have focused attention on the fact that female applicants often have to answer questions regarding their private lives which sometimes are very intimate and which have no counterpart in interviews of male applicants, for instance, regarding their behaviour during menstruation, the number of children they might plan to have, whether their husband/fiancé would be willing to move to another place if necessary, etc. In the Co-determination agreements that are taking shape under the Co-determination Act of 1976 unions sometimes try to achieve influence on how recruitment of new employees should be carried out but so far very little has been achieved in this respect.

60. Matters regarding a person's private life are more important for his or her chances of ever getting a job at all than for keeping a job once employed. As a rule, private life may not constitute a just cause for dismissal. Matters such as smoking habits, drinking habits, sexual habits, manner of dressing, length of hair etc. may threaten a person's right to stay employed only is they in any important way affect the ability to perform the job satisfactorily or if they in any crucial way would hurt the employer's business or reputation.

61. The importance - from the point of view of employment security - of drunkenness at work has been discussed in several cases brought to the Labour Court. Such behaviour is not automatically accepted as just cause for dismissal. If the drunken behaviour does not involve danger at the work site or show complete unfitness for the job, the Labour Court has ruled that the employee may not, in principle, be dismissed on this ground. On the contrary, the court has put a duty on the employer to try to help the employee socially, if the problem with alcohol is serious, for instance, by establishing contact with the social or health care authorities. Only in exceptional cases may drunkenness at work constitute a just cause for dismissal.

62. If an employee commits a crime it might influence his or her right to retain a job. A distinction is made between crimes committed outside work and crimes committed within the employment relationship. Neither leads automatically to dismissal. A crime committed outside work may lead to dismissal/discharge only if the employee thereby has showed lack of fitness for the job s/he holds or if it would hurt the image/reputation/respect that the employer enjoys among customers or clients if the employee remained with the employer. Crime committed at the work place may more easily lead to dismissal/discharge. Violent behaviour, theft, fraud etc. usually lead to immediate discharge.

200

IV. EXCEPTIONS

§1. Bona fide occupational qualification

63. A **bona fide** occupational qualification is a factor that justifies, or rather excuses, an action that would otherwise be regarded as discriminatory. To select a man to play a male role in a theatre performance or to employ a female model to show women's clothes is not sex discrimination, although sex is the factor that determines the choice. The Equal Opportunities Act prescribes restrictiveness with permitted exceptions from the fundamental principle that a person's sex shall have nothing to do with his/her right to get or hold a job. Reasons such as moral or cultural values or respect for integrity may, however, justify that only women are employed in the social home service (which implies that the social worker takes care of elderly and/or sick people in their homes). The fact that physical strength is needed to perform a certain job may be accepted as a reason for employing a man for that job, although such problems are primarily to be solved by the installation of technical equipment. It is uncertain whether an employer may select a person of a certain sex for a certain job simply because s/he believes that his or her business would benefit from having an employee of a certain sex in that particular position; s/he would probably have to have very strong underpinning for such a belief. In such a case it is not enough to refer to general stereotypes about female and male behaviour or to general assumptions about attitudes of clients or customers.

64. National origin may be a **bona fide** occupational qualification in rare cases when the job requires a certain nationality/ethnicity or certain skills that are connected with a certain nationality. As an example one can mention the need for natives in the many ethnic restaurants that have been set up in Sweden during the last decade. Of the 300-400 persons who during 1982 were admitted to the country as labour immigrants, about 100 were admitted to take employment as cooks in Chinese restaurants.

65. Similarly, political and religious opinion may be a **bona fide** occupational qualification in a case where a particular political opinion/religious belief is a prerequisite for the satisfactory performance of a certain job, for instance as political secretary of a political party, chief editor of a newspaper with a certain political profile, or ecclesiastical positions (where membership in the Church is often a formal prerequisite).

§2. Security of State

66. As has already been pointed out (see above, paragraph 35) State security is in the general labour policy regarded as one of the few acceptable reasons why foreign citizins should be treated differently with regard to rights on the labour market. Thus, foreign citizens do not, for instance, have access to employment in the military forces or to certain positions in the Department of Foreign Affairs. In addition to the limitations in rights that have already been mentioned, the Aliens Act contains a general provision (§ 27) which enables the government 'when security of the State makes it necessary' to prescribe that foreign citizens may not be employed in a certain company or in companies of a certain kind without the permission of the government or the National Immigration Board.

67. It is not only foreign citizens who are subject to special limitations on their employment rights for reasons that have to do with State security. According to the Personnel Control Ordinance of 1969 a special register is kept by the Security Policy for 'the prevention and discovery of crime against the security of the State'. Under that ordinance certain positions within the State administration which are 'essential for the total defence of the country or for the security of the State in general' may be classified as sensitive positions. A State organ that intends to employ a person for such a sensitive position shall make a personnel check on that person to check his or her civil reliability before s/he is employed. For particularly sensitive positions such personnel checks may be conducted every five years with regard to employees who hold such positions. A personnel check consists of getting information from the special register kept by the Security Police or - in particular cases - a more extensive investigation. The police decide what kind of information should be registered. The ordinance explicitly outlaws registration 'on the mere ground that somebody by membership in an organization or in any other way has simply expressed a political opinion'. The government may give instructions as to the application of the Personnel Control Ordinance. Any such instructions as well as the grounds on which the police have decided to register people are kept secret. If an employer considers terminating an employment relationship or taking any other important action with regard to an employee as a result of what has been revealed from a security check, the employer has a duty to negotiate the matter with union representatives who have been especially appointed for this task by the government.

§3. Special protective measures

68. In a welfare state such as Sweden questions of equality are constantly paramount on the political scene and several welfare programmes aim at levelling out differences in wealth, education etc. between citizens. Conditions on the labour market have not been excluded from these egalitarian efforts and, in consequence, there now exist numerous special protective measures for the purpose of compensating certain categories of employees for the shortcomings/handicaps they might have in comparison with other groups. Swedish Labour Law and labour market policy contain several provisions and schemes that constitute special protective measures for different categories of employees and here only a few of the most important will be described.

69. A category that has been subject to special protective measures with regard to their employment rights are the parents of small children. The Act regarding the Right to Parental Leave gives a parent the right to be on leave from employment on a full-time basis until the child has reached one and a half years of age and thereafter to reduce his or her working hours to 75 per cent of the normal 40 hour week until the child reaches the age of eight or has completed its first year in school (which normally occurs around the age of eight). In addition, a parent has the right to be on leave from employment for occasional care of a sick child until the child reaches the age of twelve. The parent not only has the right to leave from employment but also receives economic support in the form of social security benefits when staying with the child, in the case of childbirth (or adoption) for a total of 180 days for both parents and in the case of occasional care of a sick child for 60 days per year and per child for the parents together. A father may also take ten days off with social security benefits in connection with childbirth in the family.

70. The right to parental leave and the social security benefits connected with it are provided for male and female employees alike. The only difference is that the female employee has an unconditional right - if she wishes - to full-time leave in connection with childbirth six weeks before the estimated time of delivery and for six weeks thereafter. A mother also has the right to take time off for the purpose of breast-feeding her child.

71. An employer may not dismiss, transfer or otherwise treat an employee negatively as a result of the employee's parental leave. However, the employer may of course make adjustments in his or her organization that are necessary as a result of a parent's absence.

72. Another important special protective measure is the regulation that aims at aiding employees with short formal schooling to improve their education, namely the Act regarding the Right to Educational Leave. This act gives the employee the right to be on leave from employment for educational purposes for as long a period of time as necessary. It is the union and the employer who through negotiations decide the details of an employee's educational leave. No salary and no particular social security benefit is connected with this right to take time off from employment. The employee must find other means to support him or herself during his or her studies. The act is intended to aid employees with short formal schooling but it is not limited to this category. In practice, the rights under this act have only to a small extent been used by this category of employees; instead it has to a large extent been used by the already fairly well educated as a means to improve their education for career purposes.

73. A special protective measure for the purpose of aiding employees who do not speak Swedish to improve their ability in this respect is the Education in Swedish Act of 1972 (see above, paragraph 30).

74. A recently enforced regulation regarding the employment of young people in so-called youth teams, the Act regarding Work in Youth Teams in Public Employment of 1983, aims at providing young unemployed people between 18-20 years of age with meaningful occupational and work experience. According to the act the State and the municipalities have a duty to find employment for all these youngsters in youth teams. A youth team is a group of young people who participate as aids at work for the employer or in other useful tasks that would otherwise not be performed.

V. ENFORCEMENT

§1. Proof

75. The regular rule of evidence in Swedish Labour Law is the general rule in Civil Procedure which puts the burden of proof on the party who claims that his or her right has been violated. For a long time, the only exception in Labour Law to this rule was the burden-of-proof-rule in cases regarding violation of the right to organize. In such cases the Labour Court has lightened the burden of proof for a union which alleges that an employer has violated the right to organize of an individual employee. A similar special burden-of-proof-rule has now been introduced under the Equal Opportunities Act in sex discrimination cases (see above, paragraph 38) and is proposed in the Bill regarding ethnic discrimination that is at present pending (June, 1984).

76. If sex discrimination is alleged to have taken place, for instance with regard to an appointment to a job, the applicant who did not get the job (and who claims that sex discrimination has taken place) first has to make evident that s/he had better qualifications than the person of the opposite sex who got the job. If such is found to have been the case, the assumption is made that the employer has discriminated due to sex. The burden of proof then falls on the employer to exculpate him of herself. S/he must demonstrate that the decision was not due to the person's sex, or that it was part of a conscious affirmative action programme or that there was some other **bona fide** reason for the decision. If s/he does not manage to prove this, sex discrimination shall be found to have taken place.

§2. Enforcement agencies

77. The Equal Opportunities Act established special surveillance machinery in the form of a public body, the Equality Ombudsman, and a special Equality Commission. The Equality Ombudsman, a position that is at present held by a former female judge, has as her task to advise and persuade employers voluntarily to comply with the provisions of the act. Another task is to initiate and survey affirmative action programmes in different areas of the labour market. In practice the Ombudsman has no right to interfere with employers who are bound by Equal Opportunities collective agreements; at such work sites the question of affirmative action is handled by the union and the employer. Furthermore, the Ombudsman may take individual complaints to the Labour Court (1) if the individual permits it, (2) if the union does not take the case to court, and (3) if the Ombudsman considers the case important for the further application of the Equal Opportunities Act.

78. The policy of the Ombudsman is voluntarism and co-operation. If this soft line proves unsuccessful, the Ombudsman may ask for an injunction by the Equality Commission. So far, no such injunction has been issued or even requested.

79. An employer is obliged to provide the Ombudsman with the information that the Ombudsman asks for. An employer who refuses may be served with an injunction.

80. A particular act was enacted for the purpose of providing the employment authorities with measures that will help the so-called hard-to-place labour force to find employment or remain employed. This is the Act concerning Employment Promotion Measures of 1974. The act prescribes that co-operation shall take place between employers and the regional labour market authority regarding the possibilities of employing elderly people and people with diminished working capacity, as well as regarding possible measures to ease employment conditions for such employees. Even the unions have a right to participate in these negotiations and the activities under this act take place in what has come to be known as Adjustment Groups. These groups are set up at the work sites as voluntary bodies consisting of representatives for the labour market authority, for the employer and for the unions. At present some 5,000 such groups are in operation.

§3. Remedies

81. If an employer, a union or an employee violates Labour Law regulation, employment contract or collective agreement, the remedy is damages. A dismissal without a just cause will also lead to re-instatement of the dismissed employee. If a person is exposed to sex discrimination under the Equal Opportunities Act the discriminatory decision/measure should be declared void and the employer must also pay damages. If, however, the discriminatory decision consists of appointing a person to a job, the person appointed has a right to remain employed and the person who has been subject to discrimination receives damages only.

82. According to international standards, Swedish damages for violation of labour standards might seem rather low. A 'normal' sex discrimination violation amounts to about 20,000 Swedish crowns which equals about three month's wages for a blue-collar workers. The damages are tax deductible for the employer whereas the employee has to pay income tax on the amount of money received in damages. A government proposal has been put forward whereby - if it is passed - the employer's right to deduct labour damages from income will cease.

NOTES

1. **Immigration Policy.** Report SOU 1983:29 from the Government Committee on Immigration Policy, p. 17.
2. **Too old for work?** Report SOU 1983:62 by the Government Committee regarding Occupation for Elderly People, p. 12.
3. **In the right direction.** Report SOU 1984:55 by the Government Committee concerning Discrimination, p. 50.
4. **The Legal Status of Aliens.** Government Report DsA 1984:6 by the Government Committee concerning Discrimination, p. 125-126.

14. USA

J. Jones

I. HISTORICAL INTRODUCTION

A. Background

The goal of equality - and the prohibition of discrimination in employment a necessary element in its achievement - is inextricably linked to the historic struggle to abolish 'all badges and incidence of slavery in the United States'.[1]

Although the Declaration of Independence 'was a foundation document in the cause of freedom',[2] a clause arraigning King George III of England for forcing the slave trade upon the colonies was stricken from that document in order not to offend those, both North and South, who were involved in slavery.[3] The first federal constitution contained no prohibition of slavery and in fact encouraged it by providing for the counting of 3/5 of the Negro slaves in determining the basis for taxation and representation.[4] The slavery issue was the primary blight on the brave thesis that all men are created equal and endowed with the unalienable rights of life, liberty, and the pursuit of happiness. It was also a principal factor in continuous conflict - moral, political, social and economic - in the USA, and vestiges of those conflicts remain with us today.

The paradox of a free society dependant upon a system of slave labor generated perpetual tensions demanding resolution. After the Emancipation Proclamation, the Civil War and its attendant upheavals, a free society dependant upon intentional deprivation - by constitution, by laws, by customs and usages - was no less paradoxical. In the 120 years or more since the Emancipation Proclamation, the USA, haltingly, and moving sometimes with glacial speed, has in place in 1984 a plethora of laws and programmes directed to the prohibition of employment discrimination. From preoccupation with the legacy of slavery, the quest for equality of employment opportunity has expanded to include a multiplicity of conditions. Laws exist at all levels of government in the USA - federal, state and local. It is doubtful that there exists anywhere a complete compilation of all legal, governmental instruments seeking to prohibit discrimination in employment and to insure equality of employment opportunity.

B. Sources of EEO in the United States

1. The United States Constitution

Until ratification of the 13th Amendment, 6 December 1865,[5] the

207

Constitution of the United States was silent on the issue of employment. One has only to reflect a moment to appreciate that employment is what the 13th Amendment is about because slavery, which deprived its subjects of all rights enjoyed by free human beings, was primarily for economic purposes - a cheap, renewable source of labor.

While the Fifth Amendment to the Constitution prohibits the federal government from depriving any person of 'liberty or property without due process of law',[6] slaves were chatteled property, 'ordinary articles of merchandise'.[7] Moreover, the Fifth Amendment is a shield against federal action; it does not, without more, require the government to act. It has been contrued in recent years to prohibit discrimination by the federal government in most instances when it does act.[8]

C. Federal Statutes Prohibiting Employment Discrimination

Title VII of the Civil Rights act of 1964, as amended,[9] prohibits employment discrimination by employers and employment agencies, and membership discrimination by labour unions on the basis of race, colour, religion, sex or national origin. It established the Equal Employment Opportunity Commission as a federal agency but as originally enacted gave the Commission no enforcement powers. The act also excluded from its coverage small employers and organizations, with a decreasing number from 100 down to 25 after its first five years of existence. Additionally, the federal government, state and local governments, and private membership clubs exempt from federal taxation were also excluded.

The act did permit enforcement of pattern or practices of discrimination, principally large scale discriminatory activities, by the United States Department of Justice indepent of actions of the Equal Employment Opportunity Commission. Although the Commission had no enforcement powers and was limited to investigation and attempts to conciliate cases found to have merit, individual complainants were authorized to pursue their rights through actions in the federal courts brought on their behalf by their own attorneys.

In 1972, the Congress passed the Equal Employment Opportunity Act of 1972 which amended Title VII to broaden its coverage and gave to the EEOC the power to seek enforcement of the law in the courts. The amendments covered state and local governments as well as the executive branch of the federal government, excluding the courts and the legislative bodies, and empowered the US Attorney General to pursue suits against state and local governments. The individual complainant's right to sue in private actions was retained and extended to actions against federal, state and local governments. The act also expanded its coverage of private employers by reducing the number of employees from 25 to 15.

From its inception the act preserved existing state or local laws banning employment discrimination provided they do not conflict with the federal law. In its coverage of the federal government, however, the Supreme Court has interpreted the law to provide for exclusive resort to Title VII for vindication of the rights of federal employees.[10]

Impetus was given in the law to the states for passage of state and local laws prohibiting employment discrimination by providing that the federal commission must defer to the states, generally for 60 days, to give those entities with laws an opportunity to exercise jurisdiction.[11]

2. The Civil Rights Act of 1866 (42 USC § 1981 (1976))

Earlier in the Reconstruction Era, Congress enacted laws seeking, primarily, to protect the rights of the former slaves. One such law, among other things, attempted to protect the rights of the freemen to contract, which includes the employment relationship. The law provides all persons within the jurisdiction of the United States with the same right to make and enforce contracts as is enjoyed by white citizens. Early interpretations of it by the Supreme Court rendered it virtually useless, but in 1968 in Jones v. Alfred Mayer Co., supra, the Supreme Court resuscitated the 1866 law holding that it barred all racial discrimination, public as well as private, and that it extended to contracts of employment.[12] Unlike Title VII of the Civil Rights Act of 1964, the 1866 law grants the right to the individual and excludes no entity from its coverage. Thus private as wel as public entities would be subject to its reach. However, Brown v. GSA, supra, precludes its applicability to federal entities where such entities are subject to § 717 of the Civil Rights Act of 1964, as amended.[13]

3. The Civil Rights Act of 1871 (42 USC § 1983 (1976))

42 USC § 1983 applies to persons acting 'under color of state laws' to deprive others of federally protected rights which include employment rights. This law was also of limited utility for many years. However, in Monnel v. Dept. of social Services of the City of New York[14] the Supreme Court substantially broadened its scope by concluding that cities were indeed liable under the act. While state officials are also liable, limitations on the definition of 'person' and immunities against suits by citizens of one state against another state in the Eleventh Amendment of the Constitution of the United States render 42 USC § 1983 less viable in protecting against discrimination in employment by states than is the case in the Civil Rights Act of 1964.

The Supreme Court has determined that unlike the aforementioned statute, in Title VII Congress, acting under the Fourteenth Amendment to the Constitution, manifested its intent to override the immunity from suit granted to the states under the Eleventh Amendment.[15]

4. The Equal Pay Act of 1963[16]

The Equal Pay Act of 1963 prohibits the payment of different rates to persons for equal work on jobs that require equal skill, effort and responsibility under similar working conditions in the same establishment where such payment is based on sex. The responsibility for administration and enforcement of the law rested primarily with the United States Department of Labor until 1979 when it was transferred to the EEOC by presidential Reorganization Plan No. 1 of 1978.[17]

The Equal Pay Act, based upon the Fair Labor Standards Act model, covers employees differently and, consequently, it is possible for employers to be subject to the Equal Pay Act with less than 15 employees. FLSA had also been extended to state and local employees but its applicability to them was restricted by the Supreme Court in National League of Cities v. Usery.[18] However, there is little doubt that the Equal Pay Act is more broadly applicable to state and local employees and not subject to the limitations of National League of Cities.[19]

5. The Age Discrimination in Employment Act

The Age Discrimination in Employment Act (ADEA)[20] was also an addition to the Fair Labor Standards Act and it was passed in 1967, effective 12 June 1968. The Age Discrimination Act of 1975[21] prohibits discrimination on the basis of age in programmes or activities receiving federal financial assistance, including programmes receiving funds under the State and Local Fiscal Assistance Act of 1972.[22] The effect of its passage on enforcement of the Age Discrimination in Employment Act of 1967 is uncertain. However, in 1978 Congress amended the Age Discrimination in Employment Act and extended the protections to persons 40 to 70 years of age. The administration of this act was originally in the United States Department of Labor but Reorganization Plan No. 1 of 1978 transferred its administration to the Equal Employment Opportunity Commission effective 1 July 1979.

6. The Viet Nam Era Veterans' Readjustment Act [23]

In the aforementioned Act Congress requires employers with government contracts of $10,000 or more to take affirmative action to employ and advance disabled veterans and qualified veterans of the Viet Nam war. In addition to being applicable to government contractors, the statute also covers the employment of veterans by the federal government. Its administration is committed to the United States Department of Labor.

7. Vocational Rehabilitation Act of 1973 [24]

This statute requires contractors with the federal government for the procurement of personal property and non-personal services, including construction, to take affirmative action to employ and advance in employment qualified handicapped individuals. The requirement is imposed upon any contract in excess of $2,500. Additionally, discrimination against qualified handicapped individuals by any recipient of federal financial assistance or any federal programme or activity conducted by any federal agency is prohibited. The prohibition with regard to non-discrimination under federal grants and programmes also covers employment. [25]

The administration of the handicapped employment under federal contracts statute is in the United States Department of Labor.

8. The State and Local Federal Assistance Act of 1972, as amended

31 USC § 6716 (1982), generally referred to as the Revenue Sharing Act, prohibits any state or local government receiving federal revenues from discriminating on the grounds of race, colour, national origin, or sex, and prohibits discrimination on the basis of age or with respect to an otherwise qualified handicapped individual as defined in the federal laws.

Enforcement of this programme is committed to the Secretary of the Treasury and the prohibitions are enforced primarily by the threat of fund cut-off. However, the act authorizes the attorney general to sue in United States District Court for such relief as may be appropriate to insure the full enjoyment of the rights described in the law. [26] As a matter of general administrative law, any cut-off of funds by an administrative law judge or other administrative agency is subject to judicial review at the behest of an aggrieved party.

9. Title VI of the Civil Rights Act of 1964

A short provision in the 1964 Act prohibits discrimination on the basis of race, religion, or national origin in the participation of programmes or activities receiving federal financial assistance. Section 604 of that title restricts its applicability to employment to those grants the primary objective of which is to provide employment. Thus, Title VI has had limited applicability to employment discrimination. However, Title IX of the Education Amendments of 1972 (20 USC ch. 38, §§ 1681-1686 as amended 12 October 1976) prohibits discrimination on the basis of sex in any education programme or activity receiving federal financial assistance. Contrary to Title VI, the Supreme Court has interpreted Title IX to apply to employment. It also concluded that both Acts are subject to enforcement at the behest of the injured party in the federal courts. [27] The Supreme Court concluded that Title IX also prohibited employment discrimination generally by recipients of the subject grant but that the prohibition was limited to the programmes receiving such assistance. [28]

10. The National Labor Relations Act, as amended, (29 USC §§ 151-168 (1976))

The National Labor Relations Act, which has been on the books since the mid-1930s, is not primarily directed to the prohibition of employment discrimination on the basis of race, colour, religion, national origin or other invidious classifications. However, the NLRB has interpreted its doctrine of fair representation in cases in which there is employment discrimination caused by labour organizations to be a violation of its provision. While earlier it had exercised its control over the granting of exclusive representation rights to the union as a means of prohibiting invidious discrimination, in 1962 it asserted jurisdiction to utilize its authority to prohibit unfair labour practices to regulate such undesirable conduct. [29]

In 1964 in the Hughes Tool Co. case, 147 NLRB No. 66, the Board applied the duty to fair representation concept to a race discrimination case and its general theory was enforced by the federal courts. [30] Subsequent extension of breach of the duty of fair representation as an unfair labour practice to invidious discrimination on the basis of sex has also met with court approval. [31] The Supreme Court has not yet directly addressed this issue. [32] Except as the union and the employer are involved in activities, or the union has persuaded the employer to act against the employment interest of an employee on the basis of discrimination in breach of his duty of fair representation, the National Labor Relations Act does not apply directly to employment discrimination by the employer.

D. State Laws Providing for Equality and Prohibition of Discrimination in Employment

As of June 1983, most of the 50 states had a basic fair employment practice law covering race, color, religion, sex, age and national origin. Some states cover additional categories of discrimination. The 10 factors which state laws generally cover are race, religion, sex, national origin, age, handicapped, marital status, equal pay, arrest records, and lie detectors. Alabama only prohibited handicap discrimination and Arkansas prohibited only age, handicapped and denial of equal pay. [33]

In July of 1983 Louisiana passed a law of general applicability prohibiting intentional discrimination on the basis of race, colour, religion, sex, or national origin. [34] That state also prohibits, by other statutes, discrimination on the basis of age, alienage, sickle cell trait and handicap.

The District of Columbia and Puerto Rico, both federal entities, also have laws prohibiting discrimination. The District of Columbia covers 8 of the 10 protected classes while Puerto Rico covers only four - race, religion, sex and age.

Some states also have laws specifically covering state contractors. Just as the federal law was specifically amended to prohibit discrimination with regard to pregnancy as part of the prohibition against sex discrimination, some states have also specifically banned such discrimination. [35]

The methods of enforcement and the sanctions employed in the state laws vary greatly. Violation of some can result in monetary fines or prison terms while others provide for cease and desist orders and affirmative action requirements.

In addition to the states, many cities and countries have enacted ordinances and other laws prohibiting employment discrimination.

II. DEFINITION OF DISCRIMINATION (Direct-Indirect)

The objective of our constitutional protections and the early civil rights laws of the 1800s is to assure to all persons equal protection. The denial of equality in treatment then at least implicitly constitutes 'discrimination'. Neither 42 USC 1981, 1982 nor 1983 uses the term 'discrimination'.

In early years the dominant definition of discrimination, it has been suggested, involved 'evil motive, mens rea, or a state of mind test'.[36] Under this approach not only was it necessary to prove that the protected individual had been adversely affected but that the action was motivated by a subjective, evil motive, based upon the individual's race or classification.

The second concept flowing from the constitutional equal protection principle examined whether the individual had received unequal treatment because of the protected status.

The final concept of unequal effect without a sufficient justification emerges in the interpretation of Title VII of the Civil Rights Act by the Supreme Court in 1971.[37]

While Title VII of the Civil Rights Act of 1964, the principal federal statute, specifies a series on unlawful employment practices and it uses the term 'discriminate', nowhere in the statute is there an explicit definition of that term. What has emerged in interpretation of the law is an **ad hoc** approach to the definition of discrimination.[38] What is, perhaps, the leading desk reference on employment discrimination states

'four general categories or theories of discrimination ... listed in order of their historical development: (1) disparate treatment, (2) policies or practices which perpetuate the present the effects of past discrimination, (3) policies or practices having an adverse impact not justified by business necessity, and (4) failure to make reasonable accommodation to an employee's religious observances or practices.'[39]

There may well be a fifth category, that of reprisals taken against an individual for opposing an unlawful practice or participating in the process seeking to vindicate rights protected by the law.[40]

A case can be made for yet another concept of discrimination, that of 'pattern or practice'. One can. however, argue that pattern or practice is merely a combination of concepts already identified, but subject to a different process of proof.[41]

Both the Congress of the United States and the Supreme Court have recognized that employment discrimination is far more complex than it was in simpler times.

'In 1964, employment discrimination tended to be viewed as a series of isolated and distinguishable events, for the most part due to ill-will on the part of some identifiable individual or organization ... thus employment discrimination as viewed today is a far more complex and pervasive phenomena. Experts familiar with the subject now generally describe the problem in terms of "systems" and "effects" rather than simply intentional wrongs and the literature on the subject is replete with discussion of, for example, the mechanics of seniority and lines of progression, perpetuation of the present effects of pre-act discriminatory practices through various institutional devices, and testing and validation requirements.'[42]

Disparate treatment has been described by the Supreme Court as 'the most easily understood type of discrimination. The employer simply treats some people less favourably than others because of their race, colour, religion, sex or national origin. Proof of discriminatory motive is critical, although it can in some situations be inferred from the mere fact of differences in treatment'.[43] Disparate treatment has been referred to as different treatment and it doesn't matter whether the treatment is better or worse, or that the employee was a good or bad employee. There does have to be some causal connection between the adverse treatment and the status of the employee vis-à-vis race, sex etc.

'Disparate impact' or 'disparate effects' or the consequences theory holds that a facially non-discriminatory employment practice that disproportionately screens out a higher percentage of protected class members is an unlawful employment practice unless it can be demonstrated by the employer, or the other respondent subject to the act, that the practice is required by business necessity or has a manifest relationship to job performance.[44] The disparate impact concept has been used to invalidate a wide range of recruitment, assignment, hiring, promotion, discharge, testing and supervisory selection practices.[45]

'Pattern or practice' cases have been litigated primarily by the government, and the Supreme Court, in articulating the burden that the government had to carry in making out such a case, declared '... because it alleged a system-wide pattern or practice of resistance to the full enjoyment of Title VII rights, the government ultimately had to prove more than the mere occurrence of isolated or "accidental" or sporadic discriminatory acts. It had to establish by a preponderance of the evidence that racial discrimination was the company's standard operating procedure - the regular rather than the unusual pratice.'[46] The court noted that the term was not intended to be a term of art but to reflect its usual meaning. In the evidence submitted in both the Teamsters case and in Hazelwood, the government presented both statistical evidence of under utilization of the protected classes when compared with what would normally be expected from the general population or the labour market and specific instances of unequal treatment on the basis of race. The court did say in Hazelwood, however, that 'where gross statistical desparities can be shown, they alone may in proper case constitute a **prima facie** proof of a pattern or practice of discrimination'.[47]

The Supreme Court noted that it had repeatedly approved the use of statistical proof, where it reached proportions comparable to those in the Teamsters case, to establish **prima facie** case of racial discrimination in jury selection cases. It held statistics equally competent in proving employment discrimination.[48] The court notes that some courts frequently relied upon statistical evidence to prove a violation and in many cases the only available avenue of proof is the use of racial statistics to uncover clandestine and covert discrimination.

214

III. GROUNDS

1. Race/National Origin

Title VII of the Civil Rights Act of 1964 prohibits discrimination because of race, colour, religion, sex or national origin. Just as there is no specific definition of the term 'to discriminate' or 'discrimination' in the federal statute, it also contains no definition of the terms 'race, colour, sex or national origin'. The concept of race, both in law and practice, stems from perceptions of differences in primary stocks - Mongolian, Caucasian, Negro.[49] The harmful effects toward which the law is directed are probably more appropriately referred to as racism which can be usefully defined in an operational sense.

'Racism may be viewed as any attitude, action, or institutional structure which subordinates a person or group because of his or her colour. Even though "race" and "colour" refer to two different kinds of human characteristics, in (the USA) it is the visibility of skin colour - and of other physical traits associated with particular colour or groups - that marks individuals ar "targets" for subordination by the members of the white majority. This is true of Negroes, Puerto Ricans, Mexican-Americans, Japanese-Americans, Chinese-Americans, and Indians. Specifically, - ... members of all these groups are (subordinated) primarily because they are not white in colour, even though some are technically considered to be members of the "white race" and even view themselves as "white".[50]

Most people do not know the difference between race and ethnic group, between race and social cast, between nurture and nature. It makes for an economy of thought to ascribe pecularities of appearance, custom, values, to race. It is simpler to attribute differences to heredity than to juggle all the complex social grounds for differences that exist.'[51]

Prior to the end of the 'separate but equal' doctrine in the United States, state law defined a person as non-white depending upon the proportion of Caucasin or African blood the person supposedly had and frequently without regard to whether the individual appeared to be white.

The EEOC defines national origin discrimination to include denial of employment opportunity because of an individual's, or his or her ancestors', place of origin; or 'because an individual has the racial, cultural, or linguistic characteristics of a national origin group. It also includes consideration of whether opportunities have been denied because of marriage to or association with persons of a national origin group, or membership in or association with an organization so identified, attendance or participation in schools, churches, temples or mosques generally used by persons of a national origin group and because an individual's name or spouse's name is associated with such a group.' [52]

The federal government at one time defined Negroes as 'persons considered by themselves, by the school or by the community to be of African or Negro origin'.[53]

The operative factor in grounds for discrimination on the basis of a classification would therefore seem to be not only whether the individual discriminated against is in fact a member of such a group but whether the discriminator perceives such individual to be a member and acts because of the perception.

The term 'national origin', which is a protected class under the principal federal law, does not prohibit a private employer from discriminating on the basis of an employee's lack of citizenship. However, the failure to include the term 'ancestry' does not reduce the scope of coverage as the term national origin is considered to include ancestry. [54]

2. Sex

Title VII of the Civil Rights Act as enacted in 1964 gave little or no attention to sex except to include it as a protected class. Subsequently, litigation determined that discrimination on the basis of pregnancy was not protected and in 1978 an amendment to the law was added defining the terms 'because of sex' or 'on the basis of sex' to include, but not be limited to, because or on the basis of pregnancy, childbirth or related medical conditions. Women affected by pregnancy are required to be treated the same for all employment purposes. It is clear that the protection in the law relates to gender - male or female - and does not include sexual preferences. Some local employment discrimination laws have included sexual preference or orientation.

3. Religion and Political Opinion

The Civil Rights Act of 1964 was amended in 1972 to define the term 'religion' to include all aspects of religious observances and practice as well as belief, unless an employer demonstrates that he is unable to reasonably accommodate to an employee's or prospective employee's religious observance or practice without undue hardship.

The law also provided an exemption for an employer with respect to the employment of aliens outside any state, or the employment by religious corporations, associations, educational institutions, or societies for employment of individuals of a particular religion to perform work connected with the carrying on by such entities of their activities. The exemption permits religious entities to grant preferences to members of their faith.

This exemption also excludes from protection aliens employed by any employer outside of the United States. Thus, insofar as the alien is concerned, the law does not have any extra-territorial effect.

In an earlier age, fair employment practices laws in the United States frequently referred to 'race, creed, colour, religion and national origin'. Disputes over the meaning of creed, particularly as incorporating political beliefs rather than religious beliefs, resulted in the term generally falling into disuse. Title VII of the Civil Rights Act of 1964, as amended, does not specifically protect political opinion. Certain protections flowing from the constitutional freedom of speech and right of association protect political opinion from actions of the federal government or state and local governments; however, federal statutes of general applicability do not extend any such protections to discrimination by private employers.

The types of discriminations prohibited by the state laws as reported above also fail to include specific prohibitions on political opinions. [55]

4. Marital Status

The federal law does not specifically protect marital status. However, prohibitions against employment by married women in certain jobs where comparable single status is not required of men have been stricken as discrimination on the basis of sex. Rules prohibiting or limiting the employement of spouses in the same activities have generally met with court approval although the US Supreme Court has not yet addressed the issue. On the other hand, 21 states and the District of Columbia have statutes prohibiting discrimination on the basis of marital status. [56]

5. Age

A separate federal statute discussed above prohibits discrimination on the basis of age, which in 1978 was amended to cover age groups 40 to 69. Restricting the coverage to individuals within the time frames serves to limit the need for further definition. Generally speaking, the specific activities which are made unlawful are the same kinds of activities which are prohibited by Title VII of the Civil Rights Act. However, there are certain exceptions and exemptions in the Age Discrimination Act which do not exist in the other law.

6. Private Life

There are no protections for private life, as such, in the federal laws. Except for marital status and sexual preferences or orientation, which are covered in some state and local laws, and certain constitutional guarantees against state or federal encroachment on freedom of speech and association, the law does not specifically reach the private life of the employee.

IV. EXCEPTIONS

1. Bona fide occupational qualifications (BFOQ)

The principal law, Title VII of the Civil Rights Act of 1964, provides exemptions from the prohibitions set forth therein where the particular status is a **bona fide** occupational qualification. While it recognizes a BFOQ for religion, sex, and national origin, there is no BFOQ exemption for race or colour. The law declares that it shall not be unlawful employment practices for an employer or other covered entity to classify on the basis of religion, sex, or national origin in those certain instances where religion, sex, or national origin is a **bona fide** occupational qualification reasonably necessary to the normal operation of that particular business or enterprise. The age discrimination laws also contain specific **bona fide** occuaptional qualification exceptions.

Businesses or enterprises on or near Indian reservations in which preferential treatment is given to individuals who are Indians living on or near a reservation are excluded from the prohibited conduct which would otherwise apply (§ 703(i)). Although the term 'Indian' is not defined in the statute, it refers to Native Americans and there are other rather complicated laws and concepts which determine Native American status and entitlements, including the right to live on the reservations.

2. Security of State

The principal federal law [57] excludes from the term 'unlawful employment practice' any action taken by an employer or other covered entity with respect to an individual who is a member of the Communist Party of the United States or any other organization required to register as such under the Subversive Activities Control Act of 1950. It also exempts discrimination against an employee where the position requires activities which would be subject to requirements imposed by the United States in the interest of national security. Nothing in the statute requires an employer not to discriminate against 'security risks'.

3. Special Protective Measures

Generally speaking in the USA, special protective laws directed toward women in the employment area are relics of the past. Under Title VII of the Civil Rights Act of 1964, unless sex is a **bona fide** occupational qualification, women are entitled to seek employment on the basis of their abilities to do the job. Specific state laws which would interfere with that right would be in conflict with the federal law and therefore void under the Supremacy Clause of the US Constitution.

There are instances in which employers, often seeking to protect themselves from other kinds of liability, restrict the employment of women in the child-bearing ages from certain activities determined to be toxic or a threat to pregnant women or women capable of becoming pregnant. Occupational health and safety standards can in some instances come in conflict with a woman's right to equal employment opportunity where risk to the fetus or the capability of procreation can be demonstrated. This is a complicated area and the development of law to clarify its limits is very much in its infancy.

There have been other constitutional issues raised in which the laws either burden or benefit women. Those which the Supreme Court considers to be a burden have been stricken. Those which have been

218

considered beneficial, and to some extent make up for preexisting deprivations, the Supreme Court has permitted to stand.[58]

V. AFFIRMATIVE ACTION AND REVERSE DISCRIMINATION

Both terms 'affirmative action' and 'reverse discrimination' are of rather recent vintage. The concepts underlying them are, however, as old as the debates in the USA in 1866 over the passage of the Freedmens' Bureau Acts.[59]

Modern preoccupation with affirmative action, a concept first included as a requirement in Executive Order 10925 issued by President John F. Kennedy in 1961, begins in 1969 when the Labor Department issued its order establishing the Philadelphia Plan in the construction industry. That order, among other things, established goals and time-tables to facilitate the increased participation of Blacks in certain construction trades on government contracts in the Philadelphia area. Because the goals and timetables involved numerical targets they were immediately attacked as unconstitutional quotas and 'reverse discrimination'. Consequently, both the positive (Affirmative Action) and the negative (reverse discrimination) aspects ofthe government's attempts to enforce minority participation in employment subject to government contracts emerged in the same exercise.

It is noteworthy that Richard Nixon, as Vice President, and Chair of the Committee on Government Contracts, in his final report to President Eisenhower, asserted that the problems facing America were not generated by evil people intentionally discriminating on the basis of race, but rather by failure of employers to take positive action to eradicate the legacy of the past. John F. Kennedy's executive order requirement that contractors take affirmative action to insure equality of employment opportunity, a requirement imposed without regard to questions of guilt or specific entitlement to relief, is responsive to the problem identified in the report of Mr. Nixon.[60] The Philadelphia Plan was promptly challenged in both the courts and in the Congress as unconstitutional and illegal butit successfully withstood challenge on both fronts.[61]

Shortly after the success in defending the Philadelphia Plan, the Department of Labor generalized the application of the principles therein established. It first issued the rules applicable to government contractors in the non-construction sector as Order 4 which ultimately was published and codified in 41 CFR part 60-2 of the Code of Federal Regulations. Although varying in some particulars, the fundamental principles applied to companies in the non-construction sector were the same as had been utilized in the Philadelphia Plan. Not only do the rules require that the companies take affirmative action to insure equality of employment opportunity but they require that such covered company prepare and maintain an affirmative action plan. Essentially the plan requires self-analysis and determination of areas of under-utilization of women and minorities and the establishment of goals and timetables to achieve appropriate utilization of the excluded classes in the job categories in which they are found lacking. The order, as did the Philadelphia Plan, prohibits discrimination while at the same time encourages the employers to find and utilize qualified members of the protected classes. Despite constant complaints to the contrary, nothing in the plans require the employers to hire unqualified individuals to meet the goals or timetables. Failure to meet the goals is merely evidence to investigate causes of such failure. Meeting the goals does not insulate the contractor from discrimination charges if the facts establish that specific individuals have been discriminated against.[62] What the rules require of the contractor is that he make 'good faith effort' to achieve the goals and within the timetables specified.[63] Contrary to general assertions, it is the good faith effort which is the maximum requirement, and meeting or failing to meet the goals only establishes certain rebuttable presumptions which upon investigation and hearing may be resolved either way.[64]

So far, the Unites States Supreme Court has declined to review cases involving affirmative action plans under the presidential executive order. However, in the much discussed case of Bakke v. Regents of the University of California,[65] in the swing opinion of Mr. Justice Powell, favourable reference is made to courts of appeals cases in which the executive order requirements were sustained. Justice Powell refers to these cases as appropriate ways in which the governmental entity could establish programmes involving goals and timetables as contrasted with the attempt made by the University of California in the case before the court.[66]

Two subsequent Supreme Court decisions would seem to lay to rest most issues regarding the constitutionality of affirmative action efforts. In United Steel Workers of America v. Weber,[67] the Supreme Court approved an affirmative action programme over the protest of a white male employee alleging reverse discrimination in a programme which was 'voluntarily' entered into by a company and a union. The basis of the plaintiff's claim of reserve discrimination was Title VII of the Civil Rights Act of 1964. The Supreme Court concluded the act did not prohibit voluntary action by the parties to correct past discrimination by utilizing a programme providing for one to one black/white participation. Although the court has not addressed the specific issue in an employment setting, in Fullilove v. Klutznik,[68] the Supreme Court examined a quota programme established by the Congress of the United States. Congress provided for a 10 per cent set-aside of certain federal contracts for minority contractors. There had long existed an executive order programme attempting to facilitate the participation of minorities in government contracting activity. In a temporary programme, Congress directly addressed the issue in a statute which was challenged on fundamentally the same constitutional bases as affirmative action in employment. The Supreme Court sustained the constitutionality of the programme by a vote of 6 to 3, although there are several opinions regarding the nature of the judicial scrutiny required. Of critical significance is the Supreme Court's determination that it is not the exclusive province of the judiciary to address the effects of past discrimination. It is appropriate for elected officials, such as chief executives and appropriate legislative bodies, to establish affirmative action programmes to deal with the legacy of the past.

Significantly, Congress in the Civil Service Reform Act of 1978, § 310, established a minority recruitment programme to carry out the act's stated policy of providing the people of the United States with a competent, honest, and productive federal work force reflective of the country's diversity. The purpose is to make the federal agencies responsible for establishing recruitment programmes to eliminate under-representation of minorities and women in the federal work force. While the statute does not impose any goals or timetables as such, the policy implications of its objectives are obvious. It would be meaningless to stimulate vigorous recruitment and to require periodic reporting if recruitment were not intended to eventuate in hiring. Thus, it seems clear that in employment in the federal executive establishment Congress has endorsed the affirmative action concept. The federal EEOC has a federal affirmative action division which monitors the progress of federal agencies in the implementation of the policy with regard to under-utilization of women and minorities in federal service. [69]

Frequently cases are reported in which reverse discrimination charges are litigated against efforts to deal with past discrimination through affirmative action programmes. Until recently the Supreme Court of the United States had refused to review any of those cases and the overwhelming majority of them have sustained the programmes against attack. [70] A recent effort at derailing an affirmative action programme was an attack on a county ordinance setting aside government contracts for black contractors. [71] Although this too is not squarely on employment, the constitutional principles involved are the same. The court of appeals sustained the validity of the programme and noted that the various views expressed in Bakke and Fullilove, supra, indicated that the following standards were important in reviewing programmes of this type:

'(1) That the governmental body have the authority to pass such legislation; (2) that adequate findings be made to insure that the governmental body is remedying the present affects of past discrimination rather than advancing one racial or ethnic group's interest over another; (3) that the use of such classifications extend no further than the established need of remedying the effects of past discrimination. In short, the legislation employing the racial preferences must incorporate sufficient safeguards to allow a reviewing court to conclude that the program will be neither utilized to an extent nor continued in duration beyond the point needed to redress the effects of past discrimination.' [72]

There are affirmative action issues which seem to offer a greater possibility of Supreme Court attention. A challenge was lodged against an affirmative action plan established pursuant to a consent decree which protected the minorities employed pursuant thereto from layoff. The critical issue was that minority employees added to the rolls pursuant to the consent decree who had accumulated limited seniority in the jobs were protected from layoff while more senior white employees were not. Both constitutional and statutory challenges were made to the plan. However, before the Supreme Court could decide the matter the State of Massachusetts provided enough resources to save harmless white males affected and thereafter the Supreme Court declared the case moot. [73]

The court has heard Firefighters Local 1784 v. Stotts. [74] The critical issue in this case is the legality of a consent decree which provides affirmative action in hiring and promotion for black fire department personnel and bars proposed layoff and demotion of black employees during a financial crisis such that the affirmative action gains would be reduced or lost. Involved is the question of the court's authority to modify a consent decree which is silent regarding layoffs in a fashion which would adversely affect a seniority system requiring layoffs in the reverse order of employment - last hired first fired.[75]

It would appear that the principle of affirmative action, namely a programme of inclusion of minorities and women into the world of work by positive action on the part of private employers or governmental entities, is constitutionally secure. The issues of the future would seem to address whether the plans or programmes are appropriate under the standards which have been utilized by the Supreme Court in comparable cases. It seems clear that the seniority cases currently pending merely address the extent to which affirmative action programmes can take priority over other kinds of rights, not whether such programmes are entitled to exist.

There is one unsettling factor with regard to the use of goals or timetables and that is that the current administration has intervened into various court cases and argued against their continued use. This administration takes the rejected position that such programmes are unconstitutional and that the constitution requires colour-blind behavior. This very Supreme Court has rejected, on a number of occasions, the fundamental premise of that position.

The state of research in equal employment and affirmative action matters in the USA is such that we do not have adequate documentation of the extent to which state and local entities have embraced the Affirmative Action concept. One gets the impression that there has been substantial acceptance of affirmative action as a necessary device throughout the USA at the point of most political significance - the state and the local levels. It seems only a tiny, but powerful and shrill, minority continues to insist on the unconstitutionality of affirmative action programmes. The elected representatives of the people have gone on to other priorities.

VI. ENFORCEMENT

The mechanism provided for the enforcement of any law, and particularly for enforcement of civil rights legislation, is as important as the substantive rights sought to be protected by the legislation. A law which purports to protect certain classes from invidious or hostile treatment but is deficient in the process by which such protections are insured tends to be more symbolic than substantive. If the law is merely confirming what has become accepted social custom and practice, then deficiencies in enforcement procedures are less significant. If, however, there is less than substantial acceptance of the rights established and a greater likelihood of resistance to according the rights to the affected classes, then effective enforcement processes are critical. This is not to suggest that laws which confirm existing social practice, or laws which are essentially symbolic, are devoid of social utility. It is to suggest, however, that in the area of equal employment in the USA effective enforcement mechanisms are as important as substantive protections.

The principal equal employment law, the Civil Rights Act of 1964, when it was enacted was seriously deficient with regard to enforcement processes. The Equal Employment Opportunity Commission had no authority to enforce the law but was limited to investigations and attempts at conciliation. Although the statute provided for pattern or practice litigation by the US Department of Justice, that provision, § 707, made no necessary link between the Justice Departments' activities and the activities of the EEOC. What saved the law from being substantially sterile was the right provided to the complaining party to take the matter to the federal district courts for a trial **de novo**. Additionally, the statute provided for attorneys' fees as part of the cost for the prevailing party. This 'private attorneys general' concept has proven to be a rather effective means of enforcing the rights guaranteed in the law, despite the fact that substantial financial burdens rest on the shoulders of the plaintiffs' class.

When Congress amended the statute in 1972 and provided enforcement authority in the Commission by its own attorneys, it retained the right of the protected class plaintiffs, independently, to resort to the courts to enforce their claims. This combination, to a substantial extent, would seem to insure that neither complacency on the part of federal officials nor inadequate budgetary support for enforcement will frustrate implementation of the rights guaranteed in the law.

The difficulty with the enforcement process orginating in the federal districts courts and, therefore of necessity proceeding through three levels of the court system prior to ultimate and authoritative disposition of issues, is that it seems to be a less efficient mechanism than one modeled on the National Labor Relations Act. That act requires substantial deference to be National Labor Relations Board's 'choice of law' and limited judicial review. Title VII involves a greater number of actors and a longer period of time before authoritative law emerges. It would seem on the face of it that the NLRA process would result in a stable body of law in a shorter period of time than that adopted by the Congress under Title VII of the Civil Rights Act of 1964.

1. Proof

The multiplicity of laws prohibiting discrimination on some bases which are in place in the USA share a common concept where intentional discrimination is at issue. Unequal treatment on the basis of protected status (race, colour, religion, sex, etc.) which has come to be referred to as 'disparate treatment',[76] like the Constitution, requires a showing of 'intent' or 'purpose'. If the element of malice or bad motive is present or inferable, then violation of virtually all of the statutes may be established. In the leading case in the Supreme Court establishing the order and allocation of burdens of proof under Title VII, the Court has declared that the plaintiff in order to establish a **prima facie** case needs to show membership in a protected class, qualification for the position or promotion in question, application for consideration of same, and that he or she was passed over and some other unprotected class person accepted or that the employer continued to seek persons of the skills which the plaintiff has.[77] Once plaintiff has established a **prima facie** case, the defendant may then 'articulate a non-discriminatory reason for the action'. The burden would then shift to the plaintiff to establish that the purported reason is a pretext for discrimination or is unworthy of credence.[78]

The Civil Rights Act of 1964 includes another concept of discrimination which has become known as 'disparate impact'.[79] Violation does not require the establishment of intentional discrimination. Where a neutral test, or other employment practice or procedure, has a disparate impact upon protected class members, it violates Title VII of the Civil Rights Act unless the employer can establish that it meets the test of business necessity or is manifestly related to ability to do the job.[80] If the defendant can establish business necessity, variously articulated as necessary to the safe and efficient operation of the business, or in the case of a test, professionally validated,[81] then the plaintiff may show that there is a less discriminatory alternative way of insuring competent workers, which showing would go to establishing that the employer's defense was a pretext.[82]

The Court has determined that the 'effects or consequences test' does not apply to cases arising under the US Constitution[83] and is not applicable in cases involving 42 USC 1981.[84]

It is too early to conclude whether or not, or to what extent, the Supreme Court will interpret other federal statutes prohibiting discrimination to permit a case to be made out on the basis of disparate impact. While developing law with regard to age discrimination and handicap discrimination will, no doubt, continue to attempt to utilize that method of analysis and proof, we will have to await Supreme Court attention to those matters before clarity in the law will be established.

The Court is hopelessly divided over the issue of whether Title VI of the Civil Rights Act of 1964 requires intent as an essential element of violation, although there was a bare majority permitting regulations under Title VI to incorporate the disparate impact standard.[85]

2. Enforcement Agencies

As noted, after the 1972 Amendment, the EEOC has substantial enforcement authority through the court process both in individual cases and in pattern or practice cases in the private sector. Additionally, individuals retain the right to seek a court action on their own. Moreover, where actions involve several states or subdivisions thereof, the law provides for the Justice Department to sue on behalf of the government. The agencies, of course, have traditional authorities to investigate and hold hearings and to attempt to resolve disputed issues by conciliation. There are also substantial efforts to assist the parties voluntarily to resolve such issues.[86]

The president's Reorganization Plan of 1978 consolidated, to some extent, civil rights enforcement in the EEOC. Thus, age discrimination and equal pay enforcement were transferred to the Commission. However, the enforcement of the presidential executive order requirements regarding affirmative action and protections against discrimination on the basis of handicap, which rest in large part upon government contracting and federal assistance programmes, was left within the US Department of Labour.

Enforcement of the president's executive order rests primarily on action of the Department of Labour as the courts have consistently concluded that there is no private right of action conferred upon individual plaintiffs.[87] There is a limited right of action against the government's failure to comply with its own rules[88] and the right to participate in judicial review of the Labour Department's administrative process.[89]

There are various agencies involved in enforcing the multiplicity of laws having to do with insuring equality in the various programmes receiving federal financial assistance. Frequently, the process ends with the possibility of fund cutoff an may in some instances support action by the agencies to require specific performance.[90] In some cases the court has also implied a private right of action.[91]

3. Remedies

Under most of the laws adressing invidious discrimination in the USA, effective remedies are available when the plaintiff or the plaintiff's class prevails. Most of the statutes provide for make-whole relief, which includes reinstatement with back pay. The term 'reinstatement' also includes orders for hiring of the applicant for employment who was discriminated against in refusals to hire.[92] Where general remedial power is provided in the statute they frequently include additional authority to order such affirmative action as may be necessary to effectuate the purposes of the law. This expansive grant of equitable power frequently results in remedial action through order of the courts, or through consent decrees by the parties, establishing more comprehensive affirmative action plans to deal with systemic problems. There are disputes regarding the scope of remedial power residing in the courts which may be resolved more clearly by the US Supreme Court in the near future.[93]

The Equal Pay Act and the Age Discrimination Act provide, in addition to make-whole relief in the form of back pay, liquidated damages which double the amount in cases of willful violation of the law.

Under 42 USC 1981, the Supreme Court has said that plaintiffs may be entitled to compensatory damages, and even, in appropriate cases, punitive damages.[94]

In addition to Title VII specifically providing for a reasonable attorney's fee as part of the cost, Congress has enacted a Civil Rights Attorney's Fee Act[95] which provides generally for attorney's fees for the prevailing party in most civil rights cases. This is an inducement to attorneys to take cases, at least where plaintiffs' cases seem to be clearly within the law and provable in court.

In some cases requiring the employer to accept an employee back into the job, or into a job, would not be in the interest of anybody concerned. In those situations courts have been rather creative in designing remedies which compensate the individual for the lost opportunities. This has been particularly true in age discrimination cases in which the job was such that a close relationship at the executive level would have been required.

In the USA substantial legal instruments are in place attempting to insure equality of employment opportunity and establishing affirmative action programmes without regard to guilt or proof of specific injury. Moreover, efforts are underway to address age-old inequities between males and females in comparable jobs. However, the macro figures demonstrate clearly that much remains to be done, even almost twenty years after the enactment of the major federal law prohibiting employment discrimination. The participation rate in the various jobs by members of the principal protected class - blacks, browns, other non-whites and women - continues to reflect an unequal distribution of wages and benefits and of burdens. Black unemployment rates remain disproportionately high, female heads of households in poverty remain disproportionately high, and the extent of penetration of protected class members into the ranks of the higher paying jobs, while showing gains, remains far less than equitable.

The 'now and future' question in the USA is - will the body politic assign a high enough priority and sufficient resources to the eventual achievement of the goal of equality and persist until it is realized?

The price of equality, like liberty, is also eternal vigilence.

NOTES

1. **Jones v. Alfred H. Mayer Co.**, 392 US 409, at 439 (1968).
2. 'Freedom to the Free/Century of the Emancipation', Report to the President of the United States, Commission on Civil Rights, USGPO (1963) p. 11.
3. **Ibid**, citing 2 Ford 'The Works of Thomas Jefferson', 211 to 213 (1904); and Boyd, 'The Declaration of Independence: Evolution of the Text', 35 (1943).
4. **Id.** at 15.
5. US CONST. amend. XIII.
6. US CONST. amend. V.
7. **Dred Scott v. Sandford**, 60 US (19 How.) 393 (1857).
8. **Bolling v. Sharp**, 347 US 497 (1954), **Schneider v. Rusk**, 377 US 163 (1964).
9. 42 USC 2000e et seq. (1976).
10. Section 717 of the Civil Rights Act of 1964, as amended; **Brown v. GSA**, 425 US 820 (1976); see also **Chandler v. Roudebush**, 425 US 840 (1976).
11. See § 706 and § 708 of the Civil Rights Act of 1964.
12. 392 US 409, at 441-43 n. 78.
13. **Davis v. Passman**, 442 US 228, (1979).

14. 436 US 658 (1978).
15. Fitzpatrick v. Bitzer, 427 US 445 (1976) but see Quern v. Jordan, 440 US 332 (1979) making clear that 42 USC § 1983 does not abrogate the Eleventh Amendment immunity of the states.
16. Public Law 88-38, which is part of the Fair Standards Act of 1938, and was approved 10 June 1963, effective 11 June 1964; 29 USC 206 (1976).
17. Reorg. Plan No. 1 of 1978, 3 CFR 321 (1978), reprinted in 5 USC app. at 1155 (1982) and in 92 Stat. 3781 (1978).
18. 426 US 833 (1976).
19. See Marshall v. A & M Consolidated School District 605 F. 2d 186 (5th Cir. 1979); Marshall v. City of Sheboygan 577 F. 2d 1 (7th Cir. 1978); Usery v. Alleghany County Institution District 544 F. 2d 148 3rd Cir. 1976), cert. denied, 430 US 946 (1977).
20. 29 USC 621 et. seq. (1976), Pub. L. 90-202, 81 Stat. 602.
21. 42 USC 6101 et. seq. (1976), Pub. L. 94-135, 89 Stat. 728.
22. 31 USC 6716 et. seq. (1982), Pub. L. 92-512, 86 Stat. 919.
23. Viet Nam Era Veterans' Readjustment Act of 1974, 38 USC ch. 42 (1976).
24. Public Law 93-112 amended in 1978; 29 USC 701 et. seq. (1976), 87 Stat. 355.
25. Consolidated Rail Corp. v. Darrone, 104 S.Ct. 1248 (1984).
26. 31 USC 6720 (1982); in addition, 31 USC 6721(a) (1982) provides that a person adversely affected by the practice may bring a civil action in an appropriate court, provided that the person has exhausted the administrative remedies under 31 USC 6721(b) (1982).
27. See Lau v. Nichols 414 US 563 (1974); Cannon v. University of Chicago 441 US 677 (1979), and North Haven Board of Education v. Bell 456 US 512 (1982).
28. North Haven Board of Education v. Bell 456 US 512 at 535-539 (1982).
29. Miranda Fuel Co., 140 NLRB 181 (1962), enforcement denied, 326 F. 2d 177 (2nd Cir. 1963).
30. Local 12, Rubber Workers v. NLRB, 368 F. 2d 12 (5th Cir. 1966).
31. See e.g. Farmer v. ARA Services, 660 F. 2d 1090 (5th Cir. 1981).
32. See Vaca v. Sipes 386 US 171 (1967) at 182-183 and Del Costello v. Teamsters 103 S. Ct. 2281 at 2293 (1983).
33. Bureau of National Affairs, Fair Employment Practices Manual, Vol. 8A, p. 451:102-104.
34. Title XXIII ch. 9 Louisiana revised statute of 1950, part VIII, § 1006.
35. Section 701(k) of Title VII of the Civil Rights Act of 1964 was added in 1978 (42 USC § 2000e-12 (1976)).
36. Blumrosen, 'Strangers in Paradise: Griggs v. Duke Power and the Prima Facie Case of Employment Discrimination', 71 Michigan Law Review 59 (1972) at 67.
37. Griggs v. Duke Power, 401 US 424 (1971). For a most perceptive analysis of the concepts of discrimination see Blumrosen, 'Strangers in Paradise', ibid.
38. See Sullivan, Zimmerman, and Richards Federal Statutory Law of Employment Discrimination, Bobbs-Merrill Co., Inc. 1980 p. 3-15.

39. Footnotes omitted, Schlei and Grossman **Employment Discrimination Law** 2nd Edition 1983, The Bureau of National Affairs, Inc., Washington DC, p. 1.

40. It has been suggested that at least in reprisal or dual-motive cases a different allocation of burdens of proof may be necessary. See Drachsler, David A., 'Burdens of Proof in Retaliatory Adverse Action Cases Under Title VII', 35 **Labor Law Journal** No. 1, 28 at 32 (1 January 1984).

41. **See Teamsters v. United States,** 431 US 324 (1977); **Hazelwood School Discrict v. Unites States** 433 US 299 (1977).

42. The Supreme Court in **Franks v. Bowman Transportation Company,** 424 US 747, at 764 note 21 (1976) quoting the report of the Senate No. 92-415, 92nd Congress 1st Session, p. 5.

43. **Teamsters v. United States,** 431 US 324, 335-36 note 15 (1977).

44. **Griggs v. Duke Power Company,** 41 US 424 (1971).

45. **See** Employment Discrimination in the Civil Rights Acts, 21 Am. Jur. files sections 1 through 72 (1972).

46. **Teamsters v. US,** 431 US 324 (1977) at 336-337.

47. 433 US at 307.

48. **Teamsters v. US,** 431 US 324 (1977) at 339-340.

49. G. Allport, **The Nature of Prejudice,** Addison-Wesley, Reading, Mass. 106-108, (1954).

50. A. Downes 'Racism in America and How to Combat It', United States Commission on Civil Rights 5-6 (1970) excerpted in Bell, **Racism in American Law,** Ch. 3, p. 87-89 Little, Brown & Co., Boston, Toronto (1973).

51. G. Allport 'The Nature of Prejudice' 106-108 (1954) quoted in Bell, 'Racism in American Law' **supra** at p. 85.

52. EEOC national origin discrimination guidelines, 29 CFR 1606 (1980).

53. **See US v. Flagler County School District,** 457 F. 2d 1402 (5th Circuit 1972).

54. **Espinoza v. Farah Mfg. Co.,** 414 US 86 (1973).

55. See text accompanying notes 33-35, **supra.**

56. Bureau of National Affairs, **supra** note 33.

57. 42 US 2000e et. seq. (1976); Title VII of the Civil Rights Act of 1964 §§ 701(f) and 701(g).

58. **Reed v. Reed** 404 US 71 (1971); **Frontiero v. Richardson** 411 US 677 (1973); **Weinberger v. Wiesenfeld** 420 US 636 (1975); **Stanton v. Stanton** 421 US 7 (1975); **Graig v. Boren** 429 US 190 (1976); but see **Kahl v. Shevin** 416 US 351 (1974); **Schlesinger v. Ballard.**

59. An act to establish a bureau for the 'Relief of Freedmen and Refugees', chapter 200, 14 Stat. 177 (1866); see J. Jones, 'Reverse Discrimination in Employment - Judicial Treatment of Affirmative Action Programmes in the United States', 120 **International Labour Review** 453 (1981) and references cited therein.

60. See Jones 'Equal Employment Law in the 21st Century', 39 **Ohio State Law Journal** 700 (1978).

61. See Note, 'The Philadelphia Plan: A Study of the Dynamics of Executive Power', in 39 **University of Chicago Law Review** 723 (Summer 1972); see also **Contractors Association of Eastern Pennsylvania v. Secretary of Labor,** 442 F. 2d 159 (3rd Cir. 1971),

cert. denied, 404 US 854 (1971); see also J. Jones, 'The Bugaboo of Employment Quotas' in 1970 **Wisconsin Law Review** 341 (1970).
62. See **Furnco Construction Corp. v. Waters,** 438 US 567 (1978).
63. 41 CFR Ch. 60-2.10 (1983).
64. **Cf.** Jones, 'Bugaboo', **supra**, n. 61, at 379; **see also Associated General Contractors of Massachusetts v. Altshuler** 490 F. 2d 9 (3rd Cir. 1973) at 17-20.
65. 438 US 265 (1978).
66. Justice Powel cited **Bridgeport Guardians, Inc. v. Bridgeport Civil Service Commission** 482 F. 2d 1333 (2nd Cir. 1973); **Carter v. Gallagher** 452 F. 2d 315 (8th Cir. 1972), modified on rehearing en banc, **id.,** at. 327; **Contractors Association of Eastern Pennsylvania v. Secretary of Labor** 442 F. 2d 159 (3rd Cir.) cert. denied, 404 US 854 (1971) and **Associated General Contractors of Massachusetts, Inc. v. Altshuler** 490 F. 2d 9 (1st Cir. 1973), cert. denied, 416 US 957 (1974). Cited in **Regents of the University of California v. Bakke** 438 US 265 at 301-302 (1978).
67. 443 US 193 (1979).
68. 100 S.Ct. 2758 (1980).
69. 17th Annual Report, Equal Employment Opportunity Commission for Fiscal Year 1982 p. 42, 43.
70. See **Bratton v. City of Detroit,** 712 F. 2d 222 (6th Cir. 1983); **Williams v. City of New Orleans** 694 F. 2d 987 (5th Cir. 1982); **Association Against Discrimination v. City Bridgeport** 647 F. 2d 256 (2nd Cir. 1981) **cert. denied** 454 US 897 (1981); **Guardians Association of New York v. Civil Service** 633 F. 2d 232 (1980), cert. denied, 452 US 940 (1981); **Chance v. Board of Examiners & Board of Education** 534 F. 2d 993 (2nd Cir. 1976) (reh'g en banc), cert. denied 431 US 965 (1977); **United States v. City of Chicago** 549 F. 2d 415 (7th Cir. 1977) **cert. denied** 434 US 875 (1977); **US v. City of Miami** 614 F. 2d 1322 (1980) and cases cited therein; but see **Stotts v. Memphis Fire Department** 679 F. 2d 541 (6th Cir. 1982), **cert. granted** 103 S.Ct. 2451 (1983).
71. **South Florida Chapter of the Associated General Contractors of America, Inc. et al v. Metropolitan Dade County, Florida;** 33 EPD 34,122 (11th Cir. 1984).
72. **Id.**
73. **Boston Chapter of NAACP v. Beecher** 679 F. 2d 965 (1st Cir. 1982) **dismissed as moot** 103 S.Ct. 2076 (1983). This case is a consolidation of two related proceedings involving the Police and Fire Departments of the City of Boston. The police department proceedings are reported at **Castro et al. v. Beecher et al.** 334 Supp. 930 (D. Mass. 1971); 459 F. 2d 725 (1st Cir. 1972); 365 F. Supp. 655 (D. Mass. 1973); 386 F. supp. 1281 (D. Mass. 1975). The fire department proceedings are reported at **Boston Chapter, NAACP, Inc. et al. v. Beecher et al.** 371 F. Supp. 507 (D. Mass. 1974); 504 F. 2d 1017 (1st Cir. 1974), **cert. denied,** 421 US 910, 95 S.Ct. 1561, 43 L.Ed. 2d, 775 (1975); 423 F. Supp. 696 (D. Mass. 1976). Both the police and fire cases were reported in Chief Judge Caffrey's consolidated opinion, 522 F. Supp. 873 (D. Mass. 1981) from which this appeal arose.

74. **Stotts v. Memphis Fire Department** 679 C. 2d 541 (6th Cir. 1982), **cert.** granted 103 S.Ct. 2451 (1983).
75. There are other cases (**Arthur v. Nyquist**, 712 F. 2d 816 (2nd Cir. 1983) cert. filed 20 October 1983); which also raised the same or similar questions. See also **Morgan v. O'Bryant**, 671 F. 2d 23 (1st Cir. 1982) **cert.** denied, 103 S.Ct. 62 (1982); **cf. Oliver v. Kalamazoo Board of Education**, 706 F. 2d 757 (6th Cir. 1983) (acknowledging power to make such an order, but reversing Disctrict Court's particular order).
76. See **Teamsters v. US**, 431 US 324 at 335-336, n. 15.
77. **McDonnell Douglas v. Greene**, 411 US 792 at 802 (1973).
78. **Texas Department of Community Affairs v. Burdine**, 450 US 248 (1981); **Furnco Construction Corp. v. Waters**, 438 US 567 (1978); **Board of Trustees, Keene State College v. Sweeney**, 439 US 24 (1978); see also **Aikens v. US Postal Service Board of Governors**, 453 US 902 (1981).
79. See **Teamsters v. US**, 431 US 324 at 335-336; see also Blumrosen, **supra** n. 36, at. 67.
80. **Griggs v. Duke Power**, 401 US 424 (1971); **Dothard v. Rawlinson**, 433 US 321 (1977); **Albemarle Paper Co. v. Moody**, 422 US 405 (1975).
81. See **Albemarle Paper Co. v. Moody**, 422 US 405 (1975).
82. See **Albemarle Paper Co. v. Moody**, 422 US 405 at 425 (1975); **Dothard v. Rawlinson**, 433 US 321 at 329 (1977).
83. **Washington v. Davis**, 426 US 229 (1976).
84. **General Contractors Assn., Inc. v. Pennsylvania**, 458 US 375 at 391; 102 S.Ct. 3141 (1982); **Washington v. Davis**, 426 US 229 (1976); **cf. Personnel Administrators of Massachusetts v. Feeney**, 442 US 256, at 272 (1979).
85. See **Guardians Association v. The City Service Commission of the City of New York**, 103 S.Ct. 3221 (1983), at 3235, n. 27.
86. See **17th Annual Report of EEOC for FY 1984**, Labor Law Reports, Employment Practices No. 12112, Commerce Clearing House Inc., 25 January 1984, p. 15.
87. **Farmer v. Philadelphia Electric Company**, 329 F. 2d 3 (3rd Cir. 1964); **Farkas v. Texas Instrument, Inc.**, 375 F. 2d 629 (5th Cir. 1967), **cert.** denied, 389 US 977 (1967); **Cohen v. IIT**, 524 F. 2d 818 (7th Cir. 1975), **cert.** denied, 425 US 943 (1976); **Cap v. Lehigh University**, 433 F. Supp. 1275 (ED Pa. 1977).
88. See **Legal Aid Society v. Brennan**, 608 F. 2d 1319 (9th Cir. 1979), **cert.** denied, 447 US 921 (1980).
89. See **Hadnot v. Laird**, 463 F. 2d 304 (DC Cir. 1972); **US v. New Orleans Public Service Inc.**, 553 F. 2d 459 (5th Cir. 1977); **US v. Mississippi Power and Light Co.**, 553 F. 2d 480 (5th Cir. 1977); **Association of Data Processing Service Organizations, Inc. v. Camp**, 397 US 150 (1970); **Barlow v. Collins**, 397 US 159 (1970); **Abbott Laboratories v. Gardner**, 387 US 136 (1967); see also Jones, 'The Maturation of the Administrative Enforcement Process of the Executive Order', 69 **Chicago Kent Law Review**, 67 (1982).
90. See **US v. The City of Chicago**, 395 F. Supp. 329 (ND Ill., 1975), **aff'd US v. The City of Chicago**, 525 F. 2d 695 (7th Cir. 1975); **Green v. Connally**, 330 F. Supp. 1150 (DDC 1975), **aff'd sub nom.**

Coit v. Green, 404 US 997 (1971); Norwood v. Harrison, 413 US 455 (1974); Gilmore v. City of Montgomery, 417 US 556 (1974).

91. See Cannon v. The University of Chicago, 441 US 677 (1979); Lau v. Nichols, 414 US 563 (1974); Cort v. Ash, 422 US 66 (1975); Consolidated Rail Corp. v. Darrone, 104 S.Ct. 124 (1984).

92. See Franks v. Bowman Transportation Company, 424 US 747 (1976), Albemarle v. Moody, 422 US 405 (1975).

93. See e.g. Stotts v. Memphis Fire Department, 679 F. 2d 541 (6th Cir. 1982), cert. granted 103 S.Ct. 2451 (1983). But see Bratton v. City of Detroit, 712 F. 2d 222 (6th Cir. 1983); Williams v. City of New Orleans, 694 F. 2d 987 (5th Cir. 1982); Equal Employment Opportunity Commission v. American Telephone and Telegraph, 556 F. 2d 167 (3rd Cir. 1977), cert. denied, 438 US 915 (1978); US v. City of Alexandria, 614 F. 2d 1358 (5th Cir. 1980); US v. City of Chicago, 549 F. 2d 415 (7th Cir. 1975), cert. denied, 434 US 875 (1977); Boston Chapter, NAACP, Inc. v. Beecher, 504 F. 2d 1017 (1st Cir. 1974), cert. denied, 421 US 910 (1975).

94. Johnson v. Railway Express Co., 421 US 454 (1975) at 459-460.

95. 42 USC 1988 (1976).

15. Yugoslavia

V. Brajic

I. INTRODUCTION

It is impossible to make a brief historical survey of legal norms and practice in this area because available data is rather scarce. Yugoslavia was established as a state only after World War I. Initially she did not have her own legal system as her law at that time was a collection of legal norms of the various regions which were united into the new state. The Constitution was adopted in 1921 and then some time later it was suspended and replaced by a dictatorship.

The Constitution, and particularly practice, did not recognise the multinational character of Yugoslavia, nor consequently, the corresponding national rights, as the Constitution of 1921 proceeded from the principle that in Yugoslavia there was only one nation with a number of religious affiliations. National equality and rights were not formally recognised and the logical consequence of that fact was a real inequality.

As regards employment, one can hardly add much more to this fact, but it should be mentioned that Yugoslavia before World War II was an economically underdeveloped country with a small working class.

During World War II, simultaneously with the struggle for national liberation, the socialist revolution was taking place. The foundations of the legal system of the new state were laid down in the course of the war by the introduction of regulations which were passed by national liberation committees in the liberated parts of the country.

The foundations of the constitutional system were laid by decisions of the National Anti-fascist Liberation Council of Yugoslavia in 1943. The Constitution of the new state, the Federal People's Republic of Yugoslavia, was adopted soon after World War II, in 1946. It was one of the first constitutions adopted after the Second World War.

Under Art. 21 of that Constitution, all citizens of the Federal People's Republic of Yugoslavia were declared equal before the law and with equal rights, regardless of their nationality, race and religion. No privileges on account of birth, social position, wealth and education were recognised; any act granting citizens privileges or restricting their rights on account of their nationality, race and religion, as well as stirring up national, racial or religious hatred and discord, were declared unconstitutional and punishable by law.

The Constitutional Law of 1953 was actually the amendment to the Constitution of 1946 and did not have special provisions on human rights, but it guaranteed the right to work.

With regard to human and civil rights, the Constitution of 1963, which replaced the Constitution of 1946 and the Constitutional Law of 1953, meant considerable progress in comparison with the Constitution of 1946. The conception of human rights in the Constitution of 1963 was that they were expressions and an inalienable part of socialist and democratic relations protected by the Constitution.

Consequently, freedoms and rights became a protected and inalienable part of the constitutional system which as such could not be realised without these freedoms and rights.[1] This was a philosophy expressing an attitude towards the state, society and an individual, and a demand that all of them should proceed from the rights of man and the citizen provided for by the Constitution. Such a conception of rights and freedoms is contained also in the Constitution of 1974 which is in force now.

The Yugolav constitutional system has abandoned the concept under which the rights are given to citizens by the state and are dependable on the will of the state. On the contrary, the rights belong to man and the citizen and therefore they are constitutionally protected and represent an inalienable part of socialist self-management relations in Yugoslavia.

The Constitution of 1974, which is in force at present, has further advanced and elaborated the concept of freedoms, rights and obligations of man and the citizen. It particularly emphasises the right of workers to take part in self-managing decision-making and in self-management in general. This concept, however, does not neglect basic and classic human and civil rights, and proceeds, as a matter of principle, from equal rights, obligations and responsibilites under equal terms.

The point of departure in regulation and realisation of the rights is equality of all citizens in rights and obligations, regardless of nationality, race, sex, language, religion, education and social status. All are equal before the law (Art. 153 and 154 of the SFRY Constitution).

The constitutional provisions on the freedom to work, under which everyone is free to choose his occupation and job, should be understood in the context of these and other provisions of the Constitution pertaining to the freedoms, rights and obligations of man and the citizen (Art. 160 of the SFRY Constitution of 1974). Every citizen has access, on equal terms, to every job and function in society. The right of access to every job and occupation has also been provided for in the Associated Labour Act and the acts on labour relations of socialist republics and autonomous provinces.

In studying and interpreting the question of equality and prohibition of discrimination in employment, one may proceed from the right to work as the right to employment under equal terms.[2] Equal right to employment belongs to all on equal terms with regard to their working abilities and skills, regardless of all other differences. The right to work guarantees also equal rights for the same results of work and equal self-management rights.

This is the principle on which all other legal provisions pertaining to employment and the rights emanating from work, as well as the provisions of self-management by-laws and other acts and individual decisions, are based. In the case where a legal provision is not in accord with the Constitution, the Constional Court shall annul such a legal provision, as well as the provisions of self-management by-laws, because they also have to be in accord with the Constitution.

Self-management by-laws cannot be contrary to the law and as the

234

law has to be in accord with the Constitution, in this respect there is a clearly defined relationship between all basic legal and self-management enactments. Therefore, one can always initiate proceedings for the assessment of the constitutionality of a self-management enactment or its individual provisions. This, naturally, relates also to the provisions determining the rights, obligations and responsibilities, as well as to those pertaining to employment and the rights at work and on the basis of work. All these provisions pertaining to employment and labour may be reduced to the provisions concerning the right to work, as they have to be founded on the law and self-management by-laws and in conformity with the provisions of Art. 159 of the SFRY Constitution of 1974.

One should point out here that conventions of the International Labour Organisations become, by ratification, federal laws of the Socialist Federal Republic of Yugoslavia. It means that the relations regulated by the laws of republic and autonomous provinces, as well as by self-management by-laws, cannot be in disagreement with them. The proceedings for the assessment of legality of each self-management enactment may be instituted if it is considered to be in disagreement with the provisions of the ratified convention.

All legal and self-management acts must be in conformity with the Constitution, the law (ratified conventions) and self-management enactments. Anyone who considers that his rights have been violated by an individual decision, may seek protection of his rights at the Court of Associated Labour or at the regular court, if the matter falls within its competence. Therefore, there is no exception and it means that neither can there be any exception in regard to equality in employment, nor in connection with the work.

The procedure is specified by the law and by self-management enactments, but the rules of procedure cannot restrict anybody's right to the court protection. To be able to realise the court protection, one has to respect the following basic rules of procedure: (1) a worker has to seek protection of his rights, initially in the organisation of associated labour in which he works, and (2) if he is not satisfied with the decision passed by the workers' council in his organisation of associated labour, he can initiate proceedings for the protection of his rights at the court within thirty days from the day when he was served with the decision.

II. THE DEFINITION OF DISCRIMINATION

In legislation and theory, [3] discrimination means unequal treatment of people or groups of people, whose aim or consequence is reduction, restriction or frustration of the rights of individuals or groups on account of their race, religion, sex, language, education or social position. Under discriminatiuon we mean unequal treatment, regardless of whether a specific treatment has discrimination in view, or the discrimination is only a consequence of a specific treatment. It is true that if a specific treatment does not have discrimination in view, then we do not call it discrimination but unequal treatment. Nevertheless, such treatment is prohibited in the same way as discrimination and subject to legal sanctions, which means that each state or self-management organ is obliged to establish the equality and to protect the rights of an individual or a group.

III. EQUALITY, REGARDLESS OF RACE, COLOUR, ETHNIC, NATIONAL OR SOCIAL ORIGIN

Yugoslavia does not have a population of different races or colour in large groups and communities, though there are and there may be some coloured people who, by settling down or taking Yugolav citizenship, choose to live permanently within Yugoslavian territory. Therefore, the provisions on equality are not only of declarative nature, but they are also of current interest and may be of practical importance. Besides, there are the norms which protect man or human rights in general, because they relate also to the foreigners who take employment in Yugoslavia.

At this moment in time the number of such foreigners is small. They are mostly physicians or other specialists from African countries who after graduating from Yugolav universities do not leave Yugoslavia but take up employment in the country. Similarly, some specialists from developing countries who come to Yugoslavia for further and professional training, take temporary employment.

In view of the existing difficulties with employment, that is, the problem of surplus labour, the question of the employment of foreigners in large numbers does not arise at present. However, with economic development the need to employ workers from other countries may arise. In view of traditional and present migration of workers from the South to the North and Yugoslavia's relations with Africa and Asia, in the future one may expect the employment of workers from African and even from Asian countries. Such a trend would depend largely on the economic recovery and development of Yugoslavia. If and when the workers from these parts of the world come to Yugoslavia in larger numbers, then these constitutional and legal provisions will be of greater practical importance.

The question of employment of migrant workers is of rising practical importance for many countries and for the world in general. Today, it is usually considered as the question of employment of foreigners.

In view of the complexity of the question of employment of foreigners (migrant workers), their employment is usually viewed, both in the legislation and in theory, separately from the question of equality in employment. The question of discrimination is considered mainly as the discrimination of foreigners in relation to the citizens of the host country. However, this discrimination may take the forms of racial discrimination and discrimination on account of different colour, nationality, religion etc. The reasons for discriminatory treatment lie, to a large extent, in these differences and the fact that somebody is a foreigner is only partly the reason for such treatment, though is may be and sometimes is the only reason for discriminatory treatment. Therefore, the provisions of the Constitution of 1974 pertaining to the equality of rights, obligations and responsibilities are of broader cultural and legal importance, as the question of equality is treated in a more general way. Everybody, regardless of race, is guaranteed equality of rights, obligations and responsibilites, and that means both Yugoslav and foreign citizens.

These and other constitutional and legal provisions are in line with the advancement of rights and responsibilities, embodied in the international acts accepted and ratified by Yugoslavia as a member of the United Nations, International Labour Organisation and UNESCO, which relate directly and indirectly to the question of equality and prohibition of discrimination in employment. [4]

IV. EQUALITY OF WOMEN AND MEN IN REGARD TO EMPLOYMENT

Equality of women and men in all spheres of the state, economic and socio-political life, was specified in Art. 24 of the first Constitution of the SFRY after World War II (1946). It also provided for the right of women to equal pay for equal work with men, as well as to special care in a labour relationship. These provisions indirectly speak of the prohibition of discrimination. It was also provided that mothers would enjoy the special care of the state.

In the constitutions that followed there was no mention of prohibition of discrimination of women, as the socio-economic development and, primarily, the changes which were initiated and realised in the socialist revolution, ensured real equality of men and women. This equality was ensured by the participation of women in the revolution and in the reconstruction of the country after the war.

The conception of guaranteed equal rights, obligations and responsibilities, which prevents any discrimination in regulations and in practice, presumes also equality of women and men. Therefore, there is no need for specific provisions on prohibition of discrimination of women, as any unequal treatment is illegal and unconstitutional and, consequently, punishable by law.

Yugoslavia ratified the Convention Concerning Equal Remuneration of Men and Women Workers for Work of Equal Value and thus this convention became a federal law. Its provisions apply throughout the whole territory of Yugoslavia.

In addition to legal provisions on equality in employment and on equality of rights on the basis of work of equal value, the laws of republics and autonomous provinces also contain a number of provisions concerning special protection of women. These provisions aim to take into account the inherited inequalities and specificities of women's life and work, to ensure equal working conditions for men and women. In this regard, one should particularly emphasise provisions which relate to the work of women in heavy conditions, underground and underwater, as well as legal provisions specifying women's rights during pregnancy and maternity. [5] In addition to these rights, some other rights have been introduced recently, such as: the right of the mother (but also to the father and the foster-parent) to work half working hours until the child is five years old, or the right of the mother to have long leave until the child is three years old, etc. [6]

On the basis of the equal right of all to education and professional training and of the hitherto attained level of equality of men and

women, the number of men and women studuing at schools and universities in Yugoslavia almost corresponds to their share in the total
population of the given age group. It means that women have the same
opportunities as men for professional training. Free and equal access
to education and professional training is the essential presumption for
realisation of the right to work and employment.

Due to the limited scope of this paper, one cannot enumerate all
that is important for the realisation of equality of men and women in
regard to employment and work, but, as can be seen, there is a number
of legal provisions and other measures which represent a whole system
of legislation and rules that extend the existing rights and produce new
results, which may serve others as an inspiration and the model for
the change in the sphere of labour legislation and employment policy.

It appears that in many countries some people still do not under-
stand that there is no adequate employment policy without an adequate
and complex resolution of the issue of women's employment. As an
illustration of that, one may take the discussion which preceded the
adoption of the Recommendation Concerning Employment Policy (1984).
The fact that this recommendation does not contain enough provisions
concerning the employment of women, makes the whole employment
policy formulated in this document inadequate and deficient. The
explanation which was given that the employment of women would be
separately treated, hardly could be accepted as satisfactory.

V. PRIVATE LIFE, RELIGIOUS AND POLITICAL BELIEFS AND BEHAVIOUR

A man's private life and behaviour do not affect employment and the
rights concerning work. Exceptionally, however, some aspects of
one's private life and behaviour may come into conflict with some
specific jobs and functions. Thus, for instance, if a judge who deals
with marital disputes becomes notorious for his own irregular family
and marital life, then he has no moral authority to perform his job.

The constitutions of Yugoslav socialist republics and autonomous
provinces, as well as the Constitution of the SFRY, provide for
freedom of thought and option. In conformity with the constitutional
rights and freedoms, religious, political and ideological affiliations and
beliefs do not affect the employment position and rights at work.
These freedoms and rights of citizens are restricted only by the
equal freedoms and rights of other, and may be limited only by the
law based on the Constitution and on international acts adopted
through the system of the UN.

In view of the multinational character of the Socialist Federal
Republic of Yugoslavia, in the Constitution of the SFRY and the
constitutions of the republics and autonomous provinces and in practice,
a special importance is attached to the citizens' rights to opt for a
nation or nationality, to express their national culture and to use their
language and alphabet. To protect the realisation of these rights, the
Constitution of the Socialist Republic of Serbia provides, in Art. 194,
that propagating or practising national inequality, pressures to opt
for a nationality, as well as any incitement of national and religious

hatred and intolerance, shall be unconstitutional and punishable by law.

Freedoms and rights of citizens are guaranteed and protected as equal rights and freedoms and, as such, realised without any privileges or discrimination of any kind. Freedoms and rights determined by the Constitution and, accordingly, the right to work, can be neither taken away nor restricted due to religious, political or other beliefs.

VI. YOUTH EMPLOYMENT

Regulations concerning labour relations provide for special care for young people. This care is reflected in the obligation of organisations of associated labour to employ annually a certain number of young workers (trainees). In this way, continuous employment of a certain number of young workers is ensured.

As regards the employment and work of the workers under 18, it has been determined that they cannot be employed nor assigned to jobs and workings tasks which require heavy work, work underground and underwater, and to other jobs, which could be detrimental to their health. All these provisions aim to make the working conditions of youth comparable with the working conditions of other workers, in view of the differences that exist in the psycho-physiological structure of workers of different age groups.

VII. EMPLOYMENT OF ELDERLY WORKERS

Every worker who meets the eligibility requirements in regard to the skills and working abilities for a certain job, who is generally healthy and who has reached the age of fifteen years, may establish a labour relationship. It means that there is no specified upper age limit for establishing a labour relationship.

Every worker has the right to work until he reaches the age of 65 years, that is until he meets the conditions for retirement. It has been specified by law that workers have to retire when they reach the age of 65 years (with very few exceptions). The rules which directly or indirectly specify this age limit are under discussion at present. There have been some objections on the grounds that these provisions are not in conformity with the right to work. The prevailing opinion is that they are, as they were introduced to open opportunities for the employment of the young. If there was no employment problem, this restriction would not exist.

VIII. EMPLOYMENT OF DISABLED

In those cases where the working abilities of a worker are reduced, but when he can still carry out some specific jobs or be trained for the performance of specific jobs, such a worker has the right to a corresponding employment. If a worker becomes disabled while in a labour relationship, he will have the right to be assigned to another corresponding job; simlarly, if he becomes unemployed, he will have the right to obtain a corresponding job. Certain jobs and working tasks are even reserved exclusively for disabled persons.

IX. VOCATIONAL AND PROFESSIONAL REQUIREMENTS FOR EMPLOYMENT

In addition to general conditions for employment - normal health, over 15 years of age - in Yugoslavia only those eligibility requirements for establishing a labour relationship may be specified, which correspond to the needs of the labour process and which are essential for the successful performance of a job, or a working task at a particular working post. [7]

Therefore, every worker who wants to establish a labour relationship has to meet the requirements specified for the performance of the work at a given job or working task. The worker who does not meet these requirements can not establish a labour relationship. If a worker loses some of these required abilities in the course of the work, he cannot work at the given job or the working task, but he has the right to be assigned, according to his vocational working abilities, to other jobs and tasks.

Eligibility requirements in regard to vacational and working abilities are specified by the self-management by-laws, pursuant to the rule that these requirements have to correspond to the needs of the labour process. Only exceptionally the eligibility requirements in regard to vocational and professional abilities may also be determined by the law.

Eligibility requirements in regard to vocational and professional abilities contain the rule and express a standard that those who do not meet requirements for the performance of given jobs and working tasks, cannot establish a labour relationship, unless there are no other workers who can meet these requirements. Therefore, a labour relationship can be established only by those who can meet the eligibility requirements. This is not discrimination, but a universally recognised need and the rule which is applied **bona fide.**

X. ADDITIONAL REQUIREMENTS FOR CERTAIN JOBS

Under the Constitution and within its framework, some additional requirements may be specified for certain jobs and working tasks, as for instance for judges and citizens who take part in the administration of justice in regular courts.

Under these additional requirements are meant exceptional moral integrity and professional expertise in the performance of a job which affirms human dignity and humanism, and which presumes special obligations and responsibilities. It is assumed that everybody meets these requirements, and only in the case of justified doubts have they to be substantiated. These provisions are contained in the laws on regular courts and public prosecution and expressed through the requirement that judges, public prosecutors and policemen should have moral-political capabilities. These provisions are in conformity with the Constitution of the SFRY, Art. 230, under which 'judges of regular courts shall be elected and relieved of office in a way, under conditions and by a procedure which shall ensure professional expertise and moral-political capabilities...'.

It is not by chance that moral capabilities rank so high in these requirements, as the judges are expected to have high and, if possible, exceptional moral values. Political capability does not means that someone has to be a member of the League of Communists of Yugoslavia, but that he has not opted against the system of socialist society which he is to protect. It goes without saying that the function of the judge cannot be entrusted to a man who incites national, religious and racial hatred, who propagates violation of human rights or fascism. There is no guarantee that such a man will, as a judge, perform his job as provided by the Constitution and by the law. Here, in the matter of fact, the point is in professional incompetence, as such a judge is incapable or unwilling to administer justice. Therefore, it is a question whether this additional requirement for the office of judge should be called a moral-political capability. In the way it is understood and applied, the principal meaning of this notion is moral and professional capability.

Under Art. 511 of the Associated Labour Act, a person who has been given an unsuspended sentence of imprisonment for a crime, committed with intent, against the foundations of the socialist self-management social order or the security of the country, against the national economy, against self-management rights, against social property or against official duty, may neither be appointed sole business manager nor chairman of the business managing board, nor perform affairs falling within the province of work of such organs. The restriction in this case lasts 10 years. If a person has committed, with intent, other criminal offences than those referred to earlier, and if he has received an unsuspended sentence of imprisonment of not less than three years, the restriction concerning the performance of the mentioned jobs and working tasks shall last five years.

Every organisation of associated labour determines the conditions for establishing labour relationship by its self-management by-laws. It refers also to establishing a labour relationship of the business management organ. In practice, the additional conditions specified in Art. 511 of the Associated Labour Act, in self-management by-laws and in public competitions and advertisements for a job, are called briefly 'moral-political capability' or 'the option for self-management' or 'the self-management capability'. These are short but inadequate expressions which may cause confusion. Those who read them may get the impression that it is a new condition (and not the requirement provided for in Art. 511 of the Constitution of the SFRY), or that membership of the League of Communists of Yugoslavia is required.

We have seen that in the case of judges, where the moral-political capability is explicitly required, it does not necessarily mean membership of the LCY. This is an indisputable fact in practice. Not only is political affiliation, as an eligibility requirement, not mentioned in Art. 511 of the Associated Labour Act, but there is no mention of the moral-political capability either. However, even if it were interpreted

241

in this narrow sense, the moral-political capability would not mean, as we have seen, political affiliation to a specific organisation. What is important here is the fact that this condition (moral-political capability, the self-management orientation etc.), has been reduced in practice to the provisions of Art. 511 of the Associated Labour Act.

When a self-management orientation is required from a director, it means that he is expected to manage the self-management organisation in accordance with the existing legal system, and not as a private enterprise, to respect the rights of workers and to participate in self-management. In practice, it has been understood and applied in such a way. It appears that a special provision requiring a worker to work in accordance with the rules is not necessary as, if he does not want to or cannot, there will be no conditions for the establishment of a labour relationship and, consequently, no agreement of wills.

These problems, as well as the problems of the language and of legal and technical elaboration of self-management enactments, remind us that every subject which is authorised to make regulations strives to distinguish itself by language and by autonomous solutions. This autonomy is very often manifested by different terminology and by inserting unnecessary provisions. 'Self-management capability', as we have seen, means readiness to apply laws and self-management by-laws. This should not be explicitly specified, particularly as it may be interpreted in different ways.

It could be noticed from public competitions [8] and advertisements which were called or published at the end of the 1970s that eligibility requirements, as provided by Art. 511 of the Act, or the formulations on the self-management or moral-political capabilities, were specified also for the jobs which were not of special social interest or of interest for security of the country. This practice was the subject of criticisms, investigation and adjustments with the law. The Central Committee of the League of Communists of Yugoslavia [9] criticised that practice as well. It was evidenced that, in many instances, the eligibility requirements specified in public competitions and advertisements were not provided for in self-management enactments (only the eligibility requirements provided for in self-management enactments, are legal). [10]

Organisations of associated labour determine by their self-management by-laws the eligibility requirements for establishing labour relationships and carrying out jobs from their field of operation. They have the right and a duty to determine eligibility requirements for specific jobs, in accordance with the professionally and scientifically established labour requirements and specific interests, but within the provisions of the Constitution and the Law; from the point of equality and prohibition of discrimination in employment, it means also in accordance with the Employment and Occupation Convention and other international acts and obligations. One should recall the rule that if the provisions of self-management laws are in collision with the law, the law shall be applied. Everybody who considers that some of his rights in regard to work have been violated, may seek and realise protection at the court.

XI. PROTECTION OF EQUAL RIGHTS TO EMPLOYMENT AND WORK

Every free job and function, as explicitly provided by legal provisions (the Associated Labour Act, the laws on labour relations of the republics and autonomous provinces) has to be made public through a call for a public competition or by advertising in the information media. The call for a public competition or an advertisement has to contain the eligibility requirements for the establishment of a labour relationship, as specified by self-management by-laws or by the law.

Each applicant for a job has the right to contest the decision if he considers that eligibility requirements for carrying out given jobs or working tasks, or the procedure for establishing labour relationship were violated. It means that, in all cases where a worker considers that equality has been violated, or that discrimination can be proved, he may contest the decision. Actually, it is enough to prove that one was unequally treated to pronounce the decision illegal. It relates equally to material and formal regulations.

It is a common rule that the worker who has established a labour relationship always has the right (if he considers that some of his rights have been violated) to seek protection of his rights before the court.[11] It means that if a worker considers that he has been unequally treated, he may seek protection of his rights.

The right of a worker to seek protection of his rights consists of: (1) the right to seek re-examination of the decision from the workers' council and (2) if he is dissatisfied with the decision of the workers' council, he may seek protection of his rights from the court.

It means that any discriminatory treatment of workers in regard to any of his rights is subject to re-examination and may be brought before the court for the protection of legality.

Disputes arising from the labour relationship in associated labour are within jurisdiction of the courts of associated labour, and the disputes between a worker and a private employer are within the competence of regular courts.

Disputes arising from the violation of the workers rights by the provision of self-management enactments, or by the provision of the law, are within the competence of the constitutional court which is to assess their constitutionality and legality. The issue of equality and of equal treatment is the central one in assessing the constitutionality of legal acts and self-management by-laws. The constitutionality and legality of individual self-management acts are assessed by the courts of associated labour or by regular courts.

XII. CONCLUDING REMARKS ON THE PROTECTION OF RIGHTS TO EQUALITY IN EMPLOYMENT

As it can be seen from this text, every citizen of Yugoslavia and every alien has the right to work, has an equal right to freely choose productive employment, and equal rights on the basis of equal labour and results of labour. Protection of rights provided for by the Constitution, law (ratified conventions of the ILO) and self-management by-laws, is realised in organisations of associated labour and in the

243

courts. Protection of rights is realised without any restrictions (protection of any right or legally recognised interest). The only restriction is the procedure that a worker should seek protection of his rights within thirty days from the day when he was served with the decision violating his rights. When unconstitutionality or illegality of self-management by-laws is in question, then there is no time limit for instituting the proceedings for the protection of rights.

NOTES

1. Dr J. Djordjević, **Ustavno pravo**, Beograd, 1972.
2. Dr V. Brajić, **International Encyclopeadia for Labour Law and Industrial Relations** - Yugoslavia, Kluwer 1982, no. 192.
3. The SFRY Constitution of 1974, constitutions of socialist republics and autonomous provinces (1974); Dr J. Djordjević, **Ustavno pravo**, Beograd, 1972.
4. Universal Declaration of Human Rights; International Convenant on Economic, Social and Cultural Rights; International Convention on the Elimination of All Forms of Racial Discrimination; The United Nations Declaration on the Elimination of All Forms of Racial Discriminatiuon; The United Nations Declaration on the Elimination of Discrimination Against Women; Convention Concerning Equal Remuneration for Men and Women workers for Work of Equal Value, etc.
5. In addition to the Associated Labour Act (federal law), Sluzbeni list (Official Gazette) SFRJ, No. 53/76, the republics and both autonomous provinces have their own acts on labour relations which regulate these and other rights in labour relations: Sluzbeni list SR BiH, No. 36/77; Sluzbeni list SR Crne Gore, No. 36/77 and 31/82; Narodne novine SR Hrvatske, No. 11/78 and 40/82; Sluzbeni vesnik SR Makedonije, No. 45/77; Sluzbeni glasnik SR Srbije, No. 40/77, 56/81 and 23/84; Sluzbeni list SAP Kosovo, No. 47/77; Sluzbenmi list SAP Vojvodine, No. 31/77.
6. The Law Amending the Law on Labour Relations, Sluzbeni glasnik SR Srbije, No. 9/84.
7. The Associated Labour Act, Art. 167-168.
8. Organisations of associated labour are bound to make known their needs for workers through a call for a public competition or by advertising in the information media.
9. The 8th Plenary Session of the Central Committee of the LCY, October 1979, 'Politika', 19 October 1979.
10. The decision of the Constitutional Court of the SR of Macedonia No. U-91/78 (Membership in the League of Communists of Yugoslavia cannot be identified with the position of moral-political capabilities); The Decision of the Constitutional Court of SR Serbia, No. U-13/82.
11. The Associated Labour Act, Art. 220-226.

Comparative Labour Law and Industrial Relations

(second revised edition)

edited by R. Blanpain

Industrial Relations and legal practitioners must be aware of the developments in this area of the law because of the growth of multinational enterprises and the impact of international and regional organisations aspiring to harmonise rules. This book (in its 2nd edition) describes the salient characteristics and trends in Labour Law and Industrial Relations in the contemporary world, with special emphasis to developing countries, to the public sector and to remuneration and conditions of employment.
A very useful book not only for practitioners but also for teachers and students as a textbook and a work of reference.
Including a list of abbreviations, bibliography, authors' index, geographical index and subject index.

Topics: Labour relations in the third world; international labour law; conflict of laws; European Communities; Guidelines; International Trade Union Movement; Employers' Organisations, Workers' Participation; Quality of Working Life; Collective Bargaining, Settlement of Disputes; Security etc.

in preparation

Sales in the Netherlands subject to VAT.
Also available from your bookseller.

KLUWER
Law and Taxation Publishers

P.O. Box 23   7400 GA Deventer   The Netherlands

acta sociologica

JOURNAL OF THE SCANDINAVIAN SOCIOLOGICAL ASSOCIATION

Acta Sociologica is published quarterly by Universitetsforlaget and the Scandinavian Sociological Association. The purpose of the journal is to present research results of international standard within the fields of sociology and societal research. Articles are normally written by Scandinavian sociologists, but contributions from sociologists outside Scandinavia are also welcome.

The articles differ in scope and theoretical starting point and represent a variety of issues within the field of sociology.

CONTENTS: Vol. 28 No. 1, March 1985

ACTA SOCIOLOGICA   ORDER FORM

☐ I wish to become a subscriber from No. 1, 1985

    Subscription price 1985: USD46.00   ☐ cheque enclosed
    Postage included.   ☐ please send invoice

Name: . . . .

Address: . . . .

Issues will be sent to you as soon as payment is received.
UNIVERSITETSFORLAGET, P.O. Box 2959 Tøyen, Oslo 6, Norway   126a

UNIVERSITETSFORLAGET